Families in Business

This book offers a 'contemporary' understanding of families in business and serves as a springboard for ongoing evolution of families, their composition, transformations, and activities.

The first chapter in this volume highlights the different approaches to family and concludes that identifying and understanding the entity 'family in business' is the cornerstone to understanding behaviours of family businesses. The concept of 'family in business' as a socially constructed entity allows for not only a broader scope of the concept to include individuals who share a faith (chapter 2), but also multi-generational families and chosen families. Narratives, or stories, are means for families in business to mark the boundary of the family in business (chapter 3), because not all members of the family are necessarily members of the family in business. Families and their businesses influence each other (chapter 4) and engender the family influence on the firm ('familiness') and firm influence of the family ('enterpriseness'). The last two chapters are dedicated to transgenerational family businesses, with a focus on learning between generations—chapter 5 highlights the importance of unlearning (to learn new knowledge and different ways of conducting business) and the final chapter focuses on what knowledge is actually transferred relative to initial plans.

The chapters in this book were originally published as a special issue of *Entrepreneurship & Regional Development.*

Kathleen Randerson is Associate Professor of Entrepreneurship, Strategy and Innovation Department at Audencia, France.

Hermann Frank is a professor at WU Vienna University of Economics and Business, Austria and was director of the Research Institute for Family Business until December 2021.

Clay Dibrell is Professor of Management and the Co-Director of the Center for Innovation and Entrepreneurship at The University of Mississippi, USA. He is also holder of the Endowed Chair in Entrepreneurial Excellence and a US Fulbright Scholar.

Esra Memili is Associate Professor of Entrepreneurship with Tenure and Margaret Van Hoy Hill Dean's Notable Scholar at the Bryan School of Business and Economics University of North Carolina, Greensboro, USA.

Families in Business

The Next Generation of Family Evolution

Edited by
Kathleen Randerson, Hermann Frank, Clay Dibrell and Esra Memili

Routledge
Taylor & Francis Group
LONDON AND NEW YORK

First published 2023
by Routledge
4 Park Square, Milton Park, Abingdon, Oxon OX14 4RN

and by Routledge
605 Third Avenue, New York, NY 10158

Routledge is an imprint of the Taylor & Francis Group, an informa business

British Library Cataloguing in Publication Data
A catalogue record for this book is available from the British Library

ISBN13: 978-1-032-37989-0 (hbk)
ISBN13: 978-1-032-37990-6 (pbk)
ISBN13: 978-1-003-34294-6 (ebk)

DOI: 10.4324/9781003342946

Typeset in Myriad Pro
by Newgen Publishing UK

Publisher's Note
The publisher accepts responsibility for any inconsistencies that may have arisen during the conversion of this book from journal articles to book chapters, namely the inclusion of journal terminology.

Contents

Citation Information

The chapters in this book were originally published in the journal *Entrepreneurship & Regional Development*, volume 33, issue 5–6 (2021). When citing this material, please use the original page numbering for each article, as follows:

Chapter 1

From family to families: pushing family entrepreneurship forward
Kathleen Randerson, Hermann Frank, Clay Dibrell and Esra Memili
Entrepreneurship & Regional Development, volume 33, issue 5–6 (2021), pp. 369–382

Chapter 2

The balance that sustains benedictines: family entrepreneurship across generations
Sheila K. Hanson and Ksenia Keplinger
Entrepreneurship & Regional Development, volume 33, issue 5–6 (2021), pp. 442–456

Chapter 3

Understanding entrepreneurial opportunities through metaphors: a narrative approach to theorizing family entrepreneurship
Allan Discua Cruz, Eleanor Hamilton and Sarah L. Jack
Entrepreneurship & Regional Development, volume 33, issue 5–6 (2021), pp. 405–426

Chapter 4

Structural coupling in entrepreneurial families: how business-related resources contribute to enterpriseness
Mariana Estrada-Robles, Nick Williams and Tim Vorley
Entrepreneurship & Regional Development, volume 33, issue 5–6 (2021), pp. 457–474

Chapter 5

Entrepreneurial learning: the transmitting and embedding of entrepreneurial behaviours within the transgenerational entrepreneurial family
Eric Clinton, Maura McAdam, Jordan Robert Gamble and Martina Brophy
Entrepreneurship & Regional Development, volume 33, issue 5–6 (2021), pp. 383–404

Chapter 6

Transgenerational entrepreneurship in entrepreneurial families: what is explicitly learned and what is successfully transferred?

Junsheng Dou, Emma Su, Shengxiao Li and Daniel T. Holt

Entrepreneurship & Regional Development, volume 33, issue 5–6 (2021), pp. 427–441

Notes on Contributors

Martina Brophy, DCU Business School, Dublin City University, Dublin, Ireland.

Eric Clinton, DCU Business School, Dublin City University, Dublin, Ireland.

Allan Discua Cruz, Department of Entrepreneurship and Strategy, Lancaster University Management School, Lancaster, UK.

Clay Dibrell, Center for Innovation and Entrepreneurship, The University of Mississippi, USA.

Junsheng Dou, School of Management, Zhejiang University, Hangzhou, China.

Mariana Estrada-Robles, Centre for Enterprise and Entrepreneurship Studies, University of Leeds, Leeds, UK.

Hermann Frank, WU Vienna University of Economics and Business, Austria.

Jordan Robert Gamble, Institute of Cultural and Creative Industry, Shanghai Jiao Tong University, Shanghai, People's Republic of China.

Eleanor Hamilton, Department of Entrepreneurship, Strategy, and Innovation, Lancaster University Management School, Lancaster, UK.

Sheila K. Hanson, Nistler College of Business, University of North Dakota, Grand Forks, USA.

Daniel T. Holt, Stephenson Department of Entrepreneurship & Information Systems, Louisiana State University, Baton Rouge, USA.

Sarah L. Jack, Jacob and Marcus Wallenberg Centre for Innovative and Sustainable Business Development, House of Innovation, Stockholm School of Economics, Stockholm, Sweden.

Ksenia Keplinger, Max Planck Institute for Intelligent Systems, Stuttgart, Germany.

Shengxiao Li, College of Business and Management, Shaoxing University, Shaoxing, China.

Esra Memili, Bryan School of Business and Economics, University of North Carolina – Greensboro, Greensboro, USA.

Maura McAdam, DCU Business School, Dublin City University, Dublin, Ireland.

Kathleen Randerson, Entrepreneurship, Strategy and Innovation Department, Business & Society, Audencia Business School, Nantes, France.

Emma Su, Department of Management & Marketing, University of Dayton, Dayton, USA.

Tim Vorley, Centre for Regional Economic and Enterprise Development, University of Sheffield, Sheffield, UK.

Nick Williams, Centre for Enterprise and Entrepreneurship Studies, University of Leeds, Leeds, UK.

From family to families: pushing family entrepreneurship forward

Kathleen Randerson, Hermann Frank, Clay Dibrell and Esra Memili

ABSTRACT

The present guest editorial offers a review of the different conceptualizations of families in business used in research to date, shedding light on the unique characteristics of each type. Understanding the family through the lens of social systems theory offers a means for researchers to study contextually embedded family systems, offering a foundation for studying differences among families. We demonstrate that the family business system (ownership, business, family) is incomplete without a fourth component, that of the family in business. We then present the papers included in this special issue and highlight the collective contribution to research in the fields of family business and family entrepreneurship and provide directions for future research.

Introduction

The field of *family entrepreneurship*, at the intersection of family, family business and entrepreneurship (Randerson et al. 2015), was conceptualized to be able to better grasp the phenomenon of entrepreneurial behaviours of individuals, families and family businesses,[1] and their reciprocal influences (Bettinelli, Fayolle, and Randerson 2014).

Conceptualizing and developing the field of *family entrepreneurship* is critical since the field of *family business* delineates family firms from non-family firms by considering factors of ownership and/or control, participation in management of the firm, and/or the intention to pass on the business to the next generation (Chua, Chrisman, and Sharma 1999; Litz 2008). The latter approach does not fully capture behaviours and/or resources extending beyond the boundary of the firm to include, for example, other members of the family, which may not be formally involved in the firm (Anderson, Jack, and Dodd 2005), whereas these individuals are often key to the development of the firm or to supporting family members who are directly engaged in the business.

Research efforts directed towards defining the family firm built the foundation for the field of family business and contributed to developing and understanding of what differentiates family firms from non-family firms as well as differences among family firms, the heterogeneity of this form of enterprise (Memili and Dibrell 2019). With vanguard research shedding light on the differences among family firms through the epistemological categories of family governance, non-financial and financial dynamics, organizational behaviour and human resource management and strategies, these authors point out that the field of family business has become a 'meta-field' (Dibrell and Memili 2019, 9), scrutinizing the family firm through lenses usually applied to non-family firms, to better understand the differences among family firms. How differences among families contribute to differences among family firms is addressed, for example, relative to family values (Seaman, Bent, and Silva 2019), commitment (Pongelli, Sciascia, and Minola 2019) and power (Su, Holt, and Pollack 2019).

How the family influences the firm is a second key research question for family business scholars, and has led to the development of 'familiness' being a differentiating factor between family firms from non-family firms (Frank et al. 2010b; Pearson, Carr, and Shaw 2008; Frank et al. 2017). Mirroring this construct, other researchers point to the importance of the business family as a specific social system, distinct from those of the family and the family business, and how the 'enterpriseness' of this entity can influence the other two social systems (Frank et al. 2019).

The purpose of this special issue is to expand research dedicated to the *family* component, and to advance both *family entrepreneurship* and *family business* scholarship. As management scholars, it may seem incongruous to research families (rather than businesses), but this is important for several reasons.

Differences among families can create meaningful differences among family businesses, about which we know relatively little (Randerson et al. 2015). Extant family business research that considers the family as ubiquitous, a basic dependent variable leading to many different independent variables affecting the family business, has long been identified as hindering a better understanding of family businesses (Yu et al. 2012). Differences among institutional contexts (Randerson et al. 2020) such as systems of law (Barrédy 2016) create differences in family composition, and rights and duties of family members. Another reason to focus research on families is to better understand how informal participation of family members in entrepreneurial activities of the family firm or ventures of other family members influences the process and/or outcomes of these initiatives (Anderson, Jack, and Dodd 2005). For example, although it is well known that the family (under any form) is an individual's primary resource when starting a business (Zahra and Sharma 2004), we have a paucity of knowledge concerning the role and impact of family in effectual entrepreneurial processes (Jones and Li 2017; Sarasvathy, Ali, and Block 2016).

Our guest editorial is structured as follows. We first present the transition from family business to family, by reviewing the different forms of families in business in extant research. We then present different theoretical approaches to explain this evolution, offering a basis for family heterogeneity. We then present the articles featured in this special issue, highlight their collective contribution to the literature, and end with a brief conclusion.

From family business to family in business[2]

To study the family in business, extant research has developed a multitude of concepts: the transgenerational entrepreneurial family, family entrepreneurial teams, entrepreneurial households, business families, and entrepreneurial families.

Transgenerational entrepreneurial families

The Successful Transgenerational Entrepreneurship Project (STEP) was initiated to study the transmission of entrepreneurial behaviours from one generation to the next (Habbershon, Nordqvist, and Zellweger 2010). Although Habbershon et al. (2010, 1) define transgenerational entrepreneurship as 'the processes through which a family uses and develops entrepreneurial mindsets and family-influenced resources and capabilities to create new streams of entrepreneurial, financial and social value across generations', it is only later that Zellweger, Nason, and Nordqvist (2012) shift to the family as a level of analysis conceptualizing the 'transgenerational entrepreneurial family (TEF)'.

According to these authors, the consequence of this shift from studying the evolution of the family firm as a single entity and intra-family succession to that of "change, growth, and the creation of the new induced by the controlling families » (Zellweger et al., 140), is threefold. First, it facilitates a better understanding of family firm portfolios rather than focusing on a single firm, usually the first founded, of the family. Second, it challenges structurally and temporally the definition of « family business », encouraging future research to re-examine the concepts of « success » and « failure », in particular, relative to entrepreneurial exit. Despite the vital step towards a focus on family, (Zellweger et al. 141) underscore the limitations of their suggested approach, consisting in particular of capturing the challenges of family unity and cohesion, and adopting wealth accrual as indicator of success.

In conclusion, the main merit of this approach is its shift from transgenerational family firms to transgenerational families with multiple entrepreneurial activities. The caveats include basing the boundary of TEFs on the criteria of ownership in the diverse entrepreneurial activities without indicating *who*, and considering these owning families as homogeneous. For example, these authors (Zellweger et al. 142) 'treat a family as a unitary actor and a collective subject given the unifying forces at play, such as social norms for harmony and mutual support not to mention the factual inability to leave one's family'. Whereas we know that institutional forces for example, create differences among families, including the ability, or inability, to leave one's family (Barrédy 2016).

Family entrepreneurial teams

In their study of intra-family entrepreneurship in Honduras, Discua Cruz, Howorth, and Hamilton (2013, 20) define family entrepreneurial teams (FETs) as « two or more family members, related by kinship or marriage, who engage in the identification and pursuit of business opportunities to establish or purchase a firm, have an equity stake in the firm, and have a direct influence on the strategic choice of the firm at the time of founding ». Discua Cruz, Howorth, and Hamilton (2013) note that FETs are more likely to be formed when senior generation family members are not ready to exit the family business, and simultaneously members of the junior generation aspire to pursue their own entrepreneurial endeavours outside of the (core) family business. They find that membership in a FET is based on trust and values, rather than resources and competencies. In addition, based on the two-tiered structure resulting from senior and junior generation, FETs practice a stewardship culture focused on the (nuclear) family and its assets. Results indicate that other family members (including spouses of the junior generation) in other careers also perceived themselves as stewards of the family assets.

The FET as unit of analysis is very useful to better understand family portfolio entrepreneurship based on ownership by identified family members. Indeed, the trigger of FET formation and activity mentioned above is expected to be more and more frequent as the demographic factors such as ageing population and receding retirement age become pervasive. Further, a map of the different entrepreneurial initiatives within a family, opening the possibility of different configurations, for example, FETs among same generation siblings or cousins or FETs to the benefit of extended or blended families, can be created.

Entrepreneurial households

Alsos, Carter, and Ljunggren (2014) take the household as level of analysis to understand how and why some small businesses end up as business portfolio clusters. They note that the household is the central link between the different businesses and the entrepreneurs, providing both pools of opportunities and resources.

Using the household as unit of analysis allows including changes in the composition of the family group, due for example to the evolution in the life cycle of the family (children ageing and ultimately potentially leaving the household, adult children coming back to the household with their partners, divorce of parents or adult children). Thus, structural and temporal changes can be included and lead to a better understanding of how these changes affect entrepreneurial behaviours of the members sharing the household, impacting opportunity identification, evaluation and exploitation. Entrepreneurship can also be a mechanism of integration/inclusion in the family. This paper shows how the household encourages its members (here, the spouse of one of the children) to benefit from the household and to undertake entrepreneurial activities to address their individual needs (here, an autonomous activity to acquire rights for a later pension), while meshing the initiative within the constellation of activities of the household.

The authors of this paper highlight how new business activities are started in response to spare resources, for example additional time as the children become more autonomous, the arrival of newcomers with their idiosyncratic competencies, or the return of adult children who developed competencies while they were away from the household. These authors omit, however, to insist on the role that the household plays to absorb the shocks incurred in family composition, through entrepreneurial behaviours. They also under-emphasize how being active in the entrepreneurial household is also a mechanism of inclusion into the family.

Business families: enterpriseness perspective

According to Stamm (2013) a business family is a family that owns one or more businesses and derives income via its businesses, where the business family's life is characterized by the influence of the businesses owned and in many cases also managed and/or controlled. This definition includes quantifiable elements (ownership and income) and also an important relational component: the influence that the business has on the family, that Frank et al. (2019, 264) coin as « enterpriseness » that they define as "those structures that the business family develops based on the structural coupling with its business (or businesses) and the family ». These structures influence the family's decision-making because they represent business- and family-related expectations that are effective in the business family.

Frank et al. (2019) conceptualize enterpriseness and its sub-dimensions: involvement, essence and identity. Involvement relates to the inclusion within the business family and thus to questions such as size and diversity of members in terms of age, education, etc. Essence relates to which business-related decisions should be taken within the business family (rather than in the business together with non-family employees) and here family governance mechanisms can provide structures and decision-making processes, including those relative to formalizing the considerations according to which membership decisions (inclusion, exclusion) are based. Identity refers to the answer to the question 'who are we as a business family?'. These authors underscore that business families may not perceive themselves as such (owning multiple businesses is sufficient to categorize such families as business families), but awareness comes with the will to transmit the business(es) to the next generation.

This multi-dimensional construct is useful to understand the dynamics between the enterpriseness of the business family and the familiness of the family business(es). The concept also supports understanding of differences among business families, because each dimension can be tailored to the specific (family and business) context.

Business families: cultural perspective

Xiong, Ukanwa, and Anderson (2020) adopt as a unit of analysis the business family, which they define as a socio-economic unit of both production and consumption, a micro entrepreneurial unit. The members of these women-led entities practice entrepreneurship mainly in the informal economy to maintain daily subsistence of the group and provide means to send the children for education on short and longer-term basis. The micro-entrepreneurial unit is thus the resource for the woman entrepreneur either explicitly (labour of children, raw materials or financial resources from the husband's entrepreneurial activity) or implicitly (the husband's entrepreneurial activity offering synergies with that of the woman.) It is also the source of the impetus of entrepreneurial behaviour of the women, who are expected to generate the income necessary to raise and educate the children in a context with weak (or even absent) formal institutions; informal institutions arise to take on the role.

The business family as defined in this article can be differentiated from the entrepreneurial household above in that the business family practices entrepreneurship *because it needs to* in order for the members to survive and hopefully to go on to have a better future; members leave the business as soon as a better future is possible for them. On the contrary, entrepreneurial households and the members that compose them choose to practice entrepreneurship, entrepreneurial initiatives are sources of diversification and growth, and the members of the business family do not plan on leaving the entrepreneurial household or its constituents: the family and the business.

Taking the business family, micro-entrepreneurial unit of analysis shifts focus to how these families and their members are simultaneously producers and consumers of entrepreneurial resources, transmitters and receptors of entrepreneurial mentoring, leading them to be both conducive and restrictive to entrepreneurial behaviours embedded in the cultural context. It is perhaps in this context, where the family and entrepreneurial systems overlap perfectly, that the paradoxes that pervade family businesses are exacerbated.

Entrepreneurial families

Estrada-Robles, Williams, and Vorley (2021) study the entrepreneurial family that they define as 'a collective of individuals within a socially constructed family that operates separate ventures outside of a team structure rather than creating or generating firms together'. This collective includes individuals who do not share households with enduring relationships. The inherent social capital helps to mobilize financial and non-financial capital, enables access to external networks and foster information and knowledge exchange. Compared to individual entrepreneurs, the social capital of these wider entrepreneurial families provides them with different advantages which are especially beneficial in weak institutional contexts.

Entrepreneurial families as a collective of individuals within a socially constructed family can also operate only a single business and use the family system for the development of new products, services and processes (Frank, Güttel, and Weismeier-Sammer 2010). The business family system is used as an 'incubator' for radical innovations. The development process takes place in a protected familial context. This context offers the opportunity to develop and explore new knowledge without being exposed to an immediate pressure to succeed. In order to avoid the potential conflict of the exploration and exploitation modes, the business family system can be defined as the main innovation system and cultivates an entrepreneurial posture and identity. This approach works well in many family SMEs where the business family is still actively involved in the daily business.

The works presented reveal an interesting diversity in terms of putting more emphasis on familial structures, processes and behaviours. Yet, this line of research requires more fundamental considerations. Indeed, we see that criteria of inclusion to these families actually often relate to the family business in terms of ownership and/or management, for example. A key element that can contribute to explaining this paucity of research dedicated to differences among families can relate to definitional issues, such as what is 'family'?

Family, families

The call for more research on family is definitely not new (e.g. Combs et al. 2019; Nordqvist and Melin 2010; Yu et al. 2012; James, Jennings, and Breitkreuz 2012; Zachary 2011), yet published research showcasing different families and conceptions of family is sparse (the comparison between developed and emerging economies by Jennings et al. (2015), can be seen as a noteworthy exception). Much extant family business research, as noted previously, adopts a universal 'family' variable to understand how family affects the business. This contributes to perpetuating the underlying assumption that all families are the same, often equated to a model of family, the 'nuclear family' (i.e. a married couple and their dependent children sharing a household). This is a narrow view of the diversity of families as social units, respectively, systems, varying across cultures and over time (Aldrich and Cliff 2003; Randerson and Dossena 2016; Jaskiewicz and Dyer 2017). In most industrialized countries, the nuclear family has become a minority among other forms of families: married couples (e.g. who had been previously married to other spouses) with children, couples who are married and have no children, cohabitating partners with and without children, and extended families, including grandparents. Single-parent families, same-sex partnerships, foster families and other legal guardianships as well as adults linked by biological children are also forms of family, greatly understudied. Once seen as a stable institution, the family can now be seen as a dynamic social system incorporating organizational characteristics (Montgomery 2008; Nordqvist and Melin 2010) expressing the 'enterpriseness' of business families (Frank et al. 2019).

Institutions create differences in family composition, and rights and duties of family members (Aldrich and Cliff 2003; Randerson et al. 2020). Conceptions of family unit are influenced by religion (Thornton 1985; Xiong, Ukanwa, and Anderson 2020), legal system (Barrédy 2016), and culture, for example (Randerson et al. 2020). Different cultures embrace different references of family. In China, for example, the unit of reference for family is not the nuclear family, but the stem family: married children, their spouses and children live with their parents/grandparents; children are today at the same level as those married before the communist takeover in 1949 (Forrest Zhang 2004). In other cultures such as in East Africa (Khavul, Bruton, and Wood 2009), families comprise multiple earners, multiple generations, a large number of dependent children, sometimes sharing one household and in others with distinct households organized around each wife/mother. In the latter cases, family and community ties are strong (Murithi, Vershinina, and Rodgers 2020).

More fundamentally and theory-driven, there are currently two approaches to family: the structural view and the transactional view. Most extant research is embedded in the structural view of the family (Koerner and Fitzpatrick 2004) meaning that biological and legal ties (e.g. filiation, marriage, legal partnerships) bind together a family group constitutes the foundational assumption (Brannon, Wiklund, and Haynie 2013, 108). In the transactional view, the family is defined as 'a group of intimates who generate a sense of home and group identity, and who experience a shared history and a shared future' (Koerner and Fitzpatrick 2004, 71). It is important to note that in the transactional view, the boundaries of 'family' are socially constructed, varying over cultures, generations and ideology (Koerner and Fitzpatrick 2002).

The theory of social systems (Luhmann 1995) and its application for family business (Von Schlippe and Frank 2013) is based on a constructivist point of view. The basic elements of social systems according to this theory are acts of communication. Families as social systems are based on attachment communication, businesses are based on decision communication. The family in business has to process both logics and the challenges associated with the handling of both logics (paradox management). These systems are structurally coupled (via persons) and provide an influential context for each other in the sense of stimulating a joint co-evolution, although each of the systems processes stimuli and irritations from the different environments according to its own structure.

Who is considered as a member of each of the systems is a decision based on the rules of each of these systems. Membership rules in the family are usually based on biological and legal ties, whereas membership rules in the family in business and the family business often use ownership and management roles as criteria for membership, but can also be based on other (additional) criteria such as sharing certain values or providing certain competences that are considered as useful. Especially membership in the family in business system can apply criteria offering access to financial resources, conflict resolution competencies or an outstanding reputation in public that creates access to networks.

The papers included in this Special Issue show different approaches in regards to how to become a member and how to become influential in each of these systems.

Presentation of the articles in this special issue

This special issue offers a curated ensemble of articles that have been chosen for their individual quality and novelty. We have summarized each of the articles below and encourage readers to refer to the full articles to review the details of each study.

Understanding entrepreneurial opportunities through metaphors: a narrative approach to theorizing family entrepreneurship

The paper by Discua Cruz, Hamilton and Jack (2021), is based on a longitudinal study of four enterprising families in Honduras. Here, focus is not on defining the enterprising family, but on how families, as autopoietic, operatively closed social systems are created and maintained through communication, more specifically narratives. These authors focus on how families develop and use metaphors, as artefacts, as vehicles to establish and perpetuate the entrepreneurial legacy of the family. The key findings of this study are threefold.

First, metaphors are one of the language devices that contribute to creating boundaries of the enterprising family, creating and maintaining intra- and intergenerational cohesion and linking past, present and future interactions of the family. Only the members of the family who actually participated in the physical activities that the metaphor represented were 'insiders' – fully comprehended the metaphor and the associated heuristics.

Second, metaphors contribute to the creation of entrepreneurial opportunities, the latter 'are socially constructed through language and shared entrepreneurial family stories'. Metaphors effectively support the transmission and subsequent development of heuristics, acting as 'as basic yet powerful shared constructs for organizing knowledge of the world by relating phenomena (e.g. entrepreneurial opportunities) to something previously experienced and concrete'.

Third, metaphors are tools for entrepreneurial learning, artefacts supporting the creation, transmission and acquisition of elements of the entrepreneurial legacy of the family, and this entrepreneurial learning can profit to members of the family business as well as to members of the family in business venturing out on their own.

Structural coupling in entrepreneurial families: how business-related resources contribute to enterpriseness

The paper by Estrada-Robles, Williams, and Vorley (2021) extends the construct of 'enterpriseness'. In their study of entrepreneurial families (as defined in their previous research mentioned above), the authors go beyond the theoretical development of the components of this construct (involvement, essence and identity), and the suggested consequences of enterpriseness on both the family and the family business, to offer unique empirical insights on several respects.

First, through their qualitative study of 14 entrepreneurial families, the authors set forth constitutive elements of enterpriseness. Indeed, they find that the entrepreneurial families build and share pools of resources that they share with other members of the entrepreneurial family: human capital, social capital and financial capital. There is a longstanding literature that develops how a family brings such resources to the family business. The unique contribution of this paper is to show empirically that members of entrepreneurial families actively create such pools of resources to be shared among the members of the entrepreneurial family. The added value of this paper, relative to the longstanding literature mentioned above, is to shed light on how younger generation family members can contribute such resources to the group, including to previous generations. Other important aspects relate to considering both the formal and informal activities of the members in constituting and sharing these resources, as well as to the cooperation and independence of family members whose activities can be complimentary to those of other family members.

A second important contribution of this work is to show that entrepreneurial families have specific capabilities, specifically *how* such resources are shared brought to the family, and how they are subsequently used by members of the family for their respective businesses. This is an important first step for further research to develop the constitutive elements of enterpriseness. Indeed, this study, based in Mexico, shows how entrepreneurial families create and share pools of resources in order to mitigate risks inherent to the context of institutional voids by offering access to alternative (family) sources of human resources (labour), social capital resources (connexions) and financial resources (capital), and *how* members of the family use them. Finally, this paper shows the influence of using such resources both on the venture (growth, for example) and on the family member (expectation to stay in business to in turn grow the pool of resources).

Transgenerational entrepreneurship in business families: what is effectively learned and what is successfully transferred

Dou, Su, Li and Holt (2021) examine six dyads of first and second generation of business family members in the region of Shaoxing (Zhejiang province of China). The authors aim to better understand what knowledge is successfully transferred by the first generation and effectively learned by the second generation through the 'strategic teaching' by the first generation, including role modelling by the incumbent, and also purposefully organizing other sources of knowledge such as higher education. The main contributions of this study are twofold.

First, the second generation learns values, both moral values and competence values. Moral values include facets such as principles, to the relative importance of being a 'good person' rather than a 'successful businessperson'. Other moral values acquired concern the importance and means of sustaining interpersonal relationships such as loyalty, valuing friendship and sacrificing for friends. The authors point out that these moral values (and their relative importance) stem from Confucian principles, by which the Chinese culture is greatly influenced. Competence values identified in this study include resilience and persistency, positive thinking in face of difficulties or uncertainties, imagination, ambition and social responsibility.

Second, the new generation learns heuristics from parents; parents built these heuristics by creating their own firms after 1970 time of the transition of China' economy to accept individual initiative and private enterprise. Such heuristics concern interpersonal relationships (contract negotiation, handling customer complaints, opportunity recognition and pursuit). It is these cognitive heuristics that are actually transferred to new entrepreneurial settings, applied to practical management activities, while the values presented above were more important in the evaluation and pursuit of new entrepreneurial activities.

This paper offers important insights to understand business families in the context of China. Indeed, the findings can be linked to the cultural variables such as long-term orientation and collectivism (Hofstede 2001), as well as the characteristics such as 'face' and 'guangxi' (Jennings et al. 2015), and serve as the basis for future research integrating cultural influences of entrepreneurial archetypes.

Entrepreneurial learning: the transmitting and embedding of entrepreneurial behaviours within the transgenerational entrepreneurial family

The paper by Clinton, McAdam, Brophy and Gamble based on STEP data collected in Ireland, builds our understanding of the transgenerational entrepreneurial family (TEF). Through the longitudinal study of four Irish TEFs, the authors are able to shed light on an important aspect of (entrepreneurial) learning until now overlooked: the role of *unlearning*. The analysis of a uniquely rich data set allows the authors to identify precise critical incidents affecting the TEF and how members of the TEF actually reacted to such incidents. They show in detail that the entrepreneurial behaviours in TEFs are bi-directional and co-participative and that in order to learn, the TEF must un-learn by overtly questioning previous practices and adopting evolutions in technology and ways of working for example. This 'un-learning paradox' takes place on the individual, generational, firm and TEF levels.

The theoretical contributions of this work are first to shed light on how collective (entrepreneurial) learning actually takes place in TEFs, specifically with the intention of transmitting entrepreneurial behaviours between generations. A second contribution is their empirical support to show that, and more importantly *how*, the transfer of entrepreneurial behaviours in a TEF is represented by a bi-directional, co-participative and multi-generational learning process. Finally, this paper shows that TEFs are more flexible than previously understood relative to their strategic use of unlearning and unorthodox approaches to regeneration.

While each of these contributions is important in its own, taken collectively, this paper questions and provides insights related to the evolution of the entrepreneurial legacy over time. Indeed, although there is a longstanding literature about the importance of an entrepreneurial legacy for a TEF, and the sources of such legacies, how this legacy evolves over time is still under-explored. The paper by Clinton et al. initiates this much-needed scholarly discussion.

'The balance that sustains Benedictines: Family entrepreneurship across generations' by Hanson and Keplinger (2021), offers a novel perspective of family entrepreneurship, taking the Benedictines as a family unit to demonstrate how entrepreneurial behaviours are enacted and shared among members of such family. In this conceptual piece, the authors answer the question 'What factors influence development and maintenance of resiliency of individuals, family, and family business across generations?'. They conceptualize how values and behavioural guidelines communicated through the Rule of Saint Benedict (RSB, a code of ethics) influence on three levels: 1) the resiliency of family businesses across generations through the development of long-term orientation (LTO), 2) the resiliency of families through maintenance of a balanced family type, and 3) the resiliency of family business members through individual work-nonwork balance. These three elements are constitutive of the multi-level construct of *family entrepreneurial resiliency*.

By investigating the (unusual) context and unprecedented longevity of monastic businesses, these offer a new perspective on family entrepreneurship. Indeed, this novel context is boundary spanning in several aspects.

To our knowledge, this is the first research to study a group of individuals, very distant from how the family has been predominantly defined until now, and show that despite this perceived distance many characteristics of families in business and family business are present in this context. For example, the role played by the RSB in federating family members around values and regulating their behaviour is simply an 'exotic' example of similar mechanisms and effects of family and business governance mechanisms. By showing how these rules build capacities at the individual, family and firm levels these authors pave the path for future research on how different governance mechanisms (family retreats, family constitutions, business codes of ethics) can support the development of such capacities in other types of families and family businesses. We earnestly hope that this will encourage research on alternative acceptations of family, more and more prevalent in societies today.

This paper also opens many interesting avenues for future research, one of which is to understand how families as socially constructed groups are sustained across generations (i.e. how they attract and integrated new members over time).

The collective contribution of this special issue

With the papers featured in this special issue and the present introductory article, we offer several contributions.

Criteria of inclusion in the family in business

Building on previous research dedicated to the transactional view of the family (Koerner and Fitzpatrick 2004, 71), seen as a socially constructed group or system, this special issue offers special insights relative to the criteria of inclusion and exclusion to the family in business group.

Although there is a consensus and a large body of research dedicated to showing how family values influence the firm, the papers included in this special issue are the first, to our knowledge, that show how shared values can actually constitute *criteria of inclusion in the family*: entrepreneurial values (Estrada-Robles, Williams, and Vorley 2021) or spiritual values (Hanson and Keplinger 2021). Dou et al. (2020) find that values, rather than competencies, are effectively transmitted from the first to second generation family member in the context of China: would the non-acquisition of these values be a source of exclusion?

Finally, Discua Cruz et al. (2021) show that, and how, shared experiences and associated metaphors delineate the boundary of an entrepreneurial family and serve as artefacts to share and transmit entrepreneurial heuristics. It is important to underscore two points. First, only the members present to these experiences are considered as members of the entrepreneurial family. Second, these metaphors are the embryo of the family's entrepreneurial legacy. The paper by Clinton et al. (2021) offers insights on how entrepreneurial legacies are challenged and subsequently over time through unlearning, but does and how could this affect inclusion or exclusion to the TEF?

Mechanisms of socialization, transmission of competencies and entrepreneurial heuristics

Hanson and Keplinger (2021) show how the RSB, a code of ethics, guides members towards expected behaviours and structures relations in the social system. They also indicate that the families' goals is the sustainability of the community: social value creation before short-term profitability. The transmission of values foundational to long-term business relationships (which can be at the detriment of short-term profits) are also at the heart of mentoring relationships in the Dou et al. (2021) paper.

Entrepreneurial heuristics are at the heart of the paper by Discua Cruz et al. (2021), and count among the resource pool shared by entrepreneurial families in the Robles et al. (2020) paper. The first give a fine-grained understanding of how participation to and the metaphor of the event cement entrepreneurial heuristics in the members, heuristics which can then be used in other contexts. The latter unveil the capability of bringing resources to, and the sharing of the resources by the entrepreneurial family. This capability is developed at the level of the enterprising family and includes the transmission of tacit knowledge.

Finally, the paper by Clinton et al. (2021) challenges the extant literature dedicated to entrepreneurial legacies by introducing and proving the importance of unlearning. The consequence of this unlearning is to update entrepreneurial competencies (and as a consequence the legacy). In the cases studied in this paper, unlearning was the family's reaction to critical incidents. This paper leads to the following question: under what conditions, through which processes, and what would be the outcomes of proactively managing a family's entrepreneurial legacy?

Different systems and managing multiple identities

A conundrum shared by family business and family entrepreneurship research is the multiplication of more or less different social systems and associated identities. The famous 'three circles model' by Tagiuri and Davis (1996) and Gersick et al. (1997) and foundational to family business research, positioned this field as the overlap of the family, business and ownership systems. Our review of families in business above sheds light on an additional system to consider. In each of the conceptualizations, the family system (as primary social group, usually not defined) is differentiated from the family in business system (each conceptualization associated with a specific definition).

Frank et al. (2019) raise the question of managing different systems and balancing different expectations constituting each of the systems: the family, the family in business and the family business system with the family in business system as system that has to manage cognitive and normative expectations from both the family and the business system as well as its own 'rules of the game'. The business family system may develop its own identity. Family governance measures (e.g.

Suess-Reyes 2014) like family constitutions turn out to be helpful in this respect, because they stimulate reflection and the making of self-descriptions of what a system stands for.

Through the literature discussed and the papers in this Special Issue of *Entrepreneurship and Regional Development,* it is evident that, based on the different systems involved and the heterogeneity observed, a theory of great reach that is capable of dealing with the different logics (Von Schlippe and Frank 2013) inherent in each of the systems is especially useful. Applying different theories for different systems (and their identities) are subject to the risk that different units of analysis and different assumptions underlying each of the theories (e.g. in-house assumptions that exist within a specific school of thought or paradigmatic assumptions like ontological, epistemological and methodological assumptions; see Alvesson and Sandberg 2011; Hasenzagl, Hatak, and Frank 2018) hinder a cumulative progress of knowledge on families in business. Therefore, the combination of different theories requires a reflection on how they fit on different levels of assumptions and if they are coherent on these levels at all.

Conclusion

This special issue develops new knowledge relative to families in business: criteria of inclusion/exclusion, artefacts for socializing members and for sharing and transmitting values, competencies and entrepreneurial heuristics. We illustrate that there are at least four systems (business, ownership, family and family business), more or less overlapping and structurally coupled. Indeed, the present guest editorial demonstrates that the family system and the family in business system are distinct, structurally coupled systems. Each of these four systems brings their members to adopt different identities proper to each system; the literature dedicated to paradoxes in family businesses can thus be extended and enriched to include, along with the family, business and ownership, paradoxes in families in business.

The papers featured in this special issue show how, in order to capture how family influences entrepreneurship, researchers need to design ways to capture the micro foundations of each level as well as what happens between levels.

Our review of the different conceptualizations of families in business can help structure a potentially cumulative body of knowledge. This multiplicity of conceptualizations is not per se a hindrance to the constitution of a cumulative body of knowledge, but rather a first step. Indeed, multiplicity allows for a contextually embedded fine-grained understanding of the phenomenon; in later steps, researchers can identify (eventually) recurring patterns among these different families and how they do entrepreneurship as well as develop understandings of differences among families and how they do entrepreneurship.

One of the initial aims was also to further knowledge on alternative forms of family, the latter understood as primary social system. Same-sex partnerships or marriages, blended families, couples who are married and have no children, cohabitating partners with and without children, extended families (including grandparents and/or siblings, their spouses and eventually children), single-parent families, foster families and other legal guardianships as well as adults linked by biological children are all modern forms of family. We encourage scholars to consider and to study how these different configurations of family affect the behaviours of their members, as well as the dynamics and competitiveness of their firms.

Notes

1. The field of family entrepreneurship thus aims to include and build upon the body of knowledge generated by the field of family business and by family business scholars.
2. We use the term « family in business » as a generic umbrella to include the different conceptualizations while avoiding confusion among them.

Disclosure statement

No potential conflict of interest was reported by the authors.

References

Aldrich, H. E., and J. E. Cliff. 2003. "The Pervasive Effects of Family on Entrepreneurship: Toward a Family Embeddedness Perspective." *Journal of Business Venturing* 18 (5): 573–596. doi:10.1016/S0883-9026(03)00011-9.

Alsos, G. A., S. Carter, and E. Ljunggren. 2014. "Kinship and Business: How Entrepreneurial Households Facilitate Business Growth." *Entrepreneurship & Regional Development* 26 (1–2): 97–122. doi:10.1080/08985626.2013.870235.

Alvesson, M., and J. Sandberg. 2011. "Generating Research Questions through Problematization." *Academy of Management Review* 36 (2): 247–271.

Anderson, A., S. Jack, and S. D. Dodd. 2005. "The Role of Family Members in Entrepreneurial Networks: Beyond the Boundaries of the Family Firm." *Family Business Review* 18 (2): 135–154. doi:10.1111/j.1741-6248.2005.00037.x.

Barrédy, C. 2016. "In Search of Future Alternatives for Family Business: Family Law Contributions through Civil and Common Law Comparison." *Futures* 75 (1): 44–53. doi:10.1016/j.futures.2015.09.005.

Bettinelli, C., A. Fayolle, and K. Randerson. 2014. "Family Entrepreneurship: A Developing Field." *Foundations and Trends® in Entrepreneurship* 10 (3): 161–236. doi:10.1561/0300000049.

Brannon, D. L., J. Wiklund, and J. M. Haynie. 2013. "The Varying Effects of Family Relationships in Entrepreneurial Teams." *Entrepreneurship Theory and Practice* 37 (1): 107–132. doi:10.1111/etap.2013.37.issue-1.

Chua, J. H., J. J. Chrisman, and P. Sharma. 1999. "Defining the Family Business by Behavior." *Entrepreneurship Theory and Practice* 23 (4): 19–39. doi:10.1177/104225879902300402.

Clinton, E., McAdam, M., Brophy, X, and Gamble, J. 2020. "Entrepreneurial learning: The transmitting and embedding of entrepreneurial behaviours within the transgenerational entrepreneurial family." *Entrepreneurship & Regional Development* 33 (5-6): 383–404. https://doi.org/10.1080/08985626.2020.1727088

Combs, J. G., K. K. Shanine, S. Burrows, J. S. Allen, and T. W. Pounds. 2019. "What Do We Know about Business Families? Setting the Stage for Leveraging Family Science Theories." *Family Business Review*. doi:10.1177/0894486519863508.

Dibrell, C., and E. Memili. 2019. "A Brief History and A Look to the Future of Family Business Heterogeneity: An Introduction." In *The Palgrave Handbook of Heterogeneity among Family Firms*, edited by E. Memili and C. Dibrell, 1–15. Cham: Palgrave Macmillan.

Discua Cruz, A., C. Howorth, and E. Hamilton. 2013. "Intrafamily Entrepreneurship: The Formation and Membership of Family Entrepreneurial Teams." *Entrepreneurship Theory and Practice* 37 (1): 17–46. doi:10.1111/etap.2013.37.issue-1.

Discua Cruz, A., E. Hamilton, and S. Jack. 2021. "Understanding entrepreneurial opportunities through metaphors: A narrative approach to theorizing family entrepreneurship." *Entrepreneurship & Regional Development* 33 (5-6): 405–426. https://doi.org/10.1080/08985626.2020.1727089

Dou, J., E. Su, S. Li, and D. Holt. 2020. "Trangenerational entrepreneurship in business families: What is effectively learned and what is successfully transferred." *Entrepreneurship & Regional Development* 33 (5-6): 427–441. https://doi.org/10.1080/08985626.2020.1727090

Estrada-Robles, M., N. Williams, and T. Vorley. 2020. "Structural coupling in entrepreneurial families: how business-related resources contribute to enterpriseness." *Entrepreneurship & Regional Development* 33 (5-6): 457–474. doi:10.1108/IJEBR-05-2017-0180.

Forrest Zhang, Q. 2004. "Economic Transition and New Patterns of Parent-adult Child Coresidence in Urban China." *Journal of Marriage and Family* 66 (5): 1231–1245. doi:10.1111/jomf.2004.66.issue-5.

Frank, H., Güttel, W., and Weismeier-Sammer, D. 2010b. "Ambitexterity in Familienunternehmen." *Management for schung* 20: 183–222.

Frank, H., A. Kessler, T. Rusch, J. Suess-Reyes, and D. Weismeier-Sammer. 2017. "Capturing the Familiness of Family Businesses: Development of the Family Influence Familiness Scale (FIFS)." *Entrepreneurship Theory and Practice* 41 (5): 709–742. doi:10.1111/etap.2017.41.issue-5.

Frank, H., M. Lueger, L. Nosé, and D. Suchy. 2010a. "The Concept of "Familiness": Literature Review and Systems Theory based Reflections." *Journal of Family Business Strategy* 1 (3): 119–130. doi:10.1016/j.jfbs.2010.08.001.

Frank, H., J. Suess-Reyes, E. Fuetsch, and A. Kessler. 2019. "Introducing the Enterpriseness of Business Families: A Research Agenda." In *The Palgrave Handbook of Heterogeneity among Family Firms*, edited by E. Memili and C. Dibrell, 263–296. Cham: Palgrave Macmillan.

Gersick, K. E., K. E. Gersick, J. A. Davis, M. McCollom Hampton, and I. Lansberg. 1997. *Generation to Generation: Life Cycles of the Family Business*. Boston: Harvard Business Press.

Habbershon, T. G., M. Nordqvist, and T. Zellweger. 2010. "Transgenerational Entrepreneurship." In *Transgenerational Entrepreneurship: Exploring Growth and Performance in Family Firms across Generations*, edited by M. Nordqvist and T. Zellweger, 1–38. Cheltenham and Northampton: Edward Elgar Publishing.

Hanson, S. and Keplinger, K. 2020. "The balance that sustains Benedictines: Family entrepreneurship across generations." *Entrepreneurship & Regional Development* 33 (5-6): 442–456. https://doi.org/10.1080/08985626.2020.1727092

Hasenzagl, R., I. Hatak, and H. Frank. 2018. "Problematizing Socioemotional Wealth in Family Firms: A Systems-theoretical Refraiming." *Entrepreneurship & Regional Development* 30 (1–2): 199–223. doi:10.1080/08985626.2017.1401123.

Hofstede, G. 2001. *Culture's Consequences: Comparing Values, Behaviors, Institutions and Organizations across Nations.* Thousand Oaks: Sage publications.

James, A. E., J. E. Jennings, and R. S. Breitkreuz. 2012. "Worlds Apart? Rebridging the Distance between Family Science and Family Business Research." *Family Business Review* 25 (1): 87–108. doi:10.1177/0894486511414271.

Jaskiewicz, P., and W. G. Dyer. 2017. "Addressing the Elephant in the Room: Disentangling Family Heterogeneity to Advance Family Business Research." *Family Business Review* 30 (2): 111–118. doi:10.1177/0894486517700469.

Jennings, J. E., K. A. Eddleston, P. Devereaux Jennings, and R. Sarathy, Eds. 2015. *Firms within Families: Enterprising in Diverse Country Contexts.* Cheltenham and Northampton: Edward Elgar Publishing.

Jones, O., and H. Li. 2017. "Effectual Entrepreneuring: Sensemaking in a Family-based Start-up." *Entrepreneurship & Regional Development* 29 (5–6): 467–499. doi:10.1080/08985626.2017.1297854.

Khavul, S., G. D. Bruton, and E. Wood. 2009. "Informal Family Business in Africa." *Entrepreneurship Theory and Practice* 33 (6): 1219–1238. doi:10.1111/etap.2009.33.issue-6.

Koerner, A. F., and M. A. Fitzpatrick. 2002. "Toward a Theory of Family Communication." *Communication Theory* 12 (1): 70–91. doi:10.1111/comt.2002.12.issue-1.

Koerner, A. F., and M. A. Fitzpatrick. 2004. "Communication in Intact Families." In *Handbook of Family Communication,* edited by A. Vangelisti, 177–195. Mahwah, NJ: Lawrence Erlbaum.

Litz, R. A. 2008. "Two Sides of a One-sided Phenomenon: Conceptualizing the Family Business and Business Family as a Möbius Strip." *Family Business Review* 21 (3): 217–236. doi:10.1177/08944865080210030104.

Luhmann, N. 1995. *Social Systems.* Stanford: University Press.

Memili, E., and C. Dibrell, Eds. 2019. *The Palgrave Handbook of Heterogeneity among Family Firms.* Cham: Palgrave Macmillan.

Montgomery, A. 2008. "US Families 2025: In Search of Future Families." *Futures* 40 (4): 377–387. doi:10.1016/j.futures.2007.08.005.

Murithi, W., N. Vershinina, and P. Rodgers. 2020. "Where Less Is More: Institutional Voids and Business Families in Sub-Saharan Africa." *International Journal of Entrepreneurial Behavior & Research* 26 (1): 158–174. doi:10.1108/IJEBR-07-2017-0239.

Nordqvist, M., and L. Melin. 2010. "Entrepreneurial Families and Family Firms." *Entrepreneurship & Regional Development* 22 (3–4): 211–239. doi:10.1080/08985621003726119.

Pearson, A. W., J. C. Carr, and J. C. Shaw. 2008. "Toward A Theory of Familiness: A Social Capital Perspective." *Entrepreneurship Theory and Practice* 32 (6): 949–969. doi:10.1111/etap.2008.32.issue-6.

Pongelli, C., S. Sciascia, and T. Minola. 2019. "Do We Really Want to Cut Out the Deadwood? Family-Centered Noneconomic Goals, Restructuring Aversion, and Escalation of Commitment." In *The Palgrave Handbook of Heterogeneity among Family Firms,* edited by E. Memili and C. Dibrell, 485–505. Cham: Palgrave Macmillan.

Randerson, K., C. Bettinelli, A. Fayolle, and A. Anderson. 2015. "Family Entrepreneurship as a Field of Research: Exploring Its Contours and Contents." *Journal of Family Business Strategy* 6 (3): 143–154. doi:10.1016/j.jfbs.2015.08.002.

Randerson, K. G., and A. F. Dossena. 2016. "The Futures of Family Business: Family Entrepreneurship." *Futures* 75: 36–43. doi:10.1016/j.futures.2015.10.008.

Randerson, K., C. Seaman, J. J. Daspit, and C. Barrédy. 2020. "Institutional Influences on Entrepreneurial Behaviours in the Family Entrepreneurship Context: Towards an Integrative Framework." *International Journal of Entrepreneurial Behavior & Research* 26 (1): 1–13. doi:10.1108/IJEBR-01-2020-824.

Sarasvathy, S., I. Ali, and J. Block. 2016. "Partitioning Socioemotional Wealth to Stitch Together the Effectual Family Enterprise." In *Family Entrepreneurship: Rethinking the Research Agenda,* edited by K. Randerson, C. Bettinelli, G. Dossena, and A. Fayolle, 30–62. London: Routledge.

Seaman, C., R. Bent, and M. Silva. 2019. "Family Values: Influencers in the Development of Financial and Non-financial Dynamics in Family Firms." In *The Palgrave Handbook of Heterogeneity among Family Firms,* edited by E. Memili and C. Dibrell, 507–530. Cham: Palgrave Macmillan.

Stamm, I. 2013. *Unternehmerfamilien. Der Einfluss des Unternehmens auf Lebenslauf, Generationenbeziehungen und soziale Identität.* Opladen: Budrich Verlag.

Su, E., D. T. Holt, and J. M. Pollack. 2019. "The Distribution of Family Firm Performance Heterogeneity: Understanding Power Law Distributions." In *The Palgrave Handbook of Heterogeneity among Family Firms,* edited by E. Memili and C. Dibrell, 407–429. Cham: Palgrave Macmillan.

Suess-Reyes, J. 2014. "Family Governance – Literature Review and the Development of a Conceptual Model." *Journal of Family Business Strategy* 5 (2): 138–155. doi:10.1016/j.jfbs.2014.02.001.

Tagiuri, R., and J. Davis. 1996. "Bivalent Attributes of the Family Firm." *Family Business Review* 9 (2): 199–208. doi:10.1111/j.1741-6248.1996.00199.x.

Thornton, A. 1985. "Reciprocal Influences of Family and Religion in a Changing World." *Journal of Marriage and Family* 47 (2): 381–394. doi:10.2307/352138.

Von Schlippe, A., and H. Frank. 2013. "The Theory of Social Systems as a Framework for Understanding Family Businesses." *Family Relations* 62 (3): 384–398. doi:10.1111/fare.2013.62.issue-3.

Xiong, L., I. Ukanwa, and A. R. Anderson. 2020. "Institutional Influence and the Role of Family in Poor Women's Micropreneurship." *International Journal of Entrepreneurial Behavior & Research* 26 (1): 122–140. doi:10.1108/IJEBR-05-2017-0162.

Yu, A., G. T. Lumpkin, R. L. Sorenson, and K. H. Brigham. 2012. "The Landscape of Family Business Outcomes: A Summary and Numerical Taxonomy of Dependent Variables." *Family Business Review* 25 (1): 33–57. doi:10.1177/0894486511430329.

Zachary, R. K. 2011. "The Importance of the Family System in Family Business." *Journal of Family Business Management* 1: 26–36. doi:10.1108/20436231111122263.

Zahra, S. A., and P. Sharma. 2004. "Family Business Research: A Strategic Reflection." *Family Business Review* 17 (4): 331–346. doi:10.1111/j.1741-6248.2004.00022.x.

Zellweger, T. M., R. S. Nason, and M. Nordqvist. 2012. "From Longevity of Firms to Transgenerational Entrepreneurship of Families: Introducing Family Entrepreneurial Orientation." *Family Business Review* 25 (2): 136–155. doi:10.1177/0894486511423531.

The balance that sustains benedictines: family entrepreneurship across generations

Sheila K. Hanson and Ksenia Keplinger

ABSTRACT

The heart of family business and family entrepreneurship is the family. Challenging our current understanding of what constitutes a family is important to advance the emerging field of family entrepreneurship. In this conceptual paper, we expand previous research focus with a transactional approach to family and explore family entrepreneurship across generations using the context of Benedictine organizations. The monastic family, defined from the transactional point of view, represents approximately 1,500 years of family history and entrepreneurial activities. Considering an extraordinary example of Benedictines and integrating literature from organizational behaviour, psychology, family science, family business and family entrepreneurship, we investigate the transactional family influence on development and maintenance of resilience capacity (i.e. resiliency) at organizational, family and individual levels. In particular, we develop a theoretical model conceptualizing how values and behavioural guidelines communicated through a code of ethics influences resiliency of (1) family firms through development of a long-term orientation, (2) families through maintenance of a balanced family type, and (3) individuals through enhancement of an individual work-nonwork balance. Finally, we discuss theoretical and practical implications.

1. Introduction

What do Fuller's Brewery, an independent, family-run regional brewery established in 1845 and Ampleforth Abbey, a community of Benedictine monks established in 1802 have in common? Both organizations, founded in the UK, are still owned and governed by their respective families – the Fuller, Smith and Turner families and a monastic family (Ampleforth Abbey: The Community 2019; Fuller's Story 2019). Demonstrating a long history of entrepreneurial behaviours, both businesses exemplify sustainability of family entrepreneurship across generations. Family entrepreneurship research, a rapidly developing area, emphasizes the intersecting fields of family, family business and entrepreneurship (Bettinelli, Fayolle, and Randerson 2014). In our examples, founding families facilitated entrepreneurial behaviours and safeguarded family business survival across generations. Focusing on family business future by framing decisions and expectations towards long-term survival typifies long-term orientation (LTO) (Frank et al. 2017; Lumpkin and Brigham 2011). LTO links to competitive advantage and better family firm financial performance (Lumpkin and Brigham 2011). Importantly, family businesses demonstrate resilience by overcoming various obstacles (e.g. economic, family-related) and building resilience capacity (i.e. resiliency) by honing capabilities to avoid, respond to, and recover from situations that threaten their existence (Lengnick-Hall and Beck 2005). Developing LTO and fostering resiliency of family businesses is vital for researchers and practitioners in family entrepreneurship (Brigham et al. 2014; Lumpkin and Brigham 2011).

In this conceptual paper, we ask: 'What factors influence development and maintenance of resiliency of individuals, family and family business across generations?' Family can be defined in 1) structural and 2) transactional ways (Bettinelli, Fayolle, and Randerson 2014; Koerner and Fitzpatrick 2002). While structural family is a 'group of highly interdependent individuals who are connected by birth, marriage, or adoption' (Ding 2008, 180), transactional family is 'a group of people affiliated through bonds of joint history and a commitment to share a future together while supporting development and well-being of individual members' (Hoy and Sharma 2010, 49). Revisiting our examples, a structural family operates Fuller's Brewery while a transactional monastic family runs the Ampleforth Abbey. Though scholars traditionally focus on structural approaches to family, we expand the focus by exploring the transactional approach to family and family entrepreneurship across generations through the context of Benedictine communities. Specifically, we investigate the transactional family influence on development and maintenance of resiliency at individual, family and family business levels.

Over nearly 1,500 years, Benedictines demonstrated entrepreneurship activities across different national cultures (Keplinger et al. 2016). They facilitated fundamental changes in economic development of multiple countries (Dudley 1999), mastered incredible challenges (e.g. wars and revolutions), and stayed true to their mission and values. Benedictine colleges, retreat centres, breweries and hospitals represent a wealth of guidance for entrepreneurial activities (Chan, McBey, and Scott-Ladd 2011). Previous research (e.g. Chan, McBey, and Scott-Ladd 2011; Keplinger et al. 2016; Mercier and Deslandes 2017) suggests the monastic context may benefit the field of (family) entrepreneurship. To conceptualize the monastic family, we apply the Circumplex family systems model (Olson 2000) and propose that the typical monastic family is a transactional family balanced on dimensions of family cohesion, flexibility/adaptability and communication. Furthermore, we bridge literature on balanced families from family science, work–nonwork balance from organizational behaviour, and LTO from family business to demonstrate how resiliency is developed and maintained at individual, family and organizational levels.

Our research offers several contributions. First, we advance theory by investigating transactional family and expanding the focus of previous research predominately concentrated on structural family influence on family businesses. Second, we conceptualize how values and behavioural guidelines communicated through a code of ethics influence (1) resiliency of family businesses across generations through the development of LTO (2) resiliency of families through maintenance of a balanced family type, and (3) resiliency of family business members through individual work-nonwork balance. Third, we draw attention to the context of family entrepreneurs. By investigating the (unusual) context and unprecedented longevity of monastic businesses, we offer a new perspective on family entrepreneurship. Finally, integrating the aforementioned literature, we introduce the multi-level construct of family entrepreneurial resiliency, representing individual, family and family business capacity for resilience.

2. Who are the benedictines?

The Order of St. Benedict, a Catholic religious order, consists of local male and female monastic communities. Founded by Benedict of Nursia (480–543), Benedictine communities impacted cultural, economic and political development of many countries (Woods 2005). Nowadays, Benedictines encompass over 1,000 communities with approximately 24,000 monks and nuns (Order of St. Benedict 2019). All communities follow the Rule of St. Benedict (RSB) – the formal code of ethics (Mercier and Deslandes 2017) written almost 1,500 years ago. The RSB consists of a prologue and 73 chapters, describing Benedictine values (e.g. hospitality) and expectations in pursuit of individual, relational, spiritual and economic goals. For example, the RSB speaks about the duties and

Table 1. Values and behavioural guidelines for individuals, family, and family businesses from the Rule of St. Benedict.

Guidelines and values	Topic (Chapter Number)	Excerpt
Selection Process (Cohesion)	Four Kinds of Monks/Nuns (1), Admission of New Brothers/Sisters (58)	'Do not grant newcomers to the monastic life an easy entry'.
Values (Cohesion and Flexibility)	Obedience (5), Obedience to Each Other (71), Humility (7), Good Zeal (72)	'No one is to pursue what s/he judges better for herself/himself, but instead, what s/he judges better for someone else. To their fellow monks/nuns they show the pure love of brothers/sisters'.
Behaviours and Attitudes (Cohesion and Flexibility; Communication)	Property (32), Private Ownership (33), Necessities (34), Service in the Kitchen (35), Letters & Presents (54), Clothing & Shoes (55), Silence (6), Speaking (42)	'Let the brethren serve each other so that no one be excused from the work in the kitchen, except on account of sickness or more necessary work, because greater merit and more charity is thereby acquired'.
Communication and Decision-making (also Cohesion)	Counsel of Brothers/Sisters (3)	'Let the Abbot/Abbess call together the whole community, and make known the matter which is to be considered'.
Behaviour and Values at Work/Home [73 guidelines] (e.g, Long-term Orientation)	Instruments of Good Works (4)	'Not to love pride'. 'To honour the aged'.; ' … we shall diligently execute all these tasks is the enclosure of the monastery and *stability* in the community'.
Entrepreneurial Activities	Artisans & Craftsmen (57)	'If there be skilled workmen in the monastery, let them work at their art in all humility'.
Work-Nonwork Balance	Daily Labour (48), Sleep (22), Illness (36); Elderly and Children (37), Food (39), Drink (40), Dining (41), Travelling (50–51)	'Idleness is the enemy of the soul; and therefore the brethren ought to be employed in manual labour at certain times, at others, in devout reading'.
Extent of Rule (Long-term Orientation)	Everything is not in the Rule (73)	'Written for a beginning'. (The Rule is complemented by statutes of particular communities).

responsibilities of the monastic leader, offers guidelines for worship, conduct, discipline, organization within the monastery, and economic activities. The RSB sets forth an overall theme of harmony and balance. Aside from guidelines, it contains words of encouragement and connections to Biblical values. Taken together, the RSB serves as a message of love, devotion to God, work, moderation, obedience, humility and community. Table 1 summarizes the values and behavioural guidelines of RSB:

Benedictines take vows of stability, obedience and conversion. Stability is a lifetime commitment to a particular monastic community and place. Obedience is a commitment to a disciplined, intentional life with humility and respect for fellow monastics. Conversion requires Benedictines to keep open minds and seek continuous growth and change. Following the RSB, daily rhythm in a monastic community involves 'ora' (pray), 'labora' (work) and 'lege' (study). This combination of practical and intellectual work distinguishes Benedictines from other religious orders (i.e. Franciscan, Dominican). Each monastic contributes to the long-term development of their monastic community through manual work, community prayer and spiritual/intellectual readings (Kleymann and Malloch 2010). A self-containing economic organism, each Benedictine community must maintain autonomy. Thus, the Benedictines launch businesses and direct entrepreneurial activities towards long-term livelihood. Entrepreneurial activities serve to glorify God, provide a frugal life, and secure resources for future generations over financial performance (Keplinger et al. 2016).

3. Benedictines as an example of family entrepreneurship

Family entrepreneurship is defined as 'the research field that studies entrepreneurial behaviours of family, family members, and family businesses' (Bettinelli, Fayolle, and Randerson 2014, 164) and considers mutual influence of individuals, families and family businesses on each other (Bettinelli and Randerson 2016; Figure 2.1 in Bettinelli, Fayolle, and Randerson 2014, 169). Dual relationships of family and business may lead to inter-role conflicts, in addition to intra-role conflicts in each area and thus contribute to the complexity of family business (Frank et al. 2019). Family businesses are heterogeneous ranging from managerial firms with little family involvement to pure family firms, in which family and business are tightly intertwined (Bettinelli, Fayolle, and Randerson 2014). Exemplifying a 'pure' form of family firms, we argue that the Benedictines are a unique example of transactional family entrepreneurship that provides a controlled means to study family entrepreneurship. Possessing similar goals, values and governance mechanisms described in the RSB, the Benedictines offer a relatively homogeneous perspective on the family business. This is unique, since family businesses are typically heterogeneous in their attributes (Daspit et al. 2018; Dibrell and Memili 2019).

3.1. Approaches to define family

Scholars emphasize the need to challenge and broaden our understanding of family in both 1) structural and 2) transactional ways (Bettinelli, Fayolle, and Randerson 2014). By a structural definition, family is a nexus of emotional identity around which interdependent members connected by birth, marriage, or adoption develop psychological attachments to each other (Ding 2008, 180). Structural family may represent an individual choice (i.e. adult entering a marriage) or no choice (i.e. child born into a family). The concept of structural family varies drastically across cultures (Hoy 2014) and evolves due to legal, societal and social changes (Randerson, Fayolle, and Dossena 2016).

In contrast, members of a transactional family choose to join their family and commit to it in the long-term (Hoy and Sharma 2010). Boundaries of transactional families are socially constructed with cultural, generational and ideological variations (Koerner and Fitzpatrick 2002). Notably, transactional and structural families are not mutually exclusive; both contribute to our understanding of family (Koerner and Fitzpatrick 2002). Individual behaviours are influenced by family membership in both structural and transactional families. Structure and strength of relationships between family members depend on many factors, including family cohesion, flexibility and communication (Olson 2000). Generally, when families are cohesive, family members feel strong togetherness and social support (Olson 2000).

3.2. Family, family business and entrepreneurial behaviours in the monastic context

A Benedictine community meets Hoy and Sharma's (2010) transactional family definition criteria, since members share history, develop a strong group identity, and commit to live and work together for their lifetime. Community members choose to join a monastic community – their transactional family – and give a vow of stability committing to share a future together and support the development and well-being of individual members. They see the monastery as a 'House of God', community members as 'brothers' or 'sisters', and the monastic leader as 'father' or 'mother' (RSB, Chapter 31). The vow of stability also serves to prevent temptation to leave the monastic family during difficult times. Furthermore, selection and socialization practices of Benedictine communities contribute to developing a strong group identity. Suitability of potential community members is tested over months or even years (RSB, Chapter 58). During selection, prospective monastics learn the history and core values of a monastic community, participate in and reflect on monastic community living.

Benedictine businesses can be conceptualized as family businesses. Chua, Chrisman, and Sharma (1999, 25) defined a family business as 'a business governed and/or managed with the intention to shape and pursue the vision of the business held by a dominant coalition controlled by members of the same family or a small number of families in a manner that is potentially sustainable across generations of the family or families'. Monastic family members – a dominant coalition – shape and pursue the vision of a Benedictine business and influence its daily operations by practising participative decision-making. Fundamentally, the sustainability of the family business across generations is a guiding principle of the Benedictines. Monastic family members must provide continuous income and secure resources for future monastic family generations (Rost et al. 2010; Keplinger et al. 2016).

Stability of monastic family governance is demonstrated by institutional autonomy, non-profit orientation and life-long tenure of monastics (Rost et al. 2010) where the Benedictine communities usually own, control and manage their businesses. Important players in local economies, Benedictines own land and property (Tredget 2002), run businesses across many industries (e.g. agriculture, tourism, manufacturing, retail, education, etc.), and often employ more secular employees than monastics (Müller-Stewens, Muff, and Eberle 2014). Entrepreneurial behaviours of Benedictines contributed to developing modern concepts of profit, prices and governance structures (Inauen et al. 2010; Rost et al. 2010). Even though Benedictines may dispose of unprofitable businesses and property (Müller-Stewens, Muff, and Eberle 2014), they rarely leave those they vowed to serve. For example, the Benedictine monastery in Norcia, Italy active until 200 years ago (McKenna 2016) was re-established in 1998. Nearly destroyed by an earthquake in 2016 (Hadro 2017), the resilient Benedictines, following the guiding principle of self-sufficiency, continued monastic entrepreneurial endeavours despite external circumstances.

3.3 Mutual influences of family, family members and family business

According to Bettinelli et al.'s (2014) conceptualization of family entrepreneurship, families, family members and family businesses influence entrepreneurial behaviours of each other. The Benedictines are first influenced by structural families of their birth (Nichols and Schwartz 2004). When an individual joins a monastic transactional family and commits to it with a vow of stability, the monastic family becomes his/her priority. Individuals influence entrepreneurial behaviours of their monastic family through family culture of their birth families, lifetime commitment and community-oriented entrepreneurial activities (Bettinelli, Fayolle, and Randerson 2014; Kleymann and Malloch 2010).

The monastic family impacts entrepreneurial behaviours of individual family members through stringent selection, rigorous socialization, value transmission, and formal and informal communication (Sorenson 2014). For example, monastic families promote equality of treatment in daily life (RSB, Chapters 5, 71) to integrate new family members and foster common values (Wenger and Snyder 2000). Mentoring, consisting of initial training, socialization and ongoing support of newcomers, is another technique to transmit Benedictine values and influence (entrepreneurial) behaviours of individuals. The monastic family leader mentors each family member's development and senior monks/nuns guide juniors (Keplinger et al. 2016). Monastic families also influence entrepreneurial behaviours of individuals through formal and informal communication. For example, the monastic leader fosters open discussions about difficult subjects and encourages input from all individuals.

Furthermore, personality traits of individuals, their demographic characteristics (e.g. age, gender), and leadership styles influence entrepreneurship in family businesses (Bettinelli, Fayolle, and Randerson 2014). By giving the vow of stability, individuals commit themselves to the monastic family and its family businesses for a lifetime, unlike individuals who remain members of structural families regardless of their involvement in family business. Thus, Benedictine family business members influence entrepreneurial behaviours of Benedictine family firms through lifetime commitment and choice of entrepreneurial activities. Their influence is facilitated through the participative family business culture and professional development opportunities of their monastic family.

Due to the vow of stability and explicit focus on sustainability across generations, monastic family businesses aim to secure resources for future generations of monastics (Keplinger et al. 2016). Thus, entrepreneurial behaviours of monastic family firms focus on long-term investments and long-term relationships with stakeholders. According to the vow of conversion, Benedictines are expected to flexibly adapt to changing environments. Consequently, they abandon activities no longer contributing to long-term survival in favour of new entrepreneurial options (Müller-Stewens, Muff, and Eberle 2014). Finally, monastic businesses affect entrepreneurial behaviours of the monastic family by developing family traditions and learning processes (Bettinelli, Fayolle, and Randerson 2014;

Salvato, Chirico, and Sharma 2010). Benedictines teach monastic family history and traditions to new family members, contributing to long-term survival of both monastic family and family business (Fassler 2010).

4. What can we learn from benedictines about family entrepreneurship across generations?

Monastic families demonstrate almost 1,500 years of family entrepreneurship. This is an unprecedented example of transgenerational entrepreneurship, since family businesses rarely endure past three generations (Jaskiewicz, Combs, and Rau 2015). This long history of family entrepreneurship offers ideas applicable outside of the monastic context.

4.1 Code of ethics in family businesses

Family business values are 'explicit or implicit conceptions of the desirable in both family and business life' (Koiranen 2002, 177). Conflicts of interest between family, family members and family business necessitate clear definition and communication of common values (Koiranen 2002). Communication of values encourages people to switch from what is right (mere compliance) to what is good (value implementation) (Mercier and Deslandes 2017). Benedictines rely on the RSB, a code of ethics applicable to monastics, the monastic family, and monastic businesses (Mercier and Deslandes 2017). The RSB organizes manual and intellectual work, shapes a structured organization, emphasizes core values in business activities (i.e. moderation, stewardship, respect), and ensures long-term sustainability (Chan, McBey, and Scott-Ladd 2011; Mercier and Deslandes 2017). Fully integrated into organizational culture and Benedictine entrepreneurial activities (Mercier and Deslandes 2017), the RSB clearly communicates and encourages the implementation of common values and goals at the individual, monastic family and business levels. Although the RSB may not directly apply to secular family entrepreneurs, integrating values of family members, family unit and family business into one document is noteworthy. Based upon 1,500 years of monastic family business experience in various industries, we propose:

Proposition 1: *Rules/guidelines and values codified and communicated through a formal code of ethics, simultaneously guide behaviour and transmit values for family businesses, family units, and family members.*

4.2 Family balance

We draw upon family science research and apply the Circumplex family systems model (Olson 2000) to the monastic context. Three dimensions – cohesion, flexibility and communication – are critical for family systems (see Figure 1) (Olson 2000). The two first dimensions are assessed on a continuum from low to high levels of cohesion and from low to high levels of flexibility/adaptability. Four levels on two dimensions generate 16 family types (Olson 2000; Michael Tsabari and Lavee 2012). This typology includes four balanced family types, four unbalanced types and eight mid-range types (see Figure 1).

Family cohesion is defined as 'the emotional bonding that family members have towards one another' (Olson 2000, 145). Due to the vow of stability, the Benedictines exhibit lifelong commitment and loyalty to people who live and work in a monastic community. Relying on each other in daily activities, community members develop strong emotional connections. The importance of emotional bonding is emphasized in the RSB (Chapter 4) and strengthened through various activities (daily joint prayers, communal meals and readings) (Rost et al. 2010). Although monastic family members share values and goals, they may study and work separately. For example, some monastics

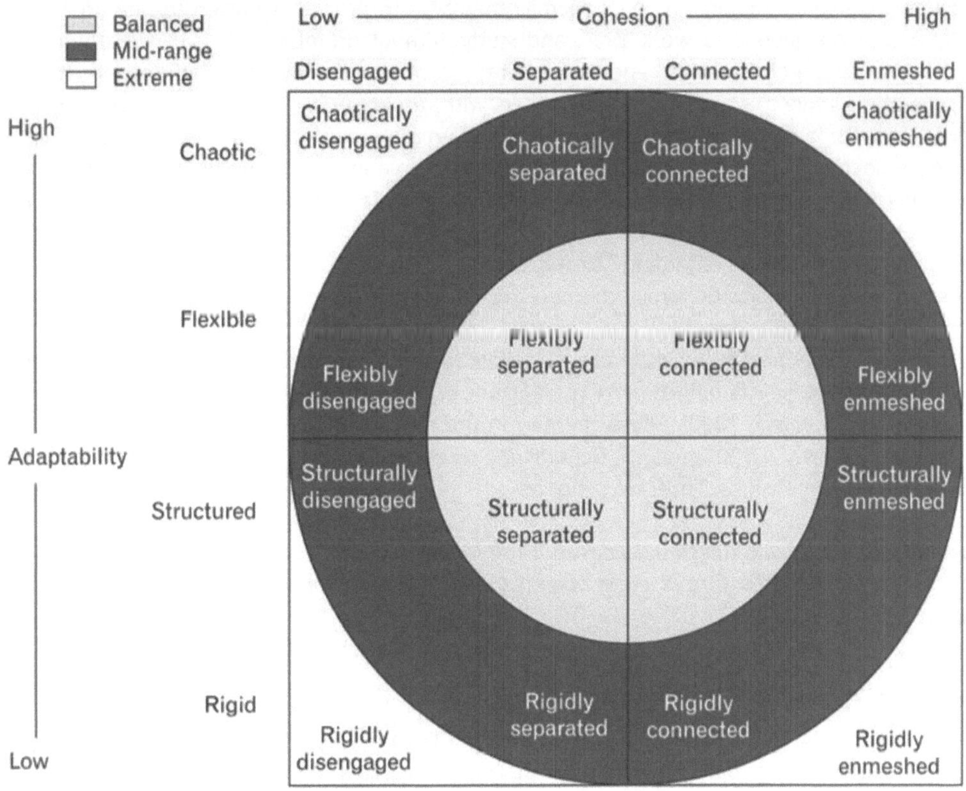

Figure 1. The Circumplex model of family systems (adapted from Olson 2000; Michael-Tsabari and Lavee 2012).

teach or farm, while others maintain the monastery or manage monastic family businesses. Following this reasoning, cohesion in a stereotypical monastic family is assessed as *connected* (moderate to high) (see Figure 1).

The second dimension of the Circumplex model describes family flexibility or adaptability – 'the amount of change in its leadership, role relationships, and relationship rules' (Olson 2000, 146). Giving the vow of conversion, monastic family members commit to proactive continuous improvement through change and personal growth. This vow requires flexibility, adapting to others' needs and living each day better than the previous one. Monastics practice adaptability by rotating jobs of menial service (e.g. kitchen work and housecleaning) to show respect to others and each individual's role in the monastic family. Given clearly defined roles, every monastic family member knows his/her place within the family (Tredget 2002). The hierarchical structure of monastic families typically consists of four main levels: leader, posts of responsibility, seniors and juniors (Inauen et al. 2010; Rost et al. 2010). The democratically elected leader governs the autonomous monastic community and nominates officials responsible for specific matters. Based on the Circumplex model, flexibility/adaptability in monastic families may be assessed as *structured*. Though heterogeneity may exist across monastic families, we argue that the RSB calls for a balanced family type. More specifically, typical monastic families exemplify *structurally connected family types*.

The third dimension of the Circumplex model – communication – facilitates family cohesion *and* flexibility/adaptability. Communication involves attentive and empathetic listening skills, speaking for oneself rather than others, sharing feelings, clarity and respect (Olson 2000). The RSB is instrumental for developing a social system with both cohesion and flexibility to withstand crisis. Specifically, it codifies and encourages to implement the values that facilitate cohesion, flexibility and balance (see Table 1).

The vow of obedience requires monastic family members to proactively listen to one another and humbly accept obligations to work, pray, and study without grumbling. Obedience is not simply submitting to authority. Receiving encouragement and reinforcement from their leaders, monastic family members strive to support and treat others with respect (RSB, Chapter 72). Through communication, monastic family members have voice in both family and business matters. As the Benedictines practice democratic decision-making, all monastics with solemn profession participate in decision-making and advise monastic leaders. Consequently, monastic family members encourage open communication about important issues and invest in the future of the monastic family (Janotík 2012). Senior monks/nuns mentor juniors regarding self-disclosure and emotions (RSB, Chapter 58). Informal communication between monastic family members is crucial to foster family cohesion and encourage flexibility/adaptability (Keplinger 2019).

In summary, the typical monastic family is a *balanced family*. This assessment of family functioning is derived from the key family dimensions of cohesion, flexibility and communication from the Circumplex Model (Olson 2000). These themes, in the form of values and guidelines found in the RSB, represent nearly 1,500 years of Benedictine experience with a continuous code of ethics espousing these dimensions. Thus, we propose:

Proposition 2: *Values and rules/guidelines that foster cohesion and flexibility in families facilitated by communication through a formal code of ethics enable development and maintenance of family balance.*

4.3 Long-term orientation

According to Frank and colleagues (2017, 730), LTO of family business 'represents a decision premise that frames decisions regarding the long-term survival and success of the business'. LTO illustrates the family's expectations towards the business and manifests itself in decision-making processes within the family business (Weismeier-Sammer, Frank, and Von Schlippe 2013). LTO, associated with competitive advantages and higher financial performance of family firms (Lumpkin and Brigham 2011), plays a pivotal role in family business. According to the Circumplex model (Olson 2000), a balanced family demonstrating high levels of cohesion and flexibility/adaptability with good communication suggests common expectations about the long-term development and success of a family business, such as LTO. As previously stated, the Benedictines are charged with economic self-sufficiency and through their entrepreneurial endeavours, they adapt for the long-run. Despite disagreements, members of a balanced family learn how to work together. For Benedictines, working together is guided by their code of ethics, the RSB. In particular, communication of values and goals 'serves as glue to communal engagement' (Ponzetti 2014, 33) in the long run encouraging the Benedictines to forego individual desires. Benedictines follow long-term interests of the monastic family and monastic businesses solving important issues by democratic discussion and active participation (Janotík 2012). Additional quantitative evidence of strong LTO is the fact that the average lifespan of Benedictine organizations in Germany/Switzerland and in Austria is 460 and 648 years, respectively (Feldbauer-Durstmüller, Sandberger, and Neulinger 2012; Inauen et al. 2010). Summarizing these arguments, we propose:

Proposition 3: *Rules/guidelines and common values fostering stability/long-term survival communicated through a formal code of ethics facilitate development and maintenance of LTO.*

4.4 Work-nonwork balance

Casper et al. (2018, 197) define work-nonwork balance as 'the extent to which employees hold a favourable evaluation regarding their combination of work and nonwork roles, arising from the belief that their emotional experiences, involvement and effectiveness in work and nonwork roles are commensurate (compatible) with the value they attach to the roles'. For Benedictines, balance between work and nonwork roles is a fundamental principle described in the RSB, which describes a balanced life of prayer and work as the ideal. Benedictines should not be consumed by work, nor should they spend so much time in prayer that responsibilities are neglected. According to the RSB, all things – eating, drinking, sleeping, reading, working and praying – should be in moderation. Therein, Benedictines learn to balance various roles (monks/nuns, monastic family members, member of local communities) with deeply held values of love and humility. They share knowledge about maintaining work-nonwork balance by welcoming guests dealing with life stressors and offering retreats and workshops (i.e. Holy Cross Monastery, New York, US).

Proposition 4: *Values and guidelines directing both work and non-work behaviours, communicated through a code of ethics facilitate work-nonwork balance at the individual level.*

4.5 Resilience and resiliency

We review concepts of resilience and resiliency from developmental and organizational psychology, family science and family business. In particular, we focus on building resilience capacity (i.e. resiliency) of family entrepreneurs against inevitable disruptions. Broadly defined, resilience is 'the capacity of a dynamic system to adapt successfully to disturbances that threaten its function, viability, or development' (Masten 2014, 10). Reflecting the multi-level nature of family systems, we distinguish between individual and family levels of resilience (Patterson 2002; Yang and Danes 2015). Family entrepreneurs who sustain family business over many generations experience the ups and downs of business. Chrisman, Chua, and Steier (2011, 1109) define family firm resilience as a 'function of how they respond to the need to infuse managerial talent in the firm without losing control, to the need to balance economic and noneconomic goals over varying time frames, to the need to use their unique governance systems to innovate, and to the need to extract maximum value from the social capital that exists among family members'. For family entrepreneurs – at the individual, family, or family business levels – resilience is associated with positive business outcomes, such as growth, success and survival (Bullough and Renko 2013).

Bullough and Renko (2013) define resilience for individual entrepreneurs as both 1) the ability to go on with life purposely (Tedeschi and Calhoun 2004) and, 2) a dynamic process involving positive adaptation (Luthar, Cicchetti, and Becker 2000) following adversity. The first definition reflects trait-like resilience while the second refers to post-traumatic growth through change and learning after hardship (Bullough and Renko 2013). In the face of adversity, resilience is necessary for individuals engaging in entrepreneurial behaviours (Bullough and Renko 2013). Resilience is conceptualized as a response or adaption to change as well as a protective factor, where resilience is developed to respond to future stressors (Patterson 2002). Resilience as a capacity is known as *resiliency.* A protective factor – for individuals, families and family businesses – resilience capacity prepares all for future stress, change and disruption, and is likely beneficial to sustainability over time. Next, we explain how resilience capacity is developed and nurtured at family business, family, and individual levels and introduce the concept of family entrepreneurial resiliency in Figure 2, our theoretical model.

4.5.1 Individual resiliency and work–nonwork balance

Individual resiliency is built in *advance* of adversity. Resilience researchers associate the feelings of connectedness and achieving work-nonwork balance with building resilience capacity (i.e. resiliency), particularly in challenging workplace conditions (Jackson, Firtko, and Edenborough 2007). Furthermore, Tusaie and Dyer (2004, 4) indicate that high levels of resiliency fit with 'a belief system that provides existential meaning, a cohesive life narrative and an appreciation of the uniqueness of oneself'. Consequently, participating in nonwork activities and finding identity outside of work roles

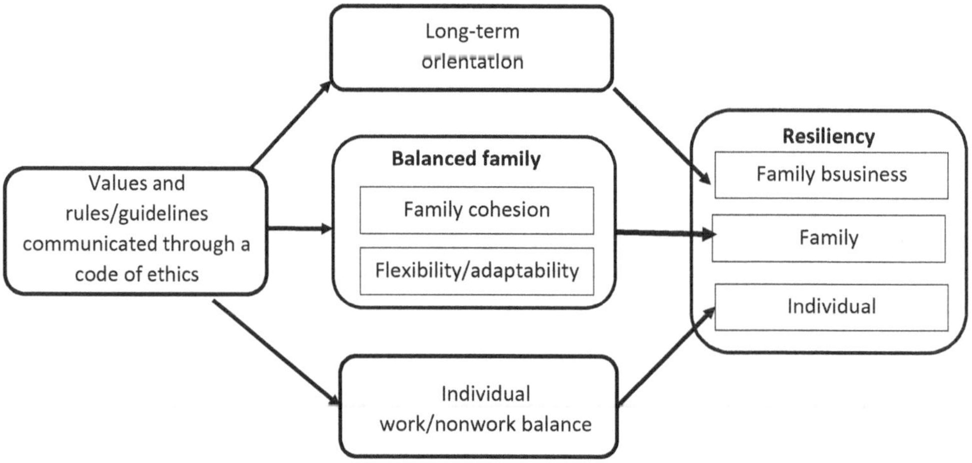

Figure 2. Factors influencing resiliency at individual, family, and organizational levels.

nurtures individuals in physical, emotional and spiritual ways and helps them build individual resiliency despite demanding work (Jackson, Firtko, and Edenborough 2007).

In the monastic context, the RSB requires Benedictines to follow the principle of 'ora' (pray), 'labora' (work) and 'lege' (study) engaging in both work and nonwork activities. Nonwork activities include regular time for thoughtful study (e.g. meditating upon RSB or scripture, exploring contemporary literature, or participating in a retreat) and recreation. These are integral practices of balanced life and spiritual journey for Benedictines. Balance between work and nonwork activities provides inner stability in changing times contributing to monastics' mental health and building resilience capacity (i.e. resiliency). However, despite clear prescriptions in the RSB, achieving work-nonwork balance is sometimes challenging for monastics (Keplinger 2019). We propose that proactive guidelines prescribing work-nonwork balance help build resiliency capacity (i.e. resiliency) at the individual level (see Figure 2):

Proposition 5: *Values and rules/guidelines calling for both work and non-work behaviours communicated through a formal code of ethics facilitate development of individual resiliency through regulation of individual work-nonwork balance.*

4.5.2 Family resiliency and family balance

Similar to individuals, families may build resilience *after* hardship; however, they may also build resilience capacity through family processes buffering them against stressors. Family scientists (Olson 2000) and developmental psychologists (Masten 2014) find that – at the family level – development and maintenance of family cohesion, closeness and belonging are key to resiliency. Previous sections described how the Circumplex Model (Olson 2000) promotes family balance through cohesion and flexibility/adaptability and how communication helps families foster these dimensions. Thus, families may improve family balance through better communication – both formal and informal. In the monastic context, the RSB prescribes the means to communicate (e.g. 'Let the Abbot/Abbess call together the whole community') and how to communicate (e.g. 'Listen with your heart'). Strong emphasis on monastic family cohesion helps the Benedictines deal with hardships at the family level. Based on the Circumplex Model (Olson 2000) and lengthy experience of the Benedictines, we propose (see Figure 2):

Proposition 6: *Values and rules/guidelines of flexibility and cohesion as communicated through a formal code of ethics build the resilience capacity of family (i.e. family resiliency) through development and maintenance of a balanced family.*

4.5.3 Family business resiliency and long-term orientation

Building resilience capacity through human resource practices is important for organizations to thrive despite uncertain or adverse conditions. Specifically for family firms, resiliency is important if family business owners intend to pass ownership and management to the next generation (Chrisman, Chua, and Steier 2011). However, literature suggests that odds are against enduring past the first few generations (Jaskiewicz, Combs, and Rau 2015). Thus, finding sources of resiliency is important to family firms (Yang and Danes 2015) as building resiliency at the organizational level enables entrepreneurship over time (Randerson et al. 2015). Lumpkin *et al.*(2010) suggested that LTO is as a source of resiliency in family businesses. In particular, family businesses with a strong LTO constantly scan their environment to identify trends and anticipate future ups and downs (Lumpkin *et al.*2010).

The RSB directs monastic family members to actively listen to outside input and attend to environmental changes. The Benedictine vow of stability and lifetime commitment to monastic family and businesses is consistent with LTO. Since Benedictines self-sustain economically and aim for long-term survival, they prepare to bounce back from adversity. As a result, Benedictine organizations have demonstrated resiliency for almost 1,500 years. Building on Lumpkin's (2010) suggestion and the example of Benedictine businesses, we propose (see Figure 2):

Proposition 7: *Rules/guidelines and values guiding behaviour towards stability/long-term survival as communicated through a formal code of ethics leads to family business resiliency through LTO.*

4.5.4 Communication through an ethics code and multi-level resiliency

We propose how to leverage an ethical code to communicate behavioural expectations and values to individuals, families and family businesses. Specifically, we delineate this through the monastic family to show how the Benedictines' ethics code encourages behaviours and transmits values leading to individual work–nonwork balance, family balance and LTO of family business. Taken together, propositions 5 to 7, lead to the following (see Figure 2):

Proposition 8: *Collectively, the rules/guidelines and values that guide behaviours leading to cohesion, flexibility, work-nonwork balance, and LTO, communicated through a formal code of ethics result in family entrepreneurial resiliency – resiliency at individual, family, and family business levels.*

5 Discussion

5.1 Theoretical contributions

In this conceptual paper, through the (unusual) context of monastic organizations, we identify factors to develop and maintain resilience capacity (i.e. resiliency) of individuals, family, and family business across generations. First, we apply a Circumplex model of family systems (Olson 2000) to conceptualize monastic family. As monastic family is an example of transactional family, we advance theory by expanding the focus of previous research concentrated on structural family and its influence on family members and family business. The transactional family view allows researchers to integrate people who are not considered part of structural family but participate in decision-making processes in family business matters, make their expertise available to family members, and thus shape the family business vision. In the monastic context, rules and values applicable to individuals, family and family businesses are combined and codified into their ethics code that facilitates communication and implementation of values. According to our conceptualization, the typical monastic family is balanced on the dimensions of cohesion and flexibility/adaptability, and characterized by open communication. Unique internal contextual factors (e.g. cohesion) enable Benedictines to simultaneously communicate business and family values, addressing typically contradictory expectations of business and family (Frank et al. 2019) and deepening our understanding of business family.

Second, we develop a theoretical model that explains the role of an ethics code in developing resilience capacity (i.e. resiliency) at individual, family and organizational levels. In particular, we propose that communication through a code of ethics contributes to developing resiliency of (1) family business members through individual work-nonwork balance, (2) business family through family balance, and (3) family business through development and maintenance of the LTO. Our theoretical work contributes to the need for research on communication and managing family in family business suggested by Yu et al. (2012). Accounting for the individual, family unit and family business levels, we introduce multi-level resiliency (a capacity) punctuating the need for multi-level research in family entrepreneurship called for by several scholars (Randerson et al. 2015; Yu et al. 2012). Third, we contribute to the literature on survival of family entrepreneurial firms past the first few generations by investigating the unique example of Benedictines. Finally, we integrate diverse literature (organizational behaviour, psychology, family science, family business and family entrepreneurship) highlighting the importance of family entrepreneurial context.

5.2 Practical implications

To safeguard family entrepreneurship across generations, it is useful to develop an ethics code for individuals, family units, and their family businesses before conflicts arise. Though entrepreneurs build resilience through responses after adversity (e.g. learning after failure), we assert they may also build resilience capacity to buffer against future disruptions through the proactive process of integrating and codifying behaviours and values in an ethics code applicable for both family and business. Previous research (e.g. Arteaga and Menéndez-Requejo 2017) suggests that developing a family constitution when a business family is already in conflict may cause even more conflicts. Thus, it is beneficial for a business family to be proactive and codify their values and expected behaviours as the process of creating a code of ethics is as important as the result.

Family entrepreneurs may also find wisdom in the 1,500 year-old RSB. At the organizational level, family entrepreneurs may facilitate resiliency by developing policies applicable to both family and business. Thus, practitioners who work with family entrepreneurs may assist in developing codes of ethics that prescribe resiliency. Specifically, work-nonwork balance is important for individuals (Casper et al. 2018). Family cohesion and flexibility facilitated and maintained by communication lead to family balance (Olson 2000). Finally, LTO (Lumpkin et al. 2010) is associated with family business resilience (Chrisman, Chua, and Steier 2011). Taken together, knowledge of these resilience-building processes is instrumental for consultants, educators and researchers working with family entrepreneurs.

5.2 Limitations and future research

We conceptualize Benedictines as a unique example of family entrepreneurship. On the one hand, they reflect homogeneity in governance and values, providing an opportunity to study aspects of family entrepreneurship under controlled conditions. On the other hand, the monastic expression of family entrepreneurship is not always generalizable to other family entrepreneurs. Yet, family entrepreneurs may learn and apply concepts of balance (individual and family) and communicate through an ethics code for both family and business systems to build resiliency. We present an arguably rare, idealized portrait of the Benedictines. Indeed, monastic family and Benedictine organizations may be 'hot spots for gossip and peer control, including lobbying and power games' (Inauen et al. 2010, 51). Shared values with extremely high family cohesion might lead to groupthink (Janis 1982) and unwillingness to change. For these reasons, organizations need tools to select and socialize appropriate employees while also challenging ideas.

We propose three factors – work-nonwork balance, family balance and LTO – to foster multi-level resiliency. Certainly, other mechanisms contribute to development and maintenance of resilience capacity of family entrepreneurs. For example, entrepreneurial education and access to social networks (Bullough and Renko 2013) are associated with resiliency and future research may investigate these sources. Further, the resiliency of communities (Steiner and Atterton 2015) is another interesting topic for family entrepreneurship, as Benedictines demonstrate the importance of communities. Quantitatively testing our conceptual model offers an interesting future research endeavour.

Our conceptual model is developed based on the assumption that the values and guidelines of RSB serve as a source of resiliency for the Benedictines predominately from our theoretical lens of the Circumplex model of family science and complimentary theory in psychology. Interestingly, when viewed as a social system, Benedictine organizations can also be viewed from the enterpriseness perspective (see Frank et al. 2019). Monastic families may develop enterpriseness in their structural coupling of business and family by accepting business-related rules codified in the RSB, as one of the structures of a business family. Further, the statutes developed by particular monastic communities provide another potential source of structure and identity. A fruitful avenue for future research may investigate enterpriseness in the Benedictine context and more specifically including the dimensions of essence, identity and involvement as a framework for studying the enterpriseness of Benedictines and other business families.

6 Conclusion: the rest of the story

Revisiting the family entrepreneurship examples, the resilient Ampleforth Abbey started anew in England after exile in France and Fuller's Brewery survived successions and unpredictable changes. As these family entrepreneurs continue their ventures, questions linger – how long will these family firms successfully endure? What about the role of work-nonwork balance, family balance and LTO? Will their ethics codes boost them with resiliency across generations?

Disclosure statement

No potential conflict of interest was reported by the authors.

ORCID

Sheila K. Hanson http://orcid.org/0000-0001-6314-2848
Ksenia Keplinger http://orcid.org/0000-0002-1727-3406

References

Ampleforth Abbey: The Community. 2019. Accessed 15 November 2019. https://www.ampleforth.org.uk/abbey/community

Arteaga, R., and S. Menéndez-Requejo. 2017. "Family Constitution and Business Performance: Moderating Factors." *Family Business Review* 30 (4): 320–338. doi:10.1177/0894486517732438.

Bettinelli, C., and K. Randerson. 2016. "Introduction: What We Know about Family Entrepreneurship." In *Family Entrepreneurship: Rethinking the Research Agenda*, edited by K. Randerson, C. Bettinelli, G. Dossena, and A. Fayolle, 1–12. London, UK: Routledge.

Bettinelli, C., A. Fayolle, and K. Randerson. 2014. "Family Entrepreneurship: A Developing Field." *Foundations and Trends in Entrepreneurship* 10 (3): 161–236. doi:10.1561/0300000049.

Brigham, K. H., G. T. Lumpkin, G. T. Payne, and M. A. Zachary. 2014. "Researching Long-Term Orientation: A Validation Study and Recommendations for Future Research." *Family Business Review* 27 (1): 72–88. doi:10.1177/0894486513508980.

Bullough, A., and M. Renko. 2013. "Entrepreneurial Resilience During Challenging Times." *Business Horizons* 56 (3): 343–350. doi:10.1016/j.bushor.2013.01.001.

Casper, W. J., J. Holliday, J. Wayne, H. Vaziri, S. DeHauw, and J. Greenhaus. 2018. "The Jingle-Jangle of Work-Nonwork Balance: A Comprehensive and Meta-Analytic Review of Its Meaning and Measurement." *Journal of Applied Psychology* 103 (2): 182–214. doi:10.1037/apl0000259.

Chan, C. C. A., K. McBey, and B. Scott-Ladd. 2011. "Ethical Leadership in Modern Employment Relationships: Lessons from St. Benedict." *Journal of Business Ethics* 100 (2): 221–228. doi:10.1007/s10551-010-0676-x.

Chrisman, J. J., J. J. Chua, and L. P. Steier. 2011. "Resilience of Family Firms: An Introduction." *Entrepreneurship Theory and Practice* 35: 1107–1119. doi:10.1111/j.1540-6520.2011.00493.x.

Chua, J. H., J. J. Chrisman, and P. Sharma. 1999. "Defining the Family Business by Behavior." *Entrepreneurship Theory and Practice* 23 (4): 19–39. doi:10.1177/104225879902300402.

Daspit, J. J., J. J. Chrisman, P. Sharma, A. W. Pearson, and R. V. Mahto. 2018. "Governance as a Source of Family Firm Heterogeneity." *Journal of Business Research* 84: 293–300. doi:10.1016/j.jbusres.2017.12.041.

Dibrell, C., and E. Memili. 2019. "A Brief History and A Look to the Future of Family Business Heterogeneity: An Introduction." In *The Palgrave Handbook of Heterogeneity among Family Firms*, edited by E. Memili and C. Dibrell, 1–15. Cham, Switzerland: Palgrave Macmillan.

Ding, B.-H. 2008. "Family Involvement in Family Firms: Antecedents and Moderators." In *Theoretical Developments and Future Research in Family Business*, edited by P. H. Phan and J. E. Butler, 177–193. Charlotte, NC: Information Age Publishing.

Dudley, L. 1999. "Communications and Economic Growth." *European Economic Review* 43 (3): 595–619. doi:10.1016/S0014-2921(97)00129-3.

Fassler, M. 2010. "Filming the Nuns of Regina Laudis: Old and New Evidence for Monastic Studies." *Religion Compass* 4 (6): 340–352. doi:10.1111/reco.2010.4.issue-6.

Feldbauer-Durstmüller, B., S. Sandberger, and M. Neulinger. 2012. "Sustainability for Centuries: Monastic Governance of Austrian Benedictine Abbeys." *European Journal of Management* 12 (3): 83–92.

Frank, H., J. Suess-Reyes, E. Fuetsch, and A. Kessler. 2019. "Introducing the Enterpriseness of Business Families: A Research Agenda." In *The Palgrave Handbook of Heterogeneity among Family Firms*, edited by E. Memili and C. Dibrell, 263–296. Cham, Switzerland: Palgrave Macmillan.

Frank, H., A. T. Kessler, J. Rusch, J. Suess-Reyes, and D. Weismeier-Sammer. 2017. "Capturing the Familiness of Family Businesses: Development of the Family Influence Familiness Scale (FIFS)." *Entrepreneurship Theory and Practice* 41 (5): 709–742. doi:10.1111/etap.12229.

Fuller's Story. 2019. Accessed 15 November 2019. https://www.fullers.co.uk/history-and-heritage

Hadro, M. 2017."Echoes of St. Benedict as Norcia Monks Rebuild after Earthquake" *Catholic News Agency*. Accessed 7 June 2018. https://www.catholicnewsagency.com/news/echoes-of-st-benedict-as-norcia-monks-rebuild-after-earthquake-84407

Hoy, F. 2014. "Entrepreneurial Venturing for Family Business Research." In *SAGE Handbook of Family Business*, edited by L. Melin, M. Nordqvist, and P. Sharma, 620–628. London, UK: SAGE Publications.

Hoy, F., and P. Sharma. 2010. *Entrepreneurial Family Firms*. Englewood Cliffs, NJ: Prentice Hall.

Inauen, E., K. Rost, M. Osterloh, and B. S. Frey. 2010. "Back to the Future – A Monastic Perspective on Corporate Governance." *Management Revue* 41 (1): 38–59. doi:10.5771/0935-9915-2010-1.

Jackson, D., A. Firtko, and M. Edenborough. 2007. "Personal Resilience as A Strategy for Surviving and Thriving in the Face of Workplace Adversity: A Literature Review." *Journal of Advanced Nursing* 60 (1): 1–9. doi:10.1111/jan.2007.60.issue-1.

Janis, I. L. 1982. *Groupthink*. Boston: Houghton Mifflin.

Janotík, T. 2012. "Benedictine Monasteries from the Point of View of Happiness Economics." *Economics Bulletin* 32 (2): 1215–1225.

Jaskiewicz, P., J. G. Combs, and S. B. Rau. 2015. "Entrepreneurial Legacy: Toward a Theory of How Some Family Firms Nurture Transgenerational Entrepreneurship." *Journal of Business Venturing* 30 (1): 29–49. doi:10.1016/j.jbusvent.2014.07.001.

Keplinger, K. 2019. "A Moral Being Is an Accountable Being: Leadership and Accountability in Monastic Organizations." In *Unternehmen Und Klöster: Wirtschaft Und Monastisches Leben Im Interdisziplinären Dialog [Entreprises and Cloisters: Business and Monastic Life in an Interdisciplinary Dialog]*, edited by B. Feldbauer-Durstmüller, T. Wolf, and M. Neulinger, 345–361. Wiesbaden, Germany: Springer.

Keplinger, K., B. Feldbauer-Durstmüller, S. Sandberger, and M. Neulinger. 2016. "Entrepreneurial Activities of Benedictine Monasteries — A Special Form of Family Business?" *International Journal of Entrepreneurial Venturing* 8 (4): 317–333. doi:10.1504/IJEV.2016.082217.

Kleymann, B., and H. Malloch. 2010. "The Rule of Saint Benedict and Corporate Management: Employing the Whole Person." *Journal of Global Responsibility* 1 (2): 207–224. doi:10.1108/20412561011079362.

Koerner, A. F., and M. A. Fitzpatrick. 2002. "Toward a Theory of Family Communication." *Communication Theory* 12 (1): 70–91. doi:10.1111/comt.2002.12.issue-1.

Koiranen, M. 2002. "Over 100 Years of Age but Still Entrepreneurially Active in Business: Exploring the Values and Family Characteristics of Old Finnish Family Firms." *Family Business Review* 15 (3): 175–187. doi:10.1111/j.1741-6248.2002.00175.x.

Lengnick-Hall, C. A., and T. E. Beck. 2005. "Adaptive Fit versus Robust Transformation: How Organizations Respond to Environmental Change." *Journal of Management* 31 (5): 738–757. doi:10.1177/0149206305279367.

Lumpkin, G. T., and K. H. Brigham. 2011. "Long-term Orientation and Intertemporal Choice in Family Firms." *Entrepreneurship Theory and Practice* 35 (6): 1149–1169. doi:10.1111/j.1540-6520.2011.00495.x.

Lumpkin, G.T, K. H Brigham, and T. W. Moss. 2010. "Long-term Orientation: Implications for The Entrepreneurial Orientation and Performance Of Family Businesses." *Entrepreneurship & Regional Development* 22 (3–4): 241-64. doi:10.1080/08985621003726218.

Luthar, S. S., D. Cicchetti, and B. Becker. 2000. "The Construct of Resilience: A Critical Evaluation and Guidelines for Future Work." *Child Development* 71 (3): 543–562. doi:10.1111/cdev.2000.71.issue-3.

Masten, A. 2014. "Global Perspectives on Resilience in Children and Youth." *Child Development* 85 (1): 6–20. doi:10.1111/cdev.2014.85.issue-1.

McKenna, J. 2016."Italy's Benedictine Monks of Norcia Look to Future after Quake." *Religious News Service*. Accessed 7 June 2018. https://religionnews.com/2016/11/03/italys-benedictine-monks-of-norcia-look-to-future-after-quake/

Mercier, G., and G. Deslandes. 2017. "There are No Codes, Only Interpretations. Practical Wisdom and Hermeneutics in Monastic Organizations." *Journal of Business Ethics* 145 (4): 781–794. doi:10.1007/s10551-016-3055-4.

Michael-Tsabari, N., and Y. Lavee. 2012. "Too Close and Too Rigid: Applying the Circumplex Model of Family Systems to First-Generation Family Firms." *Journal of Marital and Family Therapy* 38 (1): 105–116. doi:10.1111/jmft.2012.38.issue-s1.

Müller-Stewens, G., M. Muff, and T. Eberle. 2014. "Management von Klöstern: Ein Erfahrungsbericht. ." *zfo Zeitschrift Führung + Organisation* 83 (3): 184–189.

Nichols, M. P., and R. C. Schwartz. 2004. *Family Therapy: Concepts and Methods*. 6th ed. Boston: Allyn Bacon.

Olson, D. H. 2000. "Circumplex Model of Marital and Family Systems." *Journal of Family Therapy* 22 (2): 144–167. doi:10.1111/joft.2000.22.issue-2.

Order of St. Benedict. 2019. "Order of St. Benedict Atlas." Accessed 15 November 2019. http://www.osbatlas.com/default.asp?id=352

Patterson, J. 2002. "Understanding Family Resilience." *Journal of Clinical Psychology* 58 (3): 233–246. doi:10.1002/(ISSN)1097-4679.

Ponzetti, J. J. 2014. "Governance in the Cloister: Lessons from the Rule of Benedict for Sustainable Leadership in Communal Organizations." *Journal of Leadership, Accountability and Ethics* 11 (3): 25–35.

Randerson, K., A. Fayolle, and G. Dossena. 2016. "The Futures of Family Entrepreneurship." *Futures* 75: 36–43. doi:10.1016/j.futures.2015.10.008.

Randerson, K., C. Bettinelli, A. Fayolle, and A. Anderson. 2015. "Family Entrepreneurship as a Field of Research: Exploring Its Contours and Contents." *Journal of Family Business Strategy* 6 (3): 143–154. doi:10.1016/j.jfbs.2015.08.002.

Rost, K., E. Inauen, E. M. Osterloh, and B. Frey. 2010. "The Corporate Governance of Benedictine Abbeys." *Journal of Management History* 16 (1): 90–115. doi:10.1108/17511341011008331.

Rule of St. Benedict. Accessed 13 June 2019. http://archive.osb.org/rb/text/toc.html

Salvato, C., F. Chirico, and P. Sharma. 2010. "A Farewell to the Business: Championing Exit and Continuity in Entrepreneurial Family Firms." *Entrepreneurship and Regional Development* 22: 321–348. doi:10.1080/08985621003726192.

Sorenson, R. L. 2014. "Values in Family Business." In *SAGE Handbook of Family Business*, edited by L. Melin, M. Nordqvist, and P. Sharma, 463–479. London: SAGE.

Steiner, A., and J. Atterton. 2015. "Exploring the Contribution of Rural Enterprises to Local Resilience." *Journal of Rural Studies* 40: 30–45. doi:10.1016/j.jrurstud.2015.05.004.

Tedeschi, R. G., and L. G. Calhoun. 2004. "Posttraumatic Growth: Conceptual Foundations and Empirical Evidence." *Psychological Inquiry* 15 (1): 1–18. doi:10.1207/s15327965pli1501_01.

Tredget, D. A. 2002. "'The Rule of Benedict' and Its Relevance to the World of Work." *Journal of Managerial Psychology* 17 (3): 219–229. doi:10.1108/02683940210423123.

Tusaie, K., and J. Dyer. 2004. "Resilience: A Historical Review of the Construct." *Holistic Nursing Practice* 18: 3–10. doi:10.1097/00004650-200401000-00002.

Weismeier-Sammer, D., H. Frank, and A. Von Schlippe. 2013. "Untangling 'Familiness'." *The International Journal of Entrepreneurship and Innovation* 14 (3): 165–177. doi:10.5367/ijei.2013.0119.

Wenger, E. C., and W. M. Snyder. 2000. "Communities of Practice: The Organizational Frontier." *Harvard Business Review* 78 (1): 139–146.

Woods, T. E. 2005. *How the Catholic Church Built Western Civilization*. Washington, DC: Regnery Publishing.

Yang, Y., and S. M. Danes. 2015. "Resiliency and Resilience Process of Copreneurs in New Venture Creation." *Journal of Entrepreneurship Research* 5 (1): 1–30. doi:10.1515/erj-2013-0076.

Yu, A., G. T. Lumpkin, R. L. Sorenson, and K. H. Brigham. 2012. "The Landscape of Family Business Outcomes: A Summary and Numerical Taxonomy of Dependent Variables." *Family Business Review* 25 (1): 33–57. doi:10.1177/0894486511430329.

Understanding entrepreneurial opportunities through metaphors: a narrative approach to theorizing family entrepreneurship

Allan Discua Cruz, Eleanor Hamilton and Sarah L. Jack

ABSTRACT

The concept of opportunity is central to entrepreneurship theory. This article contributes to theorizing family entrepreneurship across generations by examining how entrepreneurial opportunities are constructed, communicated, and acted upon at the intersection between family and business. Drawing on the experiences of four families in different business sectors in Honduras, the study adopts a narrative perspective and argues that metaphors of entrepreneurial opportunity can enrich our understanding of family entrepreneurship. Findings also suggest that metaphors play a role in developing entrepreneurial legacy. This study of metaphors of opportunity, and how they might entail entrepreneurial legacy, opens up new avenues for theorizing intergenerational family entrepreneurship. In examining the metaphors referring to entrepreneurial practices developed and repeated in the family, this study contributes to understanding family entrepreneurship as a social and discursive process where meanings and values are communicated and maintained in everyday interactions.

Introduction

This study responds to calls to advance the field of family entrepreneurship by extending knowledge on the intersection where entrepreneurship and family meet (Randerson et al. 2015a, 144). A significant process for an entrepreneurial family is the creation of new opportunities. In constructing an entrepreneurial opportunity (Anderson 2000; Randerson, Degeorge, and Fayolle 2015b), family members often face unfamiliar and uncharted territories, thus making sense of their journey through narratives embedded in family discourse (Hamilton 2013). However, we know little about how such narratives are constructed or used in family entrepreneurship. As such, this study explores how metaphors provide a medium for a shared understanding of opportunities, and how this influences family entrepreneurship.

A metaphor is the use of a familiar image to illuminate an unfamiliar idea or institution (Clarke, Holt, and Blundel 2014; Cornelissen 2005). As a linguistic and cognitive device, it bridges diverse elements or domains by framing the unfamiliar in terms of the familiar to make its understanding easier (Lakoff and Johnson 1980). Whilst metaphors are increasingly recognized as important in entrepreneurship research (Dodd, Jack, and Anderson 2013; Gaddefors 2007; Dodd 2002), little is known about how entrepreneurial families use metaphors to understand and construct entrepreneurial opportunities and enact family entrepreneurship (Larty and Hamilton 2011; Hamilton 2013; Hamilton, Discua Cruz, and Jack 2017).

In this study, we focus on metaphors that entrepreneurial families use when they talk about entrepreneurial opportunities. We offer a qualitative longitudinal study that adopts a narrative approach to understand the way entrepreneurial families turn shared experiences into metaphors to shape how they interpret opportunities over time (Hamilton, Discua Cruz, and Jack 2017). We also draw on social systems theory as a way to build appreciation of communicative processes for family entrepreneurship (Von Schlippe and Frank 2013).

This study contributes to the field of family entrepreneurship by analysing the role of family discourse in constructing and developing entrepreneurial opportunities, thereby addressing important questions at the micro level of the intersection between family and entrepreneurship (Randerson et al. 2015a). Further, it shows how entrepreneurial opportunities are constructed through metaphors, and how the family and entrepreneurship domain intersect in the creation of opportunities and the development of family entrepreneurship. Considering opportunity in terms of family entrepreneurship and how this entails the continuous development of opportunities within and across generations, the study demonstrates that family entrepreneurship narratives rely on old, well-worn metaphors, sustained through generations to create order and stability in the face of uncertainty as family members engage in the entrepreneurial process.

Literature analysis

Family entrepreneurship and entrepreneurial opportunities

Family entrepreneurship is dependent upon entrepreneurship, family, and the family business (Randerson et al. 2015a). Central to family entrepreneurship is the core concept of entrepreneurial opportunity (McMullen 2007; Randerson, Degeorge, and Fayolle 2015b). It has been argued that opportunities emerge as an outcome of a process, and are in constant development by entrepreneurs. This is a view of entrepreneurial opportunities as a socially constructed process, influenced by the way entrepreneurs make sense of the information around them (Fletcher 2007; Korsgaard 2011), where various factors interact and are constantly modelled by the entrepreneur (Randerson, Degeorge, and Fayolle 2015b). Entrepreneurship is characterized as complex, with high levels of uncertainty and unfamiliarity, and the way opportunities are conceptualized is a key influence in the entrepreneurial process (Roscoe, Discua Cruz, and Howorth 2013; Randerson, Degeorge, and Fayolle 2015b).

The importance of family for family entrepreneurship is unequivocal (Randerson, Dossena, and Fayolle 2016). Randerson, Dossena, and Fayolle (2016, 37) highlight that while families can take a variety of forms, family remains a 'mainframe' in which entrepreneurial knowledge can be fostered and entrepreneurial dispositions nurtured. The family plays a pivotal role in both the structural (e.g. births, marriages, deaths, conflict, and succession) and transactional dimensions, i.e. the way a business influences an individual mindset about entrepreneurship (Frank et al. 2010). While the structural view focuses on a traditional portrayal, binding a family group around legal or normative aspects, the transactional view asks researchers to consider family as 'a group of intimates who generated a sense of home and group identity and who experience a shared history and a shared future' (Koerner and Fitzpatrick 2002, 71). Instead, the transactional view of family highlights that the boundaries of family are socially constructed, suggesting variations in terms of culture, generation, and ideology about who can be considered as belonging to the family (Randerson, Dossena, and Fayolle 2016). Every family, influenced by diverse dynamics, commitment, loyalty, and structure, provides a specific environment for the perception of enterprise, influencing the way family members act entrepreneurially (Frank et al. 2010).

Different studies highlight the concepts of entrepreneurial families, enterprising families, entrepreneurial households, families in business or business families (Hamilton, Discua Cruz, and Jack 2017; Nordqvist and Melin 2011; Frank et al. 2019). A common denominator in these conceptualizations is the existence of a social unit, composed of different members of a family over time who behave entrepreneurially, that is, they engage in family entrepreneurship. A family social network is informed by history and shared experiences. This network influences the entrepreneurial behaviour of its members and how entrepreneurial opportunities unfold (Randerson, Dossena, and Fayolle 2016, 39). In family firms, entrepreneurial opportunities and their construction are dependent on family members performing activities together, engaging in shared labour and conversations about what needs to be done, what is involved, and why (Roscoe, Discua Cruz, and Howorth 2013). To increase knowledge on how entrepreneurial opportunities are socially constructed, scholars call for further examination of the conversations that tie entrepreneurial families together (Konopaski, Jack, and Hamilton 2015), and the processes that allow a shared view of entrepreneurial opportunities (Randerson, Degeorge, and Fayolle 2015b) that can influence family entrepreneurship.

Understanding the way families construct entrepreneurial opportunities over time and across generations would advance knowledge of family entrepreneurship (Bettinelli, Fayolle, and Randerson 2014). Scholars acknowledge the role of family in developing several businesses over time using different combinations of family members with a shared understanding of the way to create an opportunity, but also stressing the heterogeneity of families and their approach to entrepreneurship (Discua Cruz, Howorth, and Hamilton 2013; Rosa, Howorth, and Discua Cruz 2014).

Family as a social system

Recent studies suggest that grasping how the entrepreneurial dynamics of families are shaped requires novel perspectives (Frank et al. 2010; Von Schlippe and Frank 2013; Hasenzagl, Hatak, and Frank 2018). Frank et al. (2010) adopt social systems theory (Luhmann 1995) to explain the complex relationship between family and enterprise over time. A social system is defined as an autopoietic (self-reproductive or referential), operatively closed system (all processes, such as internal rationality or schemas, are produced by the system itself) constituted through communication. A social system recursively reproduces itself through communication, which involves selecting what is being communicated (information) and why (understanding). One communication connects to another in a pattern, so the dynamic form of stability that we encounter in everyday communication emerges (Von Schlippe and Frank 2013, 389). A communication is never linked to a single event/thing but situated in the context of preceding and subsequent communications. Thus, the act of communicating becomes an interactive and co-created process, constructing common meanings and experiences. Therefore, communication cannot be attributed to any one individual, but constitutes an emergent property of the interaction between many individuals.

The key paradigmatic shift offered by this perspective emphasizes moving away from individuals as the elements of a social system to focus on the different communication logic of different fields of meaning. The theoretical advantage for research as well as practice is that it might be easier to describe the 'rules of the game' than understanding individual family members (Von Schlippe and Frank 2013, 389).

Von Schlippe and Frank (2013) explain that the kind of meaning generated to deal with complexity depends on the context in which it arises. Context determines how communication is to be framed, and the logic varies in function. In families, functional logic relates to the creation of connections for the continuation of communication. The family as a social system is orientated towards relationships, using communication mainly so that its members can confirm mutual attachment. Thus, Von Schlippe and Frank (2013) argue that family as a social system consists of relational communication. Conceptualization of an entrepreneurial family as a world of meaning-processing social systems requires research focused on understanding such communication.

Family entrepreneurship, narratives, and metaphors

Narrative is widely acknowledged as a source of knowledge for scholars engaged in theory building in entrepreneurship (Larty and Hamilton 2011; Hamilton 2014). Larty and Hamilton (2011) highlight the breadth of theories and methods applied in narrative research in entrepreneurship, calling for further development of literary approaches to theory building. Narrative research has illuminated the subtleties and complexities of entrepreneurial opportunities across generations (Hamilton 2006, 2013), challenging rationalist theoretical perspectives of opportunity discovery, evaluation, and exploitation. In contrast, it has highlighted entrepreneurial opportunity as emerging from social practice (Steyaert 2007).

A key element of narratives is found in metaphors (Semino and Demjén 2016). Metaphors are a form of linguistic device, where one thing is represented in terms of another. Metaphor has a powerful role in the development of entrepreneurship theory. Clarke, Holt, and Blundel (2014, 250) theorize the entrepreneurial growth processes through an examination of metaphor, calling for research to clarify the 'meaning and application of particular metaphors'. In the context of family entrepreneurship, Hamilton (2013, 71) argues that particular metaphors are used in family members' narratives to express the hard work experienced whilst constructing entrepreneurial opportunities. The physicality of the language emphasizes challenges or struggles faced during participation in the business. Narratives serve to capture how entrepreneurial families survive over time, both emotionally and physically.

Metaphors can constitute vivid and precise images of entrepreneurial experiences. Metaphors express complex or abstract ideas, or induce audiences to experience a particular relationship among apparently unrelated ideas – to make the unfamiliar familiar. Family stories make sense of unfamiliar concepts over time (Fiese and Pratt 2004). Metaphors facilitate the creation of situated meanings and group identity (Gberardi 2000), as they acquire and create meaning in the interactions of those who produce and uphold them. Thus, meaning resides in the situation in which the metaphor is used, in the community that uses it, and in the context of the action it generated. Moreover, a focus on metaphors of entrepreneurial opportunity, and how they might have implications for family members in the future (Semino and Demjén 2016), opens up avenues for theorizing intergenerational family entrepreneurship.

Transgenerational entrepreneurship and entrepreneurial legacy

Transgenerational entrepreneurship focuses on how entrepreneurial opportunities are created by the incumbent family generation and those who succeed them (Nordqvist and Zellweger 2010). To explain how families nurture transgenerational entrepreneurship, Jaskiewicz, Combs, and Rau (2015, 31) put forward an entrepreneurial legacy theoretical perspective, defined as 'rhetorically reconstructed narratives of the family's past entrepreneurial behaviour or resilience – that motivate and give meaning to entrepreneurship'. It is argued that early involvement (from childhood) of family members imprints the family's entrepreneurial legacy through narratives that will motivate and give meaning to their future entrepreneurial behaviour (Jaskiewicz, Combs, and Rau 2015, 41). Jaskiewicz, Combs, and Rau (2015) call for further understanding the processes through which entrepreneurial families nurture entrepreneurship across generations. In the intersection between family and enterprise in family entrepreneurship (Randerson et al. 2015a), little is known about family narratives and how they may influence the interpretation of entrepreneurial opportunities, potentially leading to the creation of several businesses (Hamilton, Discua Cruz, and Jack 2017; Barbera, Stamm, and DeWitt 2018).

Konopaski, Jack, and Hamilton (2015) in their study of continuity of family firms suggest that family members learn in the context of reflections on past events and stories, which impact the way businesses are run and how new entrepreneurial opportunities are approached in the future. Continuity in family entrepreneurship across generations is deeply intertwined with entrepreneurial opportunities (Howorth, Jackson, and Discua Cruz 2014). Knowledge of opportunities can be embedded in entrepreneurial narratives (Hamilton 2013). Hammond, Pearson, and Holt (2016, 1210) suggest that family legacy represents 'a collective or shared perception reflecting a unique and continuous stream of meanings associated with the family that are transferred to and shared most often, but not always exclusively, among generations of family members through a collection of legacy artefacts. They further suggest that forms of verbal communication can influence sense-making, and as a consequence, members of the same family are likely to share similar frameworks and patterns of understanding. One of the legacy artefacts alluded to by Hammond, Pearson, and Holt (2016) is shared family stories, yet little is known about what may be included in such stories and how they are communicated.

Research context and methodology

Latin America and Honduras

Randerson et al. (2015a) advocate exploring diverse contexts in family entrepreneurship research. Many theoretical frameworks and models developed in family business and entrepreneurship rely on an Anglo-American worldview. Instead, the present study focuses on Honduras, a developing Latin American country (World Bank 2018). Gupta et al. (2008) observe that family and business issues appear to be inseparable in the Latin American culture, with family participation in business being the norm.

Honduras is characterized by a networked society in which mutual support and common action by family members are commonplace in business. Rarely is a business in Honduras not created or influenced by a family or kinship-related group (Discua Cruz et al. 2016). Honduras is typical of the Latin American context in terms of family influence in business activities and culture in business (Gupta et al. 2008). Family ties are a vital part of business dynamics, and family business dominates the economy (Roscoe, Discua Cruz, and Howorth 2013).

Methodology

Our aim is to explore how metaphors provide a medium for shared understanding of opportunities, and how this influences family entrepreneurship. Since this study seeks to explore a phenomenon over time, we rely on qualitative longitudinal research design and the use of observation, conversations, and in-depth interviews to make sense of the situations of participants (Reay and Zhang 2014; Barbera, Stamm, and DeWitt 2018). As such, an interpretivist perspective and a focus on entrepreneurial narratives are used to theorize about family entrepreneurship (Larty and Hamilton 2011).

We purposefully selected entrepreneurial families that created several entrepreneurial opportunities over time, namely, cases with varying permutations of family involvement and with businesses in diverse sectors. While the purposive sampling method has received criticisms around distortion and insufficient breadth (Patton 1990), selecting cases using these criteria allow rich data to emerge based on the narratives of entrepreneurial families (Hamilton, Discua Cruz, and Jack 2017).

Four entrepreneurial families (Table 1) that had shaped a business portfolio over time were selected from a group of twelve that were part of a larger study on entrepreneurial dynamics. Privileged access to business networks in Honduras through the first author's family in business allowed open and rich interviews. The lead author who is familiar with the place and context identified participants relevant to our research interest and sampling approach, and conducted the interviews. Strong levels of trust between the interviewer and the families allowed extensive and open interviews over time. The lead author is theoretically sensitized with the knowledge and skills required for qualitative work (Glaser and Strauss 1967), and could thus remain neutral and non-judgemental in the interviewing process. Following Konopaski, Jack, and Hamilton (2015) and McKeever, Jack, and Anderson (2015), the other members of the research team were involved and engaged throughout the research process, constantly on hand to discuss the data, the emerging patterns and themes.

Data collection involved several in-depth interviews in the locations preferred by interviewees (e.g. business premises, vehicles, farm fields, homes), lasting between 1 and 2.5 hours with multiple respondents engaged in the creation of entrepreneurial opportunities. Interviews were recorded verbatim in Spanish (the first language of the interviewees and lead author). Initial interviews took place in 2006 with follow up interviews held in 2007, 2009, 2014, and 2016. A longitudinal approach

Table 1. Descriptive information of entrepreneurial families interviewed.

Family	Business portfolio	Size (total number of employees) April 2017	First business founded	Number of businesses currently in the portfolio	Latest business founded	Family members interviewed	Generation	Number of core interviews 2006[a], 2007[b]	Follow up interviews 2009[c], 2014[d], 2016[e]	Total interviews
Distributors	Distribution, beverages, frozen food, wholesale business, coffee export, financial services. Latest business – rehabilitation.	153	1960	8	2013	Miles	1st	2[ab]	2[cd]	4
						Julio	2nd	2[ab]	3[cde]	5
						Antonio	2nd	2[ab]	3[cde]	5
Farmers	Large agricultural export (grains, non-traditional produce), real estate, livestock, agricultural machinery, saw mills, oil extraction. Latest business – agro-tourism.	311	1900	7	2014	Enrique Sr.	2nd	2[ab]	2[cd]	4
						Enrique Jr.	3rd	2[ab]	3[cde]	5
						Luis	3rd	2[ab]	2[de]	4
Landowners	Hardware, gas stations, car replacement parts, heavy goods, transportation and real estate development, farms, household appliances. Latest business – residential construction.	190	1970	8	2016	Fernando	1st	2[ab]	2[cd]	4
						Roberto	2nd	2[ab]	3[cde]	5
						Miguel	2nd	2[ab]	2[de]	4
						Nancy	2nd	2[ab]	2[cd]	4
Transporters	Passenger and commercial transportation, real estate, food retail, express packaging, construction. Latest business – cattle farming.	256	1960	7	2012	Alberto Jr.	2nd	2[ab]	3[cde]	5
						Pedro	2nd	2[ab]	2[cd]	4
						Gerardo	2nd	2[ab]	2[de]	4

was used to understand the rationale behind the entrepreneurial processes (Table 1). Subsequent interviews provided insights into the narratives and helped triangulate data. We revisited the perspectives, inviting participants to clarify meanings around the phenomena (Stake 2008). This approach allowed addressing potential issues of retrospective accounts (Loftus and Hoffman 1989), adding rigour to the methodology.

Interviews started with a general request: Tell me about yourself and the story behind this business. This elicited the recollection of vivid and often emotional life stories. Subsequent questions focused on the way businesses emerged, allowing participants to tell a story behind every venture created or acquired. This approach is considered emergent yet promising in understanding entrepreneurial families (Reay and Zhang 2014). The interview schedule (Appendix A) did not directly ask participants to think metaphorically, but to naturally express the language they use when creating entrepreneurial opportunities. The result was the discovery that metaphorical language pervaded the discourse of family entrepreneurship. Employing a metaphor to frame some aspect of a story allowed participants to narrate family entrepreneurship across time. When metaphors were expressed directly, they were often signalled with some lexical cue, such as 'is like' (e.g. creating a new firm is . . .) (Steen et al. 2010).

Data analysis

In line with Dodd (2002, 524) the analytical approach proceeded as follows. First, all metaphors were extracted from the narrative material collected. This involved several careful word-by-word readings of the text, with metaphors placed in a separate file. A metaphor was determined under the following conditions (Schmitt 2005, 371): A word or phrase that can be understood beyond its literal meaning in the context of what is being said. The literal meaning stems from an area of physical or cultural experience (the source area) that is transferred to a second, often abstract, target area. Second, we reviewed the collection of metaphors and made notes of the vehicle and object of each metaphor (e.g. vehicle: 'connecting dots'; object/grounds: seeing a bigger picture) as shown in Table 2. This step involved evaluating the general meaning of the metaphor. Results were then collated both by vehicle and by object in tabular form directly from these annotations. Finally, a broader noun or concept was entered for each vehicle and object listed. This process resulted in the discovery of metaphors chosen to describe entrepreneurial opportunities. We adopted matrices to organize the data, collecting in-situ observation, field notes, margin notes, summaries, vignettes, diagrams, and mindmaps to support the data analysis (Miles, Huberman, and Saldana 2013), allowing us to understand the narratives of family entrepreneurship over time.

The analysis was iterative in that ideas emerging from the narrative data were compared with the literature using the constant comparative method to review data with emerging categories (Konopaski, Jack, and Hamilton 2015; McKeever, Jack, and Anderson 2015). Guided by Konopaski, Jack, and Hamilton (2015), we moved from empirical data to description, thematic categorization and interpretation, and finally, theoretical implications. This resulted in 'meaningful metaphors' used by members of the entrepreneurial families emerging from the iterative analysis of narratives (Oswick, Keenoy, and Grant 2002), arising as naturally as possible, rather than researcher-imposed (Dodd 2002).

Our methodology acknowledges that metaphors are 'culturally formed and located' (Dodd, Jack, and Anderson 2013, 76). Interpretation thus requires knowledge of the background and context (Coulson and Oakley 2005), the language used (Dobrzyńska 1995), and translation (Parker et al. 2013). Whilst translation carries risks, particularly for metaphors, such issue is often not problematized (Temple and Young 2004). Our concern was to retain the metaphorical expressions of interviewees in their original language, and to avoid misunderstandings and over-interpretation. Thus, excerpts from the narrative interviews were translated only after the initial data analysis.

The cases selected are second and third generation family firms, representing the Honduran business landscape (Discua Cruz et al. 2016). In all cases, family members owned 100% of the equity, and nonfamily members did not have an ownership stake in any of the opportunities created. To preserve confidentiality, and at the participants' request, each case was given a fictitious name based on the founding business. The case vignettes of the four cases are as follows (also see Table 1).

The *farmers* family business started 100 years ago in the agriculture sector. Antonio, founder of the *farmers* estate, acquired vast amounts of land in Honduras in the 1900s. The business passed to Enrique Sr., who diversified into mass consumption crops, agricultural machinery rental, real estate, and livestock. The junior generation, educated in marketing and agronomy, created new firms related to non-traditional agriculture for export, grain mills, vegetable oil extraction, and agro-tourism. In 2000, Enrique Sr. retired to follow a political career.

The *distributors* family business started with Miles and Sonia opening a beverage distribution venture. Additional businesses in commuter transportation, coffee exports, ceramic manufacturing, xerography, processed food distribution, and advertising were gradually developed. Sonia died in the 1990s and several of the businesses had to cease operating. The junior generation pursued university degrees in law, business administration, and medicine. Junior generation members then engaged in the existing businesses and in the re-birth of Sonia's businesses. Miles retired in 2014.

The *landowners* family business started in the 1970s with Fernando and Maria acquiring the management rights of a small petrol station. They later diversified into fuel transportation, automotive replacement parts, and real estate. The junior generation diversified further, as all members had different ambitions and education, creating businesses in agriculture, construction, equipment transportation, and appliance distribution. In 2016, the senior generation retired due to health issues.

The *transporters* family started in the sector in the 1960s. Alberto and Laura gradually expanded their business through competitor acquisitions. The junior generation studied business management, agricultural engineering, and accountancy. Alberto Sr. died suddenly in 2007, a few months before this study began. Laura retired following Alberto's death. The junior generation were already managing existing businesses and developed additional ventures in cattle farming, construction, fast-food franchising, and specialized transportation.

Findings

In this section, informed by Salvato and Aldrich (2012), Reay and Zhang (2014), and Frank and Landström (2016), we present the evidence from our findings of narratives of entrepreneurial opportunities in family entrepreneurship. Following Konopaski, Jack, and Hamilton (2015) we use 'power quotes' from the data to illustrate how family members communicate the concept of opportunity. The richness of repeated entrepreneurial experiences relied on metaphors to capture and explain the creation of opportunities. Findings highlight that metaphors assist the transfer of meanings from one generation to the next, provide a shared point of reference, create a connection between something familiar and something new, and link past, current, and future interactions. Table 2 presents the details of metaphors used to give meaning to entrepreneurial opportunities.

Metaphorical foundations: early interaction in family and business

The use of metaphorical language by entrepreneurial families was commonplace in the explanation of entrepreneurial opportunities. As Table 2 shows, the metaphors represent the underlying foundation of the entrepreneurial stories that are told and shared in the context of family businesses. Metaphors embody the environment where interaction between family members occurs, and where entrepreneurial family stories have meaning. In every narrative illustration, members of entrepreneurial families were able to convey their experience and knowledge of the entrepreneurial process, relying on knowledge of the conceptual and lexical domains in their business context (e.g. farming, transportation, logistics, real estate), supported by well-known concepts in the physical world (e.g. a journey, a game, a drawing).

The most representative power quote comes from *transporters* who illustrated a metaphor of entrepreneurial opportunities as 'being on the road, a journey'. Pedro stated:

Table 2. Sources and objects in metaphors by families in business (based on Dodd 2002).

Background	Vehicles		Grounds				Explanation
Distributors	Connecting the dots	Interpreting entrepreneurial opportunities starts with a blank sheet of paper and 'dots' without a clear picture.	Every 'drawing' has diverse features/ challenges, interconnections between 'dots' need interpretation.	Connecting 'dots' is achieved with and through others (family, nonfamily).	Interpretation of drawings may change through interactions over time.	Picture (opportunity) becomes clearer as 'dots' are connected and the content is discussed and agreed.	Metaphor associates dot-to-dot drawings with understanding opportunities. The entrepreneurial process is highly interconnected. Dots represent resources, information, and people that can be linked through knowledge and information. A clearer drawing, representing a constructed opportunity, will emerge and expand as dots are visualized and connected.
Farmers	Sowing and harvesting	Interpreting entrepreneurial opportunities reflects a process dependent on nature (environment) and people.	Every 'field' needs resources, hard work, and persistence, yet with limited control of the final outcome.	Overcoming setbacks can be achieved with the support of others inside or outside family circles.	The harvest depends on what the family knows, the environment, what they 'sow', chance and patience.	Sowing and harvesting represent natural cycles that can be engaged time and time again (nature of agriculture).	Metaphor associates the language of traditional farming and new crops with understanding opportunities. It relates to a natural progression where members plan diligently, sow and harvest based on schedules contingent on climate and weather. Opportunities are interpreted as engagement in a natural cycle.
Landowners	Playing a game	Interpreting entrepreneurial opportunities resembles playing a board game with the family.	Every 'game' has rules that need to be understood first, several people are involved with resources at hand.	The outcome of the game is uncertain every time it is played, risks and rewards are involved.	As there are limited resources/time, guidance through others is needed.	The more the game is played, the more room for adaptation and improved decision-making.	Metaphor associates playing a game with understanding opportunities. Knowing the rules (contextual aspects), resources and time, allow family members to engage in the game as they play, making decisions as the process unfolds about resources supported by others.
Transporters	Being on the road	Interpreting entrepreneurial opportunities represents a journey with family through uncharted territories.	Every 'journey' may be planned in advance, with a defined starting point, route, and destination.	Unexpected setbacks (turns, hills) are to be expected, which impact the resources used.	When lost on the road or considering alternative destinations, help from others can help get back on track.	Every journey is different, detours and setbacks in the journey can lead to great destinations.	Metaphor associates understanding opportunities as a journey, with haphazard and emergent processes. Opportunities embody shared understanding of an accompanied development that will entail change and chance.

> ... it was not until we 'were on the road', as Dad said, that we understood what business is like ... as children my brothers and I loved cars and trucks, and hey, our Dad had buses, so it was fun ... Dad made sure we went with him on trips during vacation times or the weekends .... at the end of the day, we talked about what we saw on the trip, from the start to the end of the journey, the good, the bad, what was needed, the hidden costs, the joys and even about what new roadside businesses we could start along that route.

Alberto Jr. suggested young family members had to experience what 'being on the road' meant. A bus, a route, co-pilots, detours, hills, stop-signs, movement of people, shaped a shared view of interpreting entrepreneurial opportunities as a journey. Similar accounts were found in all cases, where metaphors are used not only to define and describe an experience, but also to serve as a template or reference, relying on familiar physical objects or experiences as vehicles, rendering abstract concepts (e.g. creating entrepreneurial opportunities) concrete and familiar.

Farmers articulated entrepreneurial opportunities around a metaphor linked to 'sowing and harvesting'. The language of opportunities refers to a field ready to be cultivated, preparing the soil, planting a new crop, a tree, and the natural elements involved. Enduring natural cycles that several generations encountered shaped the metaphorical approach, turning experiences into a shared collective memory of how to interpret entrepreneurial opportunities.

Distributors relied on 'connecting dots' and childhood memories of dot-to-dot drawings, arguing that family members can visualize entrepreneurial opportunities as connections. Resources needed to create an opportunity are described in terms of dots, lines are used to describe the way products would be distributed, and colours are associated with the weight of connection between dots.

Landowners described entrepreneurial opportunities in terms of playing a property-based game (Monopoly). They defined legal or commercial challenges in terms of game rules and gameplay, in tune with the real estate properties the family acquired over time. A board game is used not only as a family pastime but also as a way to introduce a familiar language of entrepreneurship to subsequent generations.

Narrative illustrations suggest that the foundations of a metaphorical approach to entrepreneurial opportunities may be strongly dependent on the early interaction of family members, relying on a common language and vocabulary in a context that is safe, familiar, and linked to existing businesses and family spheres. Such metaphors represent collective memories shaped by positive interactions in the family and business context. Interpreting entrepreneurial opportunities through metaphors serves as an intergenerational educational device. Such shared experiences (e.g. dot-to-dot drawings, riding a bus, planting crops, playing games) create the metaphor's backstory, carrying meaning for the entrepreneurial family. Table 3 shows that the founder generation lays down a memory, perhaps unintentionally, yet highly developmental for the next generation, using a metaphorical approach to later make sense of entrepreneurial opportunities collectively.

Metaphorical association: interconnections over time

Metaphors are used not only to express meaning, but also influence how meaning of entrepreneurship as a process is constructed. Table 3 shows that a metaphorical approach allows transferring the meaning from one theme to another, acting as a vehicle to interpret several opportunities over time. Metaphors become a blueprint over time, a durable point of reference in the creation of several opportunities and the interpretation of entrepreneurship as a collective process.

A representative power quote comes from *distributors*, who highlighted that a 'connecting dots' metaphor provides a template when recreating entrepreneurial opportunities disrupted after the death of a family member. Antonio explained:

> Ok, let me show you [draws several dots in a piece of paper, different colours] ... imagine you want to create a food distribution of corn-based products ... first we need to know what we have here [in existing businesses, resources, support] and what we can get our hands on before we start, I could see some dots, and my brother can tell of you of others ... each dot we think of will have a different weight or characteristic ... then we stand back and gradually start making the connections, one of us can start from who we know, the other from what we

Table 3. Understanding opportunities through metaphors (guided by Konopaski, Jack, and Hamilton 2015).

Empirical data	Description	Thematic categorization	Thematic interpretation	Theoretical implication
Julio: … after my mom passed away 'connecting dots' had a strong meaning for us … I'd need to know a bit about every 'dot' in the map where I can distribute [products] … what is the profile of customers who live there? What prices can I charge? How am I going to get products there at the minimum costs? … That is a simple way of doing things but it works for us regardless of whether we studied medicine, law, or anything else (*Distributors*, June 2009)	Succeeding generation relates earlier experiences of 'connecting dots' to constructing opportunities. Emotional links to deceased parent guidance increased its appreciation.	Early shared experiences influenced the (re) interpretation of previous and new opportunities after critical events.	Communication from an early age allows developing common understandings about entrepreneurial opportunities, which remain imprinted after family members are no longer around.	Metaphorical vehicles are introduced based on early years' interaction: Communication and shared interpretations of opportunities.
Alberto Jr: … My Dad made sure we all had that experience [being on the road] and even though we all studied different things, we all relate to it. It is stuck in our memories forever. So now we do the same with our children, we still have the original business [passenger transport] and of course modern fleets but the thinking remains the same. They [new generations] also have to go and experience that [being on the road]. It is a way to honour our Dad's legacy. (*Transporters*, May 2007)	Succeeding generation articulates that 'being on the road' is shaped by early experiences. Social situations like in being in a bus with family members can shape a metaphorical approach in future generations. Early communication from deceased parent increased shared understanding.	Early interaction influences a shared metaphorical approach among diverse members.	Metaphor used to interpret opportunities can be shaped by early interactions, critical events (sudden death), and family social situations.	
Enrique Jr: … We [junior generation] all had to sow a crop or plant a tree, look after it, check the best way to make it grow, harvest it, and sell it. So when my Dad talked to us about starting a new business being like planting a new crop, then I can see it in my mind easier than if he said something else …. My brothers will tell you the same thing. (*Farmers*, August 2014)	Succeeding generation highlights connection to early interactions and experience to agricultural language and 'sowing and harvesting' to interpret opportunities.	Early shared experiences lead to shared understanding and communication about a metaphor based on the physical world.	Metaphors may only be interpreted by those who have engaged early and continuously in business activities.	

(*Continued*)

Table 3. (Continued).

Empirical data	Description	Thematic categorization	Thematic interpretation	Theoretical implication
Gerardo: … for us, it was as simple as recalling 'being on the road' every bit was connected: from the people that could drive the transport vehicle, knowing the best routes that can get you from here to there, to knowing how much weight the vehicle can carry … because we had used it ['being on the road' metaphor] before when looking at the fast food opportunity with Dad, it made sense again. (*Transporters*, August 2014)	Succeeding generations compare new opportunities outside existing sectors to meanings communicated repeatedly through the 'being on the road' metaphor.	Continuous family communication allows shared views about the connection of a metaphor to interpreting new opportunities.	Shared views of the meaning of a metaphor allows comparing different domains over time.	Metaphorical approach to family entrepreneurship: comparisons and connections. Shared views, collaboration, and continued communication.
Fernando: … I think because they [junior generation] see starting a firm as playing our game [monopoly], then it is easier to make sense of it for the future … when the home appliances business was first being discussed, they were able to highlight what location would be best based on the properties we owned, what were the problems along the way, and of course suggesting how they could also invest together if a particular location was chosen … I imagine they would do that again when a new business idea comes about. (*Landowners*, June 2009)	Incumbent generation articulates the way in which offspring use the 'playing a game' metaphor, specifying how a metaphor allows interpreting opportunities.	Repeated communication about the meaning of a metaphor and its meaning when creating new opportunities.	Interpreting opportunities based on collective comparisons through a shared metaphor.	
Enrique Sr: … so now I have grandchildren, most of them want to be involved in the farm and tell me about their ideas … they need to learn more about our stories and be involved in the fields … their parents know that they have to use the same examples [metaphor] I did, even if they have new firms it will bind them together, the same way my father did with me … (*Farmers*, January 2016)	Good intra-family relationships support continued communication about the 'sowing and harvesting' metaphor for new generations.	Family bonds lead to engagement with younger generations to communicate and pass on a metaphorical approach.	Interpretation of opportunities through metaphors strengthens relationships through shared experiences across generations.	

(*Continued*)

Table 3. (Continued).

Empirical data	Description	Thematic categorization	Thematic interpretation	Theoretical implication
Julio: … I still keep some of those [dot-to-dot] drawings to remind me about what mom taught me about how to start a firm … we just recently started a new rehabilitation clinic project as my brother was studying medicine when mom died. It was easy for us to sit down, even after all that time that we had not really talked about the project and start 'connecting dots' … it was a time for us to remember our mom and also realize how important making sense of it [connecting dots] is for us. (*Distributors*, August 2014)	Articulating the ways by which 'connecting dots' unites family members after the death of a business founder.	Shared views about metaphors allow reinforcing the social unit in business.	Communicating metaphor and its emotional link is appreciated by selected family members.	Metaphorical approach: Implications for inclusion (or exclusion) over time.
Gerardo: We all have different memories of Dad, but we all share one thing, we 'were on the road' with him, that is what binds us since we were kids. We were all interested in different stuff, but the way we learned about doing business based on that [metaphor] allowed us to create new ones even if they have nothing to do with transportation …. we know what that [being on the road] means for us and few people will understand it. I can tell you about it but that connection is missing if you have not done it with us. (*Transporters*, January 2016)	Articulating the way that 'being on the road' bonds members through shared experiences and excludes others of the meanings embedded.	Relevance of communication of a metaphor by family members to strengthen bonds and create a social unit.	Shared views around a metaphor include unique understanding only experienced by family members.	
Enrique Jr: … it is 'sowing and harvesting' for us … it does not matter if I studied marketing and my brother engineering, we can all relate back to it … we know what it means … it is different with our cousins, who live in the city and their parents have no farm, they come to visit us during their vacations for a few weeks … I do not think they will ever get it. (*Farmers*, June 2009)	Articulating how meanings embedded in 'sowing and harvesting' around opportunities can only be understood by those sharing experiences in business.	Communicating metaphors in particular settings allows reinforcing a shared identity.	Metaphors may only be interpreted by those who continue to be involved in business activities as family over time.	

> have, and so on .... what we experienced together from those dots is what allows us to connect them ... At the end you have a picture that makes sense to all of us ...

For *distributors*, creating entrepreneurial opportunities as 'connecting dots' entails comparing the nature of a dot-to-dot drawing and its relation to people, products, customers, or existing commercial and personal networks over time. Metaphors allow constant connections between formal and informal 'rules of the game', such as government regulations or property investments, and the chances, risks, and rewards of engaging in the entrepreneurial process.

For *landowners*, the game metaphor allows interpreting opportunities around real estate development as a monopoly game, implying a process where more than one business venture can emerge. This occurred as the senior generation acquired several real estate properties, and the junior generation was encouraged to think metaphorically about the investment and related businesses whilst playing the game. Complex concepts such as chance and luck in business, which may determine the progress (or regression) of an individual player towards the attainment of his/her goal in a game, are explained by metaphorical associations. Playing a game relates to creating entrepreneurial opportunities that sharpen business judgement, as family members have to master the rules of the game, manage resources, and plan accordingly.

The narrative illustrations highlight that whilst comparison between domains of knowledge is simplified when opportunities are created over time in areas related to existing businesses (e.g. agricultural-based ventures in *farmers*), associations between seemingly disconnected areas are also made through metaphors.

Transporters relied on 'being on the road' when a new unrelated business in fast-food restaurants was started. Ambiguity and adaptation in a new industry for all entrepreneurial families also led to drawing on the metaphorical approach. Uncertainty is associated with 'bumps' or 'road maintenance works' that may slow down the process, or 'roadblocks' that may change the route or ending up in unexpected places. Family members referred to the metaphor as they illustrated how they advanced from the starting point of the journey (e.g. fast-food restaurant idea) to a destination (e.g. start of trading), relating the process to transportation terms they had become familiar with over the years. The journey demanded diverse skills and information from others as well as resources when 'driving' in uncharted territory. The comparisons made through 'being on the road' encouraged a collective approach to anticipate unexpected 'twists' and 'turns' in the entrepreneurial process.

Metaphors allow family members to frame information (e.g. changes in customer demand, industry, etc.) and create a common reference point about what an entrepreneurial opportunity looks like in both familiar and unfamiliar business sectors, allowing wider connections over time to be made (e.g. who to contact first, which resources to use and when). Table 3 shows that metaphors represent accounts of what an entrepreneurial opportunity is, difficult to articulate otherwise, becoming part of a socially constructed meaning for entrepreneurial families.

Continuity of a metaphorical approach: reinforcing social structures and belonging

The narrative illustrations reveal that a metaphorical approach is reinforced by, and in turn reinforces, the social structures of an entrepreneurial family over time and across generations. Whilst beneficial to creating a durable and shared point of reference, this also entails unintended exclusionary features. A power quote by Gerardo from *transporters* highlights this notion:

> ... well, thinking like that [based on being on the road] when looking at new businesses works for us because we witnessed what my Dad meant, we heard it at the dinner table, when we were "on the road". He discussed it only with us – his family. He would not talk about it with anyone else. I still remember the smell of grease in the bus repair shop when we returned from a long trip over the weekend and the way he would talk about getting to a new destination and how he solved the problems on the road as they appeared ... we all remember that ... we met the other day with my mom and recalled each of our anecdotes. I mean, we can all talk about being on a journey with him and what he explained, it was the way he explained, the examples he used that we still remember and apply because they work for us.

For *transporters*, 'being on the road' was cemented as the family point of reference after their father's death, reinforcing a shared identity as an entrepreneurial family

The narrative illustrations highlight that family gatherings and other social contexts both at home and at the business reinforce a shared way of creating opportunities. The notions of exclusion highlighted in Table 3 suggest that whilst the well-accepted metaphors of entrepreneurial opportunity may appear straightforward, it is the interpretation and experiences behind the meaning of such metaphors that create a unique shared reference point for family entrepreneurship. Table 3 also shows that the role of family members in ensuring continuity of meanings associated with a metaphorical approach carries an emotional weight. Such relationships help 'establish in-group language and identity', whereby shared understanding of metaphors becomes a vehicle for the inclusion or exclusion of others (Cameron 2003, 24). Members of the same entrepreneurial family may use similar metaphors to explain their experiences and interpretations of entrepreneurial opportunities.

Table 3 further reveals that metaphors embody a 'gate-keeping role', regulating participation in family entrepreneurship activities. The narrative illustrations show members strongly associate their metaphorical approach with their shared experiences, and thus the meaning and interpretation of the metaphor for entrepreneurship would automatically exclude those who lack such experiences. Metaphors ensure the continuity of the socio-cultural dynamics of the family and shared understanding of entrepreneurial opportunities. The use of metaphors assists entrepreneurial families over time to make sense of their world and their place in it, and so assisting in the creation of a social reality for the members of the entrepreneurial family.

Discussion

Our findings indicate the significance of metaphors for theorizing family entrepreneurship, especially in line with social systems theory, entrepreneurial legacy, and the social construction of opportunity.

Metaphors and social systems theory

This study shows how metaphors allow the entrepreneurial family to make sense of the complexity of the surrounding environment (Von Schlippe and Frank 2013; Oswick, Keenoy, and Grant 2002; Lakoff and Johnson 1980), and that entrepreneurial family stories and metaphors specifically can create boundaries.

Metaphors provide meaning to entrepreneurial families, and meaning delimits a social system from its environment. As such, it creates a system-environment boundary. These meanings, created via communication (Frank et al. 2019), incorporate three dimensions: a factual one (e.g. creation of a new venture), a social one (e.g. creating a trans-generational cohesion), and a temporal dimension (e.g. providing information on how to develop an opportunity in terms of 'before-after'). Family business heterogeneity is important, as each may uniquely differ from another family business (Dibrell and Memili 2019), and these heterogeneous attributes can take many forms. However, identities of social systems, such as family business, are based on self-description and constructed through narrative (Frank et al. 2019). This reflective self-conception (Frank et al. 2019) can reinforce identity and guide behaviour. Our findings show that no one else can share the entrepreneurial family stories, because they are kept within the family. Only the family who experience the activities behind the metaphor are within the boundary, and therefore, the stories frame the boundary of the family business. Animating metaphors through shared experiences provides new understanding of what can tie members of a social group (Cameron 2003).

Entrepreneurial opportunities

In terms of entrepreneurial opportunities and family entrepreneurship, this study contributes to the view that entrepreneurial opportunities are socially constructed through language and shared entrepreneurial family stories. Metaphors facilitate the construction of entrepreneurial opportunities by providing a bridge 'from the familiar to the strange' (Cornelissen 2005; Clarke, Holt, and Blundel 2014). While the transactional view deems that opportunities are socially constructed, it says much less about how this occurs. Our findings show that opportunities are constructed through entrepreneurial family stories that develop shared understanding of opportunity recognition, evaluation, and exploitation. Language is an important part of this construction of opportunities in family entrepreneurship. There are other stories within families, but entrepreneurial family stories are about how these families engage in entrepreneurship.

Creating entrepreneurial opportunities is a process filled with unexpected turns and new experiences, and the entrepreneurial family, as a social unit, responds by making sense of the process through its own internal schema. What we see in this study is that metaphors can act as basic yet powerful shared constructs for organizing knowledge of the world by relating phenomena (e.g. entrepreneurial opportunities) to something previously experienced and concrete. In so doing, metaphors transfer 'familiness' (Frank et al. 2010) to entrepreneurial opportunities. In the process of making decisions, metaphors can allow an entrepreneurial family, as a social system, to construct future-oriented representations of entrepreneurial opportunities (Hill and Levenhagen 1995). The context that the family acts on is constructed through interaction with metaphors (Gaddefors 2007). Such interaction may facilitate an entrepreneurial family, as a social system, to act upon opportunities over time.

The narrative illustrations reveal that entrepreneurial families perceive how entrepreneurial opportunities 'come to be' rather than 'exist'. Entrepreneurial opportunities are contingent on family members in business communicating over time, existing in specific temporal and geographic contexts, and in relation to others (Roscoe, Discua Cruz, and Howorth 2013). As evidenced by the narrative illustrations, metaphors allow interpretation and action without hiding the complexity and uncertainty of the entrepreneurial process.

Learning effect of metaphors in entrepreneurial legacy

Key studies of legacy (e.g. Hammond, Pearson, and Holt 2016; Jaskiewicz, Combs, and Rau 2015; Barbera, Stamm, and DeWitt 2018) highlight the significance of family stories, but little has been said about the language of family entrepreneurship. This study shows that entrepreneurial family stories and metaphors specifically connect the family members through time, and so to legacy. Theorizing entrepreneurial legacy points to the importance of entrepreneurial family stories. This paper contributes to understanding what those stories consist of, and how they carry shared meanings through transmission and translation, that is, how they are socially constructed. Particular social practices of family entrepreneurship are embedded in metaphors, and metaphors draw upon shared experiences specific to each entrepreneurial family. Metaphors emerge as the result of a relational process, and entrepreneurial opportunities are socially constructed between and across generations. Whilst metaphors appear to be commonplace, they are the outcome of interactions and a relational process that belong to the family's private realm. This occurs from an early age, thus influencing the development of family legacy, and implying that through metaphors, transgenerational family entrepreneurship may emerge (Hamilton, Discua Cruz, and Jack 2017).

The narrative illustrations show that the purpose of metaphors is unveiled in the interaction between founding and subsequent generations. They offer a succinct method of instruction in practical ways. Metaphors invite family members to reflect on the world and their shared experiences, turning into a vehicle for entrepreneurial learning (Konopaski, Jack, and Hamilton 2015) that connects the family and enterprise realm in family entrepreneurship. While the connotations of some metaphors (e.g. journey, connecting dots) may be universal in scope (Dodd 2002), they reflect the lives of the families behind the businesses and the continuity of entrepreneurial engagement. This is not to say, we emphasize, that the metaphors discussed here are not applicable to other families. Families around the world have the same concerns about business continuity and how to go about engaging in further entrepreneurial activities (Rosa, Howorth, and Discua Cruz 2014; Howorth,

Jackson, and Discua Cruz 2014). The study reported here shows that metaphors are used to communicate entrepreneurial insight, and relayed to those who may be successors in existing firms or leaders in independent businesses in the future. The learning effect of metaphors may also influence family members who decide to establish family businesses on their own over time (Discua Cruz, Howorth, and Hamilton 2013). Metaphors as connected acts of communication and legacy artefacts allow family entrepreneurship to pass from one entrepreneurial family to other entrepreneurial families over time. Therefore, family metaphors deserve to be recognized for their impact on entrepreneurial behaviour and their potential to influence family entrepreneurship across generations.

Limitations and further research

This article has some limitations that provide opportunities for future research. First, we have examined a metaphor-based approach to family entrepreneurship at the micro level of analysis, that is, at the communication process micro level (e.g. interpersonal communication between family members). In terms of longitudinal research, such approach is challenging for reasons including cost, time, and cooperation between the researcher and the entrepreneurial family under study (Hassett and Paavilainen-Mäntymäki 2013). When conducting longitudinal research, many unpredictable events may occur that can affect the entire research process. In the course of this study, two families decided to sell most of their businesses and migrate overseas, while others stopped establishing new firms after the 2009 political coup in Honduras (Ruhl 2010). This poses a limitation for progressive approaches, particularly in uncertain and unstable contexts (Gupta et al. 2008). Future studies might focus on a narrative approach to study metaphors that have either survived or eroded in long established family firms in the same industry and country beyond the 5th or 6th generation (Nordqvist and Zellweger 2010), or in newly formed firms around the world (Zhang and Reay 2018). Further studies might also look at different levels of analysis, for example, a metaphorical approach to understand the ways family members communicate in the context of corporate entrepreneurship (Bettinelli et al. 2017). A wider view of family and its extensions is also of interest. For instance, for social systems theory, an underlying question might relate to who is part of the business family and who is not (see Frank et al. 2019).

Second, metaphors in this article are portrayed as largely unproblematic, but we acknowledge the ambiguity and elusiveness of metaphors (Inns 2002). Hence, we do not claim that these metaphors are universal, rather that they are part of the everyday language of entrepreneurial families and appear to influence the approach to family entrepreneurship. Nevertheless, narrative illustrations can shed light on our understanding of entrepreneurial families over time and help further decipher the language of family entrepreneurship. Important to note is that we do not suggest that metaphors presented in this article can be generalized to entrepreneurial families around the world, yet we believe that metaphors, as a way to interpret entrepreneurial opportunities, are transferable to engagement in family entrepreneurship in any setting.

A further limitation is that metaphors may be solely linked to elements of the actual phenomenon where it can provide a better illustration of the process. Ritchie (2013) cautions that the underlying meanings of metaphors may be ambiguous, and may be interpreted differently by different people based on their own unique experiences. Such underlying meanings may also change over time, as familiar metaphors may be reinterpreted in light of new cultural experiences, or in the case of entrepreneurial families creating new businesses, or when succession is disrupted. The embodiment of metaphors is often influenced by cultural beliefs and practices, and it is thus important to consider culture in any account of metaphors used by entrepreneurial families. Randerson, Dossena, and Fayolle (2016) highlight that the differences among families across cultures, legal systems, and religions merit attention.

To address these concerns, further studies would benefit from exploring items related to emotions, intentions, and cultural diversity in the study of metaphors. For instance, emotional features of metaphors remain largely unexplored in the context of entrepreneurial families (Shepherd 2016).

The use of narrative analysis, metaphors specifically, is fruitful and promising in theorizing family entrepreneurship. Narratives are a way to look at phenomena in family entrepreneurship. We build on the work of Anderson, Drakopoulou Dodd, and Jack (2009), and Larty and Hamilton (2011) to provide a guiding framework for future methodological approaches. However, we also show that further reflections on the emotional features of metaphors are needed (Dodd 2002). Conflicts or issues within entrepreneurial families working together may hinder the appreciation of metaphors and affect the approach to entrepreneurial opportunities (Discua Cruz, Howorth, and Hamilton 2013), and thus family entrepreneurship (Randerson et al. 2015a). Future studies could explore to what extent metaphors emerge 'deliberately' in the context of entrepreneurial families (Dodd 2002).

Finally, in most entrepreneurship and metaphor studies, English is the *lingua franca*, yet we suspect metaphors are used by entrepreneurial families around the world. The underlying processes of metaphor are a basic human skill, but different languages construct metaphors differently. Every language has lexical resources to bring together two ideas. Different languages have a particular set of conventionalized metaphors, partly linked to culture and partly the result of historical accident. Primary conceptual metaphors occur in all languages, but the linguistic expressions are likely to differ. Future research could expand on how family members give meaning to their metaphorical expressions in diverse cultures and contexts through narratives and metaphors (Semino and Demjén 2016). Metaphors may provide clues to deeper layers of meaning and unusual cultural translations of entrepreneurial families. Some metaphors may be universal and thus common in language, not just in Spanish or English, but also in cultures around the world (Anderson, Drakopoulou Dodd, and Jack 2009).

Moreover, as well as the potential limitations of type of respondent and interview content, future interviews may be fruitfully conducted by groups of researchers (e.g. Johannisson et al. 2007). This may be appropriate in contexts where cultural and language similarities are found, particularly for qualitative work (Bechhofer, Elliott, and McCrone 1984).

Conclusion

In examining how metaphors provide a medium for shared understanding of opportunities, this study contributes to knowledge on family entrepreneurship as a social and discursive process where meanings and values are communicated and maintained in everyday interactions. In enhancing understanding of the processes through which entrepreneurial families nurture entrepreneurship across generations, it also contributes to theorizing transgenerational family entrepreneurship (Randerson et al. 2015a). This study contributes to family entrepreneurship theory by demonstrating how metaphors of entrepreneurial opportunity are shared with and 'imprinted' on family members. Metaphors of entrepreneurial opportunity are a vehicle for conveying the unique and continuous stream of meanings identified by Hammond, Pearson, and Holt (2016). This study demonstrates metaphors are a significant feature of entrepreneurial legacy.

Metaphors, as legacy artefacts, are important in the everyday language of family entrepreneurship. We have provided evidence that entrepreneurial legacy may become purposeful through narrative elements such as metaphors. Metaphors are developed, communicated, and then translated into forms of family entrepreneurial action.

Our study shows that the way entrepreneurial families communicate about entrepreneurial opportunities is replete with metaphors, and that the language of family entrepreneurship may appear simple, yet is a highly complex and coordinated exercise. Some metaphors are enduring and form part of the entrepreneurial legacy. A key contribution of this study is that analysing metaphors and patterns of metaphor use contribute both to our understanding of family entrepreneurship and the contexts in which metaphors are used. Metaphors are the symbolic language of a process, of change, of a metamorphosis, narrating processes of family entrepreneurship across generations.

The practical implications of this study suggest that through metaphors, as the outcome of connected communication, family members in business may be able to simplify approaches to entrepreneurial opportunities and make them familiar over generations. Metaphors can have the same effect as a full story because they already have stories associated with them that are embedded in the minds of the members of the entrepreneurial family. The main contribution of this article is therefore establishing the link between metaphor as a narrative element and family entrepreneurship and opening up new avenues for further studies in the field of family entrepreneurship.

Disclosure statement

No potential conflict of interest was reported by the authors.

ORCID

Allan Discua Cruz http://orcid.org/0000-0002-0069-3092
Eleanor Hamilton http://orcid.org/0000-0002-9617-2020
Sarah L. Jack http://orcid.org/0000-0001-9459-6455

References

Anderson, A. R. 2000. "Paradox in the Periphery: An Entrepreneurial Reconstruction?" *Entrepreneurship & Regional Development* 12 (2): 91–109. doi:10.1080/089856200283027.

Anderson, A. R., S. Drakopoulou Dodd, and S. L. Jack. 2009. "Aggressors; Winners; Victims and Outsiders: European Schools' Social Construction of the Entrepreneur." *International Small Business Journal* 27 (1): 126–136. doi:10.1177/0266242608098349.

Barbera, F., I. Stamm, and R.-L. DeWitt. 2018. "The Development of an Entrepreneurial Legacy: Exploring the Role of Anticipated Futures in Transgenerational Entrepreneurship." *Family Business Review* 31 (3): 352–378. doi:10.1177/0894486518780795.

Bechhofer, F., B. Elliott, and D. McCrone. 1984. "Safety in Numbers: On the Use of Multiple Interviewers." *Sociology* 18 (1): 97–100. doi:10.1177/0038038584018001009.

Bettinelli, C., A. Fayolle, and K. Randerson. 2014. "Family Entrepreneurship: A Developing Field." *Foundations and Trends® in Entrepreneurship* 10 (3): 161–236. doi:10.1561/0300000049.

Bettinelli, C., S. Sciascia, K. Randerson, and A. Fayolle. 2017. "Researching Entrepreneurship in Family Firms." *Journal of Small Business Management* 55 (4): 506–529. doi:10.1111/jsbm.12347.

Cameron, L. 2003. *Metaphor in Educational Discourse*. London: Bloomsbury Academic.

Clarke, J., R. Holt, and R. Blundel. 2014. "Re-Imagining the Growth Process: (Co)-evolving Metaphorical Representations of Entrepreneurial Growth." *Entrepreneurship & Regional Development* 26 (3–4): 234–256. doi:10.1080/08985626.2014.888099.

Cornelissen, J. P. 2005. "Beyond Compare: Metaphor in Organization Theory." *The Academy of Management Review* 30 (4): 751–764. doi:10.2307/20159166.

Coulson, S., and T. Oakley. 2005. "Blending and Coded Meaning: Literal and Figurative Meaning in Cognitive Semantics." *Journal of Pragmatics* 37: 1510–1536. doi:10.1016/j.pragma.2004.09.010.

Dibrell, C., and E. Memili. 2019. "A Brief History and A Look to the Future of Family Business Heterogeneity: An Introduction." In *The Palgrave Handbook of Heterogeneity among Family Firms*, edited by E. Memili and C. Dibrell, 1–15. Cham: Palgrave Macmillan.

Discua Cruz, A., C. Howorth, and E. Hamilton. 2013. "Intrafamily Entrepreneurship: The Formation and Membership of Family Entrepreneurial Teams." *Entrepreneurship Theory and Practice* 37 (1): 17–46. doi:10.1111/j.1540-6520.2012.00534.x.

Discua Cruz, A., C. R. Rodas, C. Raudales, and L. Fortin. 2016. "Large Family Businesses in Honduras: The Influence of State Intervention and Immigration in the Twentieth Century." In *Evolution of Family Businesses: Continuity and Change in Latin America and Spain*, edited by P. Fernández Pérez and A. Lluch, 196–215. Cheltenham: Edward Elgar.

Dobrzyńska, T. 1995. "Translating Metaphor: Problems of Meaning." *Journal of Pragmatics, Literary Pragmatics: Cognitive Metaphor and the Structure of the Poetic Text* 24 (6): 595–604. doi:10.1016/0378-2166(95)00022-K.

Dodd, S. 2002. "Metaphor and Meaning, a Grounded Cultural Model of US Entrepreneurship." *Journal of Business Venturing* 17: 519–535. doi:10.1016/S0883-9026(01)00072-6.

Dodd, S. D., S. L. Jack, and A. R. Anderson. 2013. "From Admiration to Abhorrence: The Contentious Appeal of Entrepreneurship across Europe." *Entrepreneurship & Regional Development* 25 (1–2): 69–89. doi:10.1080/08985626.2012.746878.

Fiese, B. H., and M. W. Pratt. 2004. "Life Course and Systems Perspectives on Narrative." In *Family Stories and the Life Course: Across Time and Generations*, edited by M. W. Pratt and B. H. Fiese, 401–418. London, UK: Routledge.

Fletcher, D. 2007. "'Toy Story': The Narrative World of Entrepreneurship and the Creation of Interpretive Communities." *Journal of Business Venturing* 22 (5): 649–672. doi:10.1016/j.jbusvent.2006.10.001.

Frank, H., and H. Landström. 2016. "What Makes Entrepreneurship Research Interesting? Reflections on Strategies to Overcome the Rigour–relevance Gap." *Entrepreneurship & Regional Development* 28 (1–2): 51–75. doi:10.1080/08985626.2015.1100687.

Frank, H., M. Lueger, L. Nosé, and D. Suchy. 2010. "The Concept of 'Familiness': Literature Review and Systems Theory-Based Reflections." *Journal of Family Business Strategy* 1 (3): 119–130. doi:10.1016/j.jfbs.2010.08.001.

Frank, H., J. Suess-Reyes, E. Fuetsch, and A. Kessler. 2019. "Introducing the Enterpriseness of Business Families: A Research Agenda." In *The Palgrave Handbook of Heterogeneity among Family Firms*, edited by E. Memili and C. Dibrell, 263–296. Cham: Palgrave Macmillan.

Gaddefors, J. 2007. "Metaphor Use in the Entrepreneurial Process." *International Journal of Entrepreneurial Behaviour & Research* 13 (3): 173–193. doi:10.1108/13552550710751049.

Gberardi, S. 2000. "Where Learning Is: Metaphors and Situated Learning in a Planning Group." *Human Relations* 53 (8): 1057–1080. doi:10.1177/0018726700538002.

Glaser, B. G., and A. L. Strauss. 1967. *The Discovery of Grounded Theory: Strategies for Qualitative Research*. Chicago: Aldine Press.

Gupta, V., N. Levenburg, L. Moore, J. Motwani, and T. Schwarz. 2008. "Culturally Sensitive Models of Family Businesses in Latin America." In *A Compendium on the Family Business Models around the World*, edited by V. Gupta, N. Levenburg, L. Moore, J. Motwani, and T. Schwarz, 244–264. Hyderabad: ICFAI University Press.

Hamilton, E. 2006. "Whose Story Is It Anyway? Narrative Accounts of the Role of Women in Founding and Establishing Family Businesses." *International Small Business Journal* 24 (3): 253–271. doi:10.1177/0266242606063432.

Hamilton, E. 2013. *Entrepreneurship across Generations: Narrative, Gender and Learning in Family Business*. Cheltenham: Edward Elgar.

Hamilton, E. 2014. "Entrepreneurial Narrative Identity and Gender: A Double Epistemological Shift." *Journal of Small Business Management* 52 (4): 703–712. doi:10.1111/jsbm.12127.

Hamilton, E., A. Discua Cruz, and S. L. Jack. 2017. "Re-Framing the Status of Narrative in Family Business Research: Towards an Understanding of Families in Business." *Journal of Family Business Strategy* 8 (1): 3–12. doi:10.1016/j.jfbs.2016.11.001.

Hammond, N. L., A. W. Pearson, and D. T. Holt. 2016. "The Quagmire of Legacy in Family Firms: Definition and Implications of Family and Family Firm Legacy Orientations." *Entrepreneurship Theory and Practice* 40 (6): 1209–1231. doi:10.1111/etap.12241.

Hasenzagl, R., I. Hatak, and H. Frank. 2018. "Problematizing Socioemotional Wealth in Family Firms: A Systems-theoretical Reframing." *Entrepreneurship & Regional Development* 30 (1–2): 199–223. doi:10.1080/08985626.2017.1401123.

Hassett, M. E., and E. Paavilainen-Mäntymäki. 2013. *Handbook of Longitudinal Research Methods in Organisation and Business Studies*. Cheltenham: Edward Elgar.

Hill, R. C., and M. Levenhagen. 1995. "Metaphors and Mental Models: Sensemaking and Sensegiving in Innovative and Entrepreneurial Activities." *Journal of Management* 21 (6): 1057–1074. doi:10.1177/014920639502100603.

Howorth, C., J. Jackson, and A. Discua Cruz. 2014. "Entrepreneurship in Family Businesses." In *Handbook of Research in Small Business and Entrepreneurship*, edited by E. Chell and M. Karatas-Ozkan, 333–357. Cheltenham: Edward Elgar.

Inns, D. 2002. "Metaphor in the Literature of Organizational Analysis: A Preliminary Taxonomy and A Glimpse at A Humanities-Based Perspective." *Organization* 9 (2): 305–330. doi:10.1177/1350508402009002908.

Jaskiewicz, P., J. G. Combs, and S. B. Rau. 2015. "Entrepreneurial Legacy: Toward a Theory of How Some Family Firms Nurture Transgenerational Entrepreneurship." *Journal of Business Venturing* 30 (1): 29–49. doi:10.1016/j.jbusvent.2014.07.001.

Johannisson, B., L. Centeno Caffarena, A. F. Discua Cruz, M. Epure, E. Hormiga Pérez, M. Kapelko, K. Murdock, et al. 2007. "Interstanding the Industrial District: Contrasting Conceptual Images as a Road to Insight." *Entrepreneurship & Regional Development* 19 (6): 527–554. doi:10.1080/08985620701671882.

Koerner, A. F., and M. A. Fitzpatrick. 2002. "Toward a Theory of Family Communication." *Communication Theory* 12 (1): 70–91. doi:10.1111/j.1468-2885.2002.tb00260.x.

Konopaski, M., S. L. Jack, and E. Hamilton. 2015. "How Family Business Members Learn About Continuity." *Academy of Management Learning & Education* 14 (3): 347–364. doi:10.5465/amle.2014.0244.

Korsgaard, S. 2011. "Entrepreneurship as Translation: Understanding Entrepreneurial Opportunities through Actor-Network Theory." *Entrepreneurship & Regional Development* 23 (7–8): 661–680. doi:10.1080/08985626.2010.546432.

Lakoff, G., and M. Johnson. 1980. "Conceptual Metaphor in Everyday Language." *The Journal of Philosophy* 77 (8): 453–486. doi:10.2307/2025464.

Larty, J., and E. Hamilton. 2011. "Structural Approaches to Narrative Analysis in Entrepreneurship Research Exemplars from Two Researchers." *International Small Business Journal* 29 (3): 220–237. doi:10.1177/0266242611401796.

Loftus, E. F., and H. G. Hoffman. 1989. "Misinformation and Memory: The Creation of New Memories." *Journal of Experimental Psychology: General* 118 (1): 100–104. doi:10.1037/0096-3445.118.1.100.

Luhmann, N. 1995. *Social Systems*. Stanford, CA: Stanford University Press.

McKeever, E., S. Jack, and A. Anderson. 2015. "Embedded Entrepreneurship in the Creative Re-Construction of Place." *Journal of Business Venturing* 30 (1): 50–65. doi:10.1016/j.jbusvent.2014.07.002.

McMullen, J. S. 2007. "What Is an Entrepreneurial Opportunity?" *Small Business Economics* 28 (4): 273–283. doi:10.1007/s11187-006-9040-z.

Miles, M. B., A. M. Huberman, and J. Saldana. 2013. *Qualitative Data Analysis: A Methods Sourcebook*. 3rd ed. Thousand Oaks, CA: SAGE.

Nordqvist, M., and L. Melin. 2011. "Entrepreneurial Families and Family Firms." *Entrepreneurship & Regional Development* 22 (3–4): 211–239. doi:10.1080/08985621003726119.

Nordqvist, M., and T. Zellweger. 2010. *Transgenerational Entrepreneurship : Exploring Growth and Performance in Family Firms across Generations*. Cheltenham: Edward Elgar.

Oswick, C., T. Keenoy, and D. Grant. 2002. "Note: Metaphor and Analogical Reasoning in Organization Theory: Beyond Orthodoxy." *Academy of Management Review* 27 (2): 294–303. doi:10.5465/AMR.2002.6588045.

Parker, M., R. Thomas, C. Steyaert, and M. Janssens. 2013. "Multilingual Scholarship and the Paradox of Translation and Language in Management and Organization Studies." *Organization* 20 (1): 131–142. doi:10.1177/1350508412460998.

Patton, M. Q. 1990. *Qualitative Evaluation and Research Methods*. 2nd ed. Newbury Park, CA: Sage.

Randerson, K., C. Bettinelli, A. Fayolle, and A. R. Anderson. 2015a. "Family Entrepreneurship as a Field of Research: Exploring Its Contours and Contents." *Journal of Family Business Strategy* 6 (3): 143–154. doi:10.1016/j.jfbs.2015.08.002.

Randerson, K., J.-M. Degeorge, and A. Fayolle. 2015b. "Entrepreneurial Opportunities: How Do Cognitive Styles and Logics of Action Fit In?" *International Journal of Entrepreneurship and Small Business* 27 (1): 19–39. doi:10.1504/IJESB.2016.073353.

Randerson, K., G. Dossena, and A. Fayolle. 2016. "The Futures of Family Business: Family Entrepreneurship." *Futures* 75: 36–43. doi:10.1016/j.futures.2015.10.008.

Reay, T., and Z. Zhang. 2014. "Qualitative Methods in Family Business Research." In *The SAGE Handbook of Family Business*, edited by L. Melin, M. Nordqvist, and P. Sharma, 573–593. London: SAGE.

Ritchie, L. D. 2013. *Metaphor*. Key Topics in Semantics and Pragmatics. Cambridge: Cambridge University Press. doi:10.1017/CBO9781139136822.

Rosa, P., C. Howorth, and A. Discua Cruz. 2014. "Habitual and Portfolio Entrepreneurship and the Family in Business." In *The SAGE Handbook of Family Business*, edited by L. Melin, M. Nordqvist, and P. Sharma, 364–382. London: SAGE.

Roscoe, P., A. Discua Cruz, and C. Howorth. 2013. "How Does an Old Firm Learn New Tricks? A Material Account of Entrepreneurial Opportunity." *Business History* 55 (1): 53–72. doi:10.1080/00076791.2012.687540.

Ruhl, J. M. 2010. "Honduras Unravels." *Journal of Democracy* 21 (2): 93–107. doi:10.1353/jod.0.0170.

Salvato, C., and H. E. Aldrich. 2012. "'That's Interesting!' In Family Business Research." *Family Business Review* 25 (2): 125–135. doi:10.1177/0894486512446327.

Schmitt, R. 2005. "Systematic Metaphor Analysis as a Method of Qualitative Research." *The Qualitative Report* 10 (2): 358–394. https://nsuworks.nova.edu/tqr/vol10/iss2/10

Semino, E., and Z. Demjén. 2016. *The Routledge Handbook of Metaphor and Language*. New York: Routledge.

Shepherd, D. A. 2016. "An Emotions Perspective for Advancing the Fields of Family Business and Entrepreneurship Stocks, Flows, Reactions, and Responses." *Family Business Review* 29 (2): 151–158. doi:10.1177/0894486516634943.

Stake, R. E. 2008. "Qualitative Case Studies." In *Strategies of Qualitative Inquiry*, edited by N. Lincoln and Y. Denzin, 119–150. 3rd ed. London: SAGE.

Steen, G. J., A. G. Dorst, J. B. Herrmann, A. A. Kaal, and T. Krennmayr. 2010. "Metaphor in Usage." *Cognitive Linguistics* 21 (4): 765–796. doi:10.1515/cogl.2010.024.

Steyaert, C. 2007. "Entrepreneuring as A Conceptual Attractor? A Review of Process Theories in 20 Years of Entrepreneurship Studies." *Entrepreneurship & Regional Development* 19 (6): 453–477. doi:10.1080/08985620701671759.

Temple, B., and A. Young. 2004. "Qualitative Research and Translation Dilemmas." *Qualitative Research* 4 (2): 161–178. doi:10.1177/1468794104044430.

Von Schlippe, A., and H. Frank. 2013. "The Theory of Social Systems as a Framework for Understanding Family Businesses." *Family Relations* 62 (3): 384–398. doi:10.1111/fare.12010.

World Bank. 2018. "Doing Business in Honduras - World Bank Group." Accessed 20 April 2018. http://www.doingbusiness.org/data/exploreeconomies/honduras

Zhang, Z., and T. Reay. 2018. "Managing the Yin and Yang of Family Capital: A Study of Chinese Immigrant Entrepreneurs." *Entrepreneurship & Regional Development* 30 (7–8): 722–748. doi:10.1080/08985626.2018.1457085.

Appendix A.

Selection of interviewee questions (initial and follow-up)

Area	Question
Business portfolio development	Beginning and development of the business portfolio (who was involved and why?). Influences of the development of the business portfolio (who, what, how, why?). Are nonfamily members involved in this process (who, how, why)?
General dynamics	How did this business emerge? How was the business opportunity identified, evaluated, and exploited? Why this business opportunity? Who was involved and how was it approached? Who manages and controls this business (has it changed over time?)
Composition of the family unit in business	Who are the key members of the family in business, why? Are there any other external nonfamily members, who, why? Reason(s) for the participant to be involved in the creation or acquisition of a business (any specific personal role? Has it shifted or changed over time?)
Approach to entrepreneurial opportunities	Do you approach the creation of a new firm as a team (who does what and why)? If a team is involved: Are there any underlying rules when working together in the creation/acquisition of new businesses or management of existing businesses? What guides you in the creation of a new business? Do you to share the same views as a family when approaching a business opportunity? If so, how, why? How are existing assets (financial, plant, human, social) used in the emergence of new businesses or in the operations of existing ones (who influences such dynamics, why)?

Structural coupling in entrepreneurial families: how business-related resources contribute to enterpriseness

Mariana Estrada-Robles, Nick Williams and Tim Vorley

ABSTRACT

This paper examines how family members support each other's entrepreneurial activities through sharing resources created at the business-level. Drawing on the concept of 'enterpriseness' the study examines the flows between a family and the business and how it influences the impacts of the businesses on the family (enterpriseness). We capture the enterpriseness by focusing on entrepreneurial families where more than one member is an owner-entrepreneur. Through in-depth interviews with entrepreneurial families in Mexico, we show how different forms of capital resources emerging from multiple businesses flow back into the family and contribute to enterpriseness. The entrepreneurial family enables access to human, social and financial capital resources that are easily mobilized and combined by other members for their multiple firms, showing a subsequent effect to the business-level. Consequently, enterpriseness influences entrepreneurial behaviours which have a variety of consequences for the entrepreneurial family and their businesses. The paper concludes with a number of contributions to theory.

1. Introduction

Despite emerging studies which have sought to examine the intersection of family, family business and entrepreneurship (Randerson et al. 2015,), understanding of the reciprocal impact of the family and the business is still limited (Rau 2014; Hasenzagl, Hatak, and Frank 2018). Typically, the household is the focus in examining the resource portfolio of family businesses (i.e. Alsos, Carter, and Ljunggren 2014; Danes et al. 2009; Rodriguez, Tuggle, and Hackett 2009). While this research is highly valuable, it also leaves significant gaps, as the family can be socially constructed beyond the boundaries of a single household or nuclear family (Koerner and Fitzpatrick 2002; Von Schlippe and Frank 2013). The nuclear family is, in fact, becoming a minority in most industrialized countries over other types of families (Randerson, Dossena, and Fayolle 2016).

In this study, we focus on entrepreneurial families, where more than one member is an owner/entrepreneur who interact with other entrepreneurs members of the same family. In examining the entrepreneurial family we focus on members that are related by blood ties but that may not be part of the same nuclear family, consequently, we look at the family beyond the nuclear family and single household. As such, this conceptualization of the family adds to both structural and transactional views of the family (Koerner and Fitzpatrick 2002). Entrepreneurial families may be bound by biological and/or legal ties (structural view), but also by sharing family history and a sense of identity (transactional view) of being entrepreneurs. Entrepreneurial families operate within the intersection between family, family business and entrepreneurship, as such there is a need to look into the system where all entrepreneurs are embedded. This has thus far been neglected in family business and entrepreneurship research (Aldrich and Cliff 2003; Randerson et al. 2015). Therefore, our paper seeks to fill this important gap in the literature through the examination of the impact that businesses have on families (Frank et al. 2019).

As the entrepreneurial family has multiple owner/entrepreneurs, it not only allows the influence of the family on the firms (familiness) but also the influence of these multiple businesses on the 'entrepriseness' on the family. Frank et al. (2019, 264) define enterpriseness as 'those structures that the business family develops based on the structural coupling with its business and the family'. Enterpriseness is vital in entrepreneurial families because the support given to different members in the family normally comes from other existing firms owned by members of the family (Estrada-Robles, Williams, and Vorley 2018). As such the directionality also occurs from business to family and not only from family to business (Frank et al. 2010). Further examination is needed to explore how the resources brought from enterprising members influence enterpriseness to keep the family functioning (Frank et al. 2019). As such, we explore two key research questions:

RQ1. How do business-related resources flow to the entrepreneurial family and to other businesses owned by members of the family?

RQ2. How does the availability and use of these resources contribute to enterpriseness in entrepreneurial families?

Beyond business families with one or more businesses, our study contributes to family entrepreneurship by providing a fine-grained understanding of how enterpriseness induces entrepreneurial behaviours of family members and the consequences of those behaviours by examining families with multiple entrepreneurs. These consequences may include joining the core family business, diversifying the core family business, creating their own businesses either within the formal or informal economy, and supporting other businesses within the entrepreneurial family. They are thus not restricted to the household level or within one family business, but rather multiple opportunities and developing various entrepreneurial behaviours. The enterpriseness of the family considers the resources and decisions which the business family develops for itself as a result of the structural coupling between the family and the family business (Frank et al. 2019). While it has been acknowledged that families may own multiple firms (Habbershon and Pistrui 2002; Sieger et al. 2011; Michael-Tsabari, Labaki, and Zachary 2014; Steier, Chrisman, and Chua 2015), the processes that occur in the entrepreneurial family with multiple firms are under-researched (Rosa, Howorth, and Discua Cruz 2014).

We focus on the structural coupling between the entrepreneurial family and the multiple businesses within the family. We contribute to the literature by addressing enterpriseness in entrepreneurial families focusing on the different resource pools (human, social and financial capitals) emerging from the business setting that are available to family members through their interactions, in two key ways. First, we extend previous research on enterpriseness in business families (Frank et al. 2019) to show that the outcomes of having multiple owner/entrepreneurs contribute to the availability of business-related resources in the entrepreneurial family. The impacts of the flow of resources also leads to a wider resource availability in the family and to expectations of the family to keep inducing entrepreneurial behaviours.

Second, we further research on the involvement and essence approach of enterpriseness (Frank et al. 2019) by unveiling the boundaries of the family and the decisions that lead to a two-way interaction between the business and the family. The study identifies not only the sources of capital but also the decisions behind their use for further development of enterpriseness of the entrepreneurial family. We show how the entrepreneurial family uses enterpriseness to act upon either family or business logic depending on the family's objectives and specificities of the context they operate in, in our case Mexico. This builds on the recurrent paradox that families in business live where decisions benefit one logic over another (Frank et al. 2019). In our entrepreneurial families this is highly related to the setting where they are embedded: pressing institutional challenges frame the priorities and objectives within the family (Estrada-Robles, Williams, and Vorley 2018).

The remainder of the paper is structured as follows. First, we highlight the flow of resources in entrepreneurial families, the current state of enterpriseness and its link to entrepreneurial behaviours in entrepreneurial families. We then set out the empirical focus of our study and the methods employed. The findings are then presented, followed by the discussion and conclusions which offer a number of implications for academic theory. Finally, limitations and suggestions for future research are presented.

2. Literature review

2.1. Enterpriseness and capital resources in entrepreneurial families

This research explores the enterpriseness of 'entrepreneurial families', where multiple entrepreneurs and businesses exist within a single family. Entrepreneurial families are unique because they are a result of the integration of family and business, and thus enterpriseness may influence members of such families differently to those within a traditional family business.

To understand enterpriseness it is needed to acknowledge familiness (Frank et al. 2010). The construct of 'familiness' was initially defined as the idiosyncratic firm-level of resources and capabilities resulting from the interactions between the family, its individual members, and the business to create competitive advantage and wealth (Habbershon and Williams 1999; Habbershon, Williams, and MacMillan 2003). However, highlighting only one side of influence may lead to overlooking the complexity of dynamics between family and business (Frank et al. 2019). Further to familiness, the enterpriseness of business families expresses itself in the expectations of the business which are considered as meaningful in the business family, enterpriseness is defined as 'those structures that the business family develops based on the structural coupling with its business and the family' (Frank et al. 2019, 264). It is important to note that the two concepts are not a mirror image, as influences are perceived and processed according to the structures of each system (business and family).

Enterpriseness should not only assess the impact of business in family, or defining whether it is weak or strong but also highlighting the types of enterpriseness, these might include the rules and expectations behind managing both the business and family influences (Frank et al. 2010). Beyond rules and expectations, there is a need to analyse the consequences of enterpriseness on the members of the family and any subsequent effects to the business (Frank et al. 2019). Some consequences can cause paradoxical decisions because of the different expectations in the family and the business (Zahra and Sharma 2004); moreover, family structures are dependent on the business system (Frank et al. 2010).

Emerging research on enterpriseness has focused on employing a conceptual approach through the components of involvement and essence approach, and identity approach (Frank et al. 2019). The identity approach considers how the business family defines itself. The components of involvement approach addresses the boundaries, size and diversity of the family in business while the components of essence approach considers the behaviours and unique resources. Through the entrepreneurial family this study addresses both the involvement and essence dimension to enterpriseness through the social construction of the family and the particular behaviours exercised by their members as a consequence of enterpriseness.

Enterpriseness can be influenced by the range and amount of resources that the members in the family contribute to the operations of the entrepreneurial family (Frank et al. 2019). These resources can be financial but also come in other forms such as experience, capabilities or maintaining cohesion within the family. The portfolio of resources and decisions based on those resources are important to the interaction of the family and the business (Sirmon and Hitt 2003), and include different forms of capital resources (Hoy and Sharma 2010; Irava and Moores 2010). Entrepreneurial families make decisions together related to their businesses and entrepreneurial behaviours while keeping the cohesion in the family (Estrada-Robles, Williams, and Vorley 2018). The entrepreneurial family provides an ideal setting to study the two-way flow of resources from the family (different entrepreneurs) to their various firms; and vice versa the use of resources acquired from different firms that serve to other entrepreneurs in the family.

The dimensions of different forms of capital resources are not consistent across families and may influence the creation of capabilities in entrepreneurial families (Discua Cruz, Howorth, and Hamilton 2013). These capabilities are the result of the unique combination of those dimensions of resources and the decisions that are made based on them (Pearson, Carr, and Shaw 2008). It is of particular interest in this study to identify the specific combination of capital resources in entrepreneurial families that lead to the flow of business related resources that support enterpriseness among the family members and their other businesses. Considering that different forms of capital coexist simultaneously (Sharma 2008), their flow can take the form of a two-way transmission between family owner/entrepreneurs and their businesses, showing the enterpriseness of the family (Frank et al. 2010). The availability and flow can be a result of the informal participation of family members, even those not employed in the business (Sorenson and Bierman 2009). In the case of entrepreneurial families, owner/entrepreneurs can be formally or informally involved in other businesses in the family and belong to different households.

As a result of the simultaneous participation of family members in business and family relationships, human capital is complex and unique to business families. Within the family context, human capital can have both positive and negative effects (Sirmon and Hitt 2003), depending on the life-cycle stage of the family and the firms (Danes et al. 2009), or the quality of relationships in the family (Sorenson and Bierman 2009). A unique feature of human capital is that stocks of this type of capital, when needed, can flow through the business, the family or governance systems (Sharma 2008).

Sorenson and Bierman (2009) suggest that family relationships, derived from social capital, can attract family human and financial capital to the business. Relationships are the heart of the family, hence it is important to focus on them while studying the family (Aldrich and Cliff 2003). The strength and structure of relationships in the family can influence entrepreneurial behaviour of its family members through decisions made based on social capital (Randerson, Dossena, and Fayolle 2016) while also motivating the mobilization of different forms of capital to help other members in need (Dyer, Nenque, and Hill 2014).

In addition to human and social capital, financial capital refers to the sharing of financial resources or investments made by members in the family (Sharma 2008; Sorenson and Bierman 2009). In this study, financial support is not exclusive on the wealth and income of one household for the creation of new ventures (Kim, Aldrich, and Keister 2006). Financial resources may flow from different businesses to multiple households in the entrepreneurial family.

2.2. Enterpriseness and entrepreneurial behaviour in entrepreneurial families

The interactions between members provide support within entrepreneurial families (Estrada-Robles, Williams, and Vorley 2018) showing that family relationships and interactions among members are key points where entrepreneurship meets the family (Randerson et al. 2015). This disentangles family entrepreneurship (Bettinelli, Fayolle, and Randerson 2014) by examining the entrepreneurial family and allows exploration for the interactions between the members in the family, the behaviour of the family acting together as a result of enterpriseness and its effect back to the firms within the entrepreneurial family.

We thus extend the focus of Frank et al. (2019) on business families to examining entrepreneurial families where not only the existence of multiple businesses impacts the family but also the existence of multiple entrepreneurs. By doing so, we are able to examine the behaviours and processes within the entrepreneurial family resulting from the available resources that every entrepreneur provides to the family and the way the entrepreneurial families as a unit decide to act upon these. In many cases, that results in portfolio entrepreneurship. There is growing recognition in investigating entrepreneurial activities that lead to a portfolio of businesses in the family (Schjoedt et al. 2013). which has been conducted mainly from the individual lead entrepreneur perspective (Plate, Schiede, and von Schlippe 2010) rather than from the collective. In other cases, entrepreneurial processes may result in growing the family business or creating new ventures (Discua Cruz, Hamilton, and Jack 2012); however, there is more complexity to this and entrepreneurial families provide an avenue to examine other types of entrepreneurial behaviour. Families in business may engage in a diversity of ventures at a time or simultaneously; however, the nature and amount of support influencing entrepreneurial activity is little understood (Lumpkin, Steier, and Wright 2011).

The literature review demonstrates that there are distinct gaps within the family entrepreneurship literature, and how a focus on entrepreneurial families can integrate the family dimension into family business research. We add to research on enterpriseness (Frank et al. 2019) by exploring multiple entrepreneurs within a family structure that is not limited to the household. In doing so, we examine the dynamic state of entrepreneurial families that are socially constructed and offer suggestions for how theory can be advanced.

3. Methodology

3.1. Research design

In order to examine enterpriseness in entrepreneurial families, we utilize an in-depth qualitative approach as it has the ability to explore new depths in entrepreneurship that are in constant change and shaped by the experiences and behaviours of entrepreneurs (Neergaard and Ulhøi 2007). In the family business field, there are still several underdeveloped areas that could be answered with in-depth studies (Hall, Nordqvist, and Melin 2005; Chrisman et al. 2009; Bettinelli, Fayolle, and Randerson 2014). Thus, qualitative approaches have the potential to provide significant insights regarding the interaction between family and business (Reay 2014). Furthermore, richer descriptions are needed in developing economies to explain the complex relationships between the particular institutional environment, the impact on the business and the perceptions of the owner (Doern 2009).

3.2. Empirical setting

Previous research has shown that entrepreneurial families play an important role in supporting their members in navigating the complex institutional environment in Mexico (Estrada-Robles, Williams, and Vorley 2018). Entrepreneurial families act as an intermediary through which social capital gives family members access to resources which enable them to overcome institutional challenges. Often, this support occurs through informal agreements originated from trust and shared language within the family (Estrada-Robles, Williams, and Vorley 2018).

The importance of family values such as trust, cohesion and support are instilled in Mexican families even when new constructions of family are arising as a consequence of social changes (Arriagada 2002). Shared vision and purpose to maintain family wealth is common in Latin American countries such as Mexico, this enables family members to act together in the decisions they make (Mani and Lakhal 2015). As such, by examining entrepreneurial families in Mexico we are able to explore whether the country and cultural context impacts on the enterpriseness of entrepreneurial families.

Our study is focused on Toluca, the capital of the State of Mexico. The State itself is one of the economic and social engines of the country, and contains the largest focus of economic activity outside of Mexico City (INEGI 2014). Toluca is characterized by its strategic location, close proximity to Mexico City and other key economic centres in the country, and is one of the most industrialized cities in the country. In addition, Toluca has been the focus of State and municipal policy attention with regards to the promotion and facilitation of entrepreneurship, including support for family entrepreneurship (Gobierno Toluca 2015). The purpose of these programmes is to create 'strong' families that wish to create a new venture and/or grow their existing one to foster employment generation in the city. The Institute of the Entrepreneur in the city aims to provide support to families to start and grow businesses, 'Generating an entrepreneurial culture' is one of the priority policies to develop and consolidate businesses. In summary, because of the richness and uniqueness qualities of the locality, the city was deemed suitable for the empirical focus of the study. In addition, because of the stress on policy to promote entrepreneurship in families, the city of Toluca is an ideal setting to understand the processes within entrepreneurial families.

3.3. *Participants*

Using the definition of entrepreneurial families outlined above, contacts from the Enterprise Incubator in Toluca were employed as an initial step to make the first contact with entrepreneurial families. Through this first stage, eight entrepreneurial families were contacted and invited to take part in the research; further to this, because entrepreneurial families are hard to locate in the sense that there is no single database for them, snowball or chain sampling was employed as sampling instrument to help mitigate this limitation, with the respondents asked if they knew other families whose different members owned a business. The use of snowball sampling technique is consistent with that of past family business studies which have been limited by the unavailability of a database on family firms (i.e. Farrington, Venter, and Boshoff 2012; Bettinelli 2011; Lambrecht and Lievens 2008). Once an entrepreneurial family was identified, they were invited to participate in the research study, and in total 14 families were selected as being suitable for the study as they fulfilled our entrepreneurial family definition. We acknowledge that snowball sampling is not fully random and subject to selection bias; however, this technique also allows the researchers' high level of attentiveness to the focus of the study as they become immersed in the research area (Biernacki and Waldorf 1981). According to Creswell (2013) in qualitative studies a general guideline for sample size is not only about the study of a few individuals but also to gather extensive detail about them. We ultimately examined 14 entrepreneurial families which fit our definition and interviewed 36 individuals and who offered extensive elucidation about the phenomena in question. The number of owner/entrepreneurs within the families ranged from 2 to 5 members within the same family. The total number of participants allowed us to achieve a deep understanding of how member entrepreneurs interact with each other in terms of their businesses and the family where they belong. As we progressed in our research, taking each entrepreneurial family at a time, we found that we reached a saturation level showed by interviewees who expressed recurring responses; hence collecting sufficient high-quality data (Reay 2014). All respondents' businesses were based in Toluca. To highlight the heterogeneity of families and businesses (Dibrell and Memili 2019), we also took into account the number of entrepreneurs in the family, size of firms, age of business and diversity in firm sectors. Table 1 provides an overview of the participants regarding these dimensions. Interviews were conducted from February to May 2015 and lasted an hour on average. All interviews were conducted in Spanish, the first language of the interviewees and the interviewer, and then translated into English for analysis.

3.4. *Procedure*

While much existing research in the field has normally depicted a single respondent, in-depth semi-structured interviews were conducted with multiple respondents of each entrepreneurial family. The use of interviews allowed the study to discover implicit and ambiguous connections within the family unable to gather employing quantitative methods (Hall, Nordqvist, and Melin 2005). All interviews were conducted in person following an interview guideline, this guideline was iteratively modified throughout the data collection process. The nature of semi-structured interviews allowed

Table 1. Profile of participants.

Respondent	Family	Relationship	Business type	Size of business (Number of employees)	Age of business
1	1	Daughter	Shoe manufacturing	1–10	1–5 years
2	1	Father	Construction (Non-residential for government)	11–50	10+ years
3	1	Daughter	Beauty Services	1–10	1–5 years
4	1	Mother	Construction (Residential)	11–50	10+ years
5	1	Daughter	Textiles	Self-employed	1–5 years
6	2	Sibling	Construction (Non-residential for government)	11–50	10+ years
7	2	Sibling	Marketing Services	1–10	10+ years
8	3	Father	Pharmaceutical	11–50	10+ years
9	3	Daughter	Media	1–10	1–5 years
10	3	Son	Construction (Non–residential for government)	1–10	1–5 years
11	3	Mother	Informal	Self-employed	6–10 years
12	4	Father	Construction materials (Paints)	11–50	10+ years
13	4	Son	Construction materials (Sealers)	11–50	10+ years
14	4	Son	Construction materials (Sheetrock)	1–10	10+ years
15	5	Father	Construction (Residential)	11–50	1–5 years
16	5	Mother	Financial Services	1–10	Less than a year
17	5	Sibling (to father)	Construction equipment rental	1–10	Less than a year
18	5	Daughter	Informal	1–10	1–5 years
19	6	Father	Automobile Services	51–250	10+ years
20	6	Son	Petrol services and distribution	1–10	1–5 years
21	7	Father	Legal Services	11–50	10+ years
22	7	Daughter	Education	11–50	10+ years
23	8	Sibling	Automobile parts retailing (Ford)	1–10	10+ years
24	8	Sibling	Automobile parts retailing (Chrysler)	1–10	1–5 years
25	9	Father	Graphic design services and merchandising	1–10	10+ years
26	9	Son	General retailing	1–10	1–5 years
27	10	Sibling	Residual waste recycling (Plastic with transformation processes)	11–50	1–5 years
28	10	Sibling	Residual waste recycling (Plastic)	11–50	6–10 years
29	11	Sibling	Food services	1–10	10+ years
30	11	Sibling	Education	11–50	1–5 years
31	12	Father	Petrol services and distribution	51–250	10+ years
32	12	Son	Real state	1–10	1–5 years
33	13	Sibling	Education	51–250	10+ years
34	13	Sibling	Baking industry	11–50	10+ years
35	14	Father	Petrol services	11–50	10+ years
36	14	Son	Venue rental and event organization	1–10	1–5 years

the emergence of relevant topics not in the interview guideline but mentioned by respondents and further explored in the study (Hatch 2002). Flexibility during the interviews allowed the interviewer to encourage interviewees to share their thoughts and stories through open-ended questions. Written consent was obtained, interviews were recorded and transcribed, then thematically analysed and coded focusing on emergent topics. Transcripts resulted in a total of 412 pages alongside the notes made after each interview. Multiple respondents were fundamental in this research to gain into insight the experiences and perspectives within an entrepreneurial families. It also contributed to understand better family interactions of the entrepreneurs and to mitigate flawed memory limitation.

3.5. Data analysis

The inductive nature of the study aimed to discover themes and patterns. In line with Bryman (2012) the reliability of the coding was consistent and structured to avoid coder bias. Firstly, we analysed the data by creating individual entrepreneurial family summaries, analysing and comparing interview transcripts along with notes gathered after each interview.

Transcripts, summaries and notes were used employing an open coding process undertaken independently by the authors until predominant thematic categories emerged based on key themes (Creswell 2013). The open coding process supported the interpretative approach of the study and continuous iteration throughout the process (Hall, Nordqvist, and Melin 2005). As such, this coding scheme was conducted by the authors, comparing results and identifying any discrepancies between the coders so that they could be revisited and agreed upon. This comparative method ensured inter-coder reliability and involved continually identifying emergent themes against the interview data and employed analytic induction to identify the nature of a relationship and develop the narrative (Silverman 2000). A comparative method allowed to identify and analyse emerging themes against the data collected through an analytic induction process (Miles and Huberman 1994). The methodological techniques contributed to gain a meaningful analysis of the entrepreneurial families embedded in the specific institutional context and allowed an in-depth understanding on how families can support each other's entrepreneurial activity. In the findings section, quotes were employed to provide insightful nuances and give voice to the study. The remainder of the article focuses on business-related resources within entrepreneurial families that have an effect on the family to keep being entrepreneurial.

4. Findings

This section advances the discussions outlined in the literature review by presenting an in-depth analysis of in the process by which entrepreneurial families utilize resources and contribute to enterpriseness. The findings are developed from the empirical data generated in the interviews and are presented in two sections: the first identifies the types of business-related resources in entrepreneurial families showing the way they are derived from the intersection of the family and the business in entrepreneurial families, showing how capital resources support other entrepreneurs in the family. The second section focuses on entrepreneurial activity in entrepreneurial families by examining how enterpriseness is created and its consequences. Figure 1 shows the model emerging from the results where the two-way flow is shown from familiness to enterpriseness through the resource availability and use of human, social and financial capital, and how that availability enables the family to make decisions that contribute to enterpriseness. As such, the outcomes of entrepreneurial activity through different businesses in the entrepreneurial family create enterpriseness

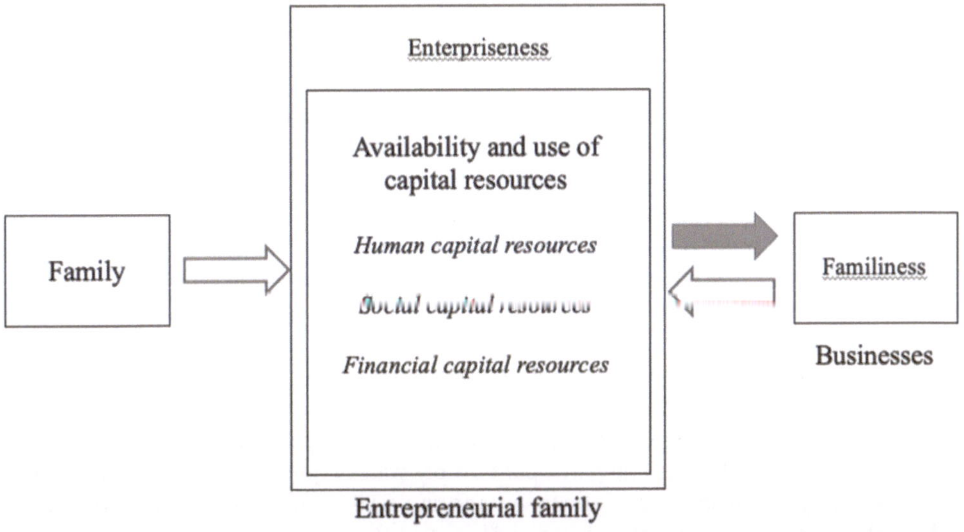

Figure 1. The availability and sharing of resources between the family, the entrepreneurial family and the businesses.

which is transferred back to the family leading to a wider resource availability in the family to be shared by their members. Such resource availability may not be replicated in family businesses which lack this wider resource pool.

4.1. Forms of capital and enterpriseness in entrepreneurial families

4.1.1. Human capital resources

We find that human resources manifest in entrepreneurial families and further on how enterpriseness is developed. Knowledge from family members coming from the different businesses is shared within the family through the multiple experiences of their members, and where there is trust and accessibility it is natural to approach other family members for support. For example: 'At a family dinner we can discuss things about our businesses. My dad or my mum ask us, how are things going with the business, either the one I run with my sister or my own' [INT1/FAM1]. It is an advantage in the entrepreneurial family that other entrepreneurs are easily reached as they are family members, even if they do not share the same household. As one participant stated, 'We have direct communication (with my son) around three to four times a week even when we don't live together. We are independent in a way but we help each other with our businesses' [INT21/FAM6]. This extends on research on household endowments (Alsos, Carter, and Ljunggren 2014; Danes et al. 2009; Rodriguez, Tuggle, and Hackett 2009), as we find that resource accumulation and mobilization occurs in entrepreneurial families that not necessarily share the same household. This also reinforces suggestions on the importance of strong ties and stable family relationships for sharing resources across the family for entrepreneurial endeavours (Sorenson and Bierman 2009). It also shows how the strength and structure of relationships in the family can influence the entrepreneurial behaviour of its family members (Randerson, Dossena, and Fayolle 2016). In Latin American countries, these relationships are affected by the nature and size of the family which may complicate the relationship between the family and business (Botero and Betancourt 2016).

In contexts such as Mexico, some entrepreneurial families may not fulfil all of the legal requirements; thus, engage in informal economic activity. Some of the respondents stated that this occurred when they have projects alongside their main business that do not require them to have a registered business. Our research finds that informality often happens when the financial sustenance in the family comes from the main family business or other entrepreneurial ventures within the family. One interviewee commenting: 'my mum has always liked selling things (informally) and is always spotting opportunities … she was the one who gave me the idea for my business [INT9/FAM3]. Another participant in the family agreeing from his perspective 'One of my biggest support to make decisions in the business is my wife, even when she only sells things informally she has given us (entrepreneurs in the family) a lot of advice' [INT8/FAM3]. In this way, human capital also emerges from informal economic activity that supports further formal business activity in the entrepreneurial family. This highlights the involvement dimension of enterpriseness where the boundaries of the entrepreneurial family are socially constructed including the members that add value to the entrepreneurial activity of other members.

Families are able to transfer resources across generations (Dyer, Nenque, and Hill 2014). In our entrepreneurial families, it also happens in the same generation, sharing enterprise knowledge and skills are common through generations but also between sibling entrepreneurs. That is the case of two siblings each owning their enterprise in the same sector, 'My brother and I share information, yes we do. We are in the same industry so we talk a lot but each one is also very independent [INT27/FAM10]. The strong ties of being family nurture the constant communication between siblings albeit they might be competing against each other with their businesses. Business skills are also transferred from generation to generation as one participant simply states I guided my son on how to run his business. [INT21/FAM6]. Offspring can obtain enterprising skills in the family business during childhood through exposure and experience (Lane and Lubatkin 1998). Such is the case of this participant. 'As kids we would come during our school holidays to help in the business. It wasn't an obligation we went because we liked it. Being involved helped me know the business well. If we didn't come as kids, it wouldn't be the same nowadays, perhaps I would be working for a company' [INT12/FAM3]. This shows how human capital feeds enterpriseness, the new generation not only helping in the family business but being able to leverage on that knowledge obtained in the family business to their own entrepreneurial endeavours.

The flow of resources from the business, or different businesses in the case of entrepreneurial families, goes back to the family and its members. Such is the case when policies are changing in the country, entrepreneurial families share information with other members who seek for, for advice on ways to deal with new policies. Entrepreneurs in the family choose to deal and manage with regulations together across all the businesses in the family. Sometimes new generations are the ones who guide the senior, an example of this: 'my dad has never done the new processes, my mum has never been registered in the tax office, so they didn't really know and I had to show them from what I went through with my business' [INT3/FAM1]. Entrepreneurs share information and transfer knowledge to the rest in the family on how they have dealt with the everyday management of their firms and reforms in the country. It becomes a capability of the entrepreneurial family in which their involvement provides a way to complement for the lack of guidance in the reforms; members take part in shaping the experiences of others on a day-to-day basis, this shows a clear benefit of enterpriseness to family members in entrepreneurial families.

In Mexico, sometimes the operation of a business can create implications of risk and insecurity to entrepreneurs. In fact, business owners in Mexico try to protect themselves from theft and expropriation while suffering the burdens of corruption and bureaucracy (Acemoglu and Robinson 2012). The existence of multiple entrepreneurs in the family and business-related resources helps prevent other family members trying to protect both the family and their firms. This protection coming from the family is common in Mexico where the institutional environment is inadequate to provide the structures for business owners to navigate such challenges (Estrada-Robles, Williams, and Vorley 2018). Hence, this task is delegated to the family where the values of trust and cohesion enable involvement and support in each other's firms. As stated by one respondent: 'You notice that in Mexico there are bad things like insecurity but because we live here we get used to it. If I advise my children with their businesses is because I don't want them to live all sort of trouble you have when operating a business like frauds or other insecurity issues. I want them to know how to protect themselves' [INT2/FAM1]. Overall these are examples of distinctive enterpriseness, a positive influence that the entrepreneurial family has over the family itself and over the multiple firms.

4.1.2. Social capital resources

Social capital in entrepreneurial families is shown in the existence of interactions, shared visions, trust, and networks. Trust is shown, for example, when an entrepreneur is suffering the instability of running a construction business, and then he is integrated into the family business to open independent branches as a plan of expansion. He reflects on the benefits ' … many advantages from the support in the family, this comes from the trust we all have in each other and more than trust is because we are all part of it so we have to take care of it' [INT10/FAM3]. There is a reciprocity of support among the members in the entrepreneurial families, the son manages now the branches to gain more income for his own nuclear family while the father resolves the need for someone 'trustable' to manage the branches. This means that there are gains to both family members, the father and the son, showing the availability of options in the family to conduct different entrepreneurial behaviours, in this case joining and growing the family business. This creates a strong sense of cohesion of members being able to help in diverse ways which facilitates resource mobilization (Granovetter 2005). As one respondent stated: 'When you work with family you live in peace knowing that … you [can] trust them' [INT 13/FAM4]. Trust within members in the family is crucial to share resources and collaborate with each other across the multiple businesses (Alsos, Carter, and Ljunggren 2014).

Networks and connections play an important resource for entrepreneurial families when gaining contracts or opening a certain type of businesses. One respondent stated that *'in Mexico it is all about contacts, depending on the government in place, we see if we have contacts or not, we do better when we have' [INT12/FAM4]*. Connections to the government provide entrepreneurs with the opportunity to operate their firms with exclusive licences. These firms offer certain services or products that are directly related to government processes that citizens need to comply with. As such, being able to operate these particular firms with concessions from the government. The way to get these concessions is by using connections and networks, in most of the cases, these connections are formed at the business level with the previous generation or through another firm in the family. This is the case of FAM6 and FAM7, the connections come from two and three generations back and they have been maintained in the family to serve the businesses of new generations. A respondent mentioning 'with friends in the government my father had the opportunity for me to continue with this business; we do the same now and my daughter will continue with my business' [INT21/FAM7]. Family networks emerging from other firms play an important role to find new connections within the public sector. As it can be noted, business and politics are highly intertwined, and the use of connections or influences is a common practice.

The way enterpriseness is developed in the entrepreneurial family is through the 'appropriability' characteristic of social capital, that is the existence of networks for one purpose may be used for others (Coleman 1988). As such, showing enterpriseness, for example, commercial networks are also employed by entrepreneurial families, the father sharing networks of customers with his son, 'I only told him (if you open your business) it should be in a field that is compatible and not competitive to my sector. I said, 'I will promote you with my business directing people to go and buy from you'. [INT13/FAM4]. The path of the family has driven the foundation of new lines of business. Another example between two siblings with complementary businesses, 'with my sister we make a good team. She kept my father's business which is similar to mine but I am independent, we share customers and suppliers sometimes' [INT25/FAM7]. External ties are brought to the family pool of resources for others to utilize. These bridges then facilitate achievement of goals through information, opportunities and favourable negotiations (Adler and Kwon 2002), and act as a form of distinctive enterpriseness.

4.1.3. Financial capital resources

Entrepreneurial families pool financial resources together, members seek support in the family to ask for loans instead of going to a bank. About this a participant mentioning the benefits, 'I have been able to grow my business faster with my sister's support' [INT33/FAM13]. Sharing of financial resources include, for example, profit created in a business in the family turned into an investment for another business to get earnings over the longer-term or informally investing in real estate properties to maintain family wealth. On this a participant stated: 'I am selling real state to my son, the money he could pay to the bank he can give it to me without interest' [INT11/FAM4]. The father is flexible when his son occasionally asks to skip a month of payment and afterwards pay for 2 months together; different from contract terms with a bank. Enterpriseness here has an impact on both the business and the family dimension in order to maintain wealth in the entrepreneurial family.

Financial resources originated in firms go back to the family and later turned into support to different firms in the entrepreneurial family. Enterpriseness enacts depending on the needs of the family or individual members with their own firms. An example is a formal education of how resources move in a loop from business to family and back from family to business. Financial resources obtained from the family business have made possible formal education for younger generations. When the younger generation grows it wants to give back to the family business. Such is the case of potential successor in case FAM5 where this member is studying a master's degree abroad, he is trying to demonstrate his father that he has the knowledge to contribute to the business. The son opts to contribute with his formal education to the family business because he knows he is the potential successor of the firm, and moreover he is interested in taking over it someday. This shows how the impact of enterpriseness on the family and its retroactive impact on the firm.

Another way resources are kept in the family is when owner/entrepreneurs in entrepreneurial families pool financial resources together making them available to other owner/entrepreneurs who need them instead of going to a bank. For example, 'my sister and I have invested money with my dad. We will receive more profit from my dad's business than if we had that money saved in the bank. We have the money working'. [INT2/FAM1]. Family entrepreneurs invest their business profits in other firms belonging to the family because they conceive it is an unsafe practice to keep the money in the bank and that the return of investment in the bank is much lower than to have it 'working' in another business in the family, while other owner/entrepreneurs struggle with money matters in their businesses and can benefit from this lack of trust on formal financial institutions.

The analysis of the entrepreneurial family brings out the enterpriseness, resources developed through businesses serve other family owner/entrepreneurs for their firms regardless of their involvement in a particular business. This reinforces the family as an entrepreneurial family and the enterpriseness within. This also contributes to understanding the process of portfolio entrepreneurship in the family business context that is still unexplored (Plate, Schiede, and von Schlippe 2010). The quality of the resources is also shaped by the enterpriseness; business knowledge is formed experientially in the management of the firms and from the interactions with other members in the family. That knowledge evolves so that when it comes back to the family the business advice from an owner/entrepreneur to another is more valuable. The outcomes of those capabilities rely in the enterpriseness of the family.

4.2. How capital resources contribute to enterpriseness

The reciprocity shows the distinctiveness of entrepreneurial families, with a two-way flow of resources from the businesses to the family (see Figure 1). Members benefit from the enterprising knowledge existing in the family. This represents a safety net for nascent entrepreneurs, 'it was an advantage that my father had his own business. I see it with my friends, for example, they started from zero because their parents were not entrepreneurs, they are now at level 2 or 3. With my dad's help, perhaps I am in level 5 or 6 compared to those fiends. [INT22/FAM6]. Having a pool of business-related resources available to other members builds on enterpriseness and keeps the flow moving back and forth from/to family and business while resource availability increases simultaneously. Moreover, this safety net feeds enterpriseness when members in the family know that if something goes wrong with their business they will have the support from the other members and their businesses. A respondent mentioning: "my family has my back, they have told me if you fail with your business nothing will happen, we will continue forward. Then, you have the security and trust in your family that if you fall, it's OK nothing bad will happen" [INT2/FAM1]. This notes that members of the family are encouraged to undertake entrepreneurial behaviours even when the outcome might not be a positive one. In this family, one of the members mentions: "what I put into my daughters" businesses I see it as lost, if I get profit out of that then great' [INT1/FAM1]. Here, the need to maintain the family structure as being entrepreneurial is important, beyond the success of the businesses.

What might be considered business competition among siblings also creates enterpriseness with each sibling trying to achieve their goals with their own business; however within the same industry, they share resources when they collaborate with each other sharing knowledge for the benefit of both their businesses. This example is illustrated, 'Even in the same industry, I don't consider my brother as a competitor. We both learn from each other; we help each other as much as we can but we understand we have independent businesses' [INT28/FAM20].

Entrepreneurial families decide how they use their available resources, their capability is fostered from the combination of resources mainly internal resources mobilized and applied through the strong bonds. Trust and cooperation have made possible to refine the managerial experience, 'we are well organized, we have managed to achieve this organization on the go, exploiting each individual's knowledge' [INT35/FAM14]. The son complements in his interview 'our secret is our excellent service combined with our team work' [INT36/FAM14]

The family business provides stability to the family, which enables opportunity for the family to diversify which is not only strategical but also related to family well-being benefiting both business and family logic This is consistent with diversification decisions taken for strategic because of the interests of family members (Dodd, Anderson, and Jack 2015), which also reduces risk of over-specialization. Entrepreneurial members are able to pursue their own interests, for example in case of FAM5 the wife and daughter have their own business, unrelated to the core family firm, although the daughter is selling merchandise incurring in the informal economy. Regardless the type of business, more income comes to the family thus providing stability and diversification in some cases. The same happens with FAM8 where both sisters [INT23 and INT24] own their company and additionally they choose to sell informally extra things not related to the core business using the facilities and exposure to clients to incur in informal economic activity. This shows the complexity of the variety of entrepreneurial behaviours but also the interplay with formality and informality. Also, the complexity between cooperation and independence in entrepreneurial families, while INT23 and INT24 work independently in their own firms, they work together to create the products that they sell informally.

Family firms are often related to firm-specific knowledge or industry-specific knowledge (Sieger et al. 2011), while this is still true when looking at the specific core family business, when looking at the entrepreneurial family it is found that knowledge becomes more generic for the use in different firms and industries. Diversification in entrepreneurial families occurs in different forms (Rosa, Howorth, and Discua Cruz 2014) and for diverse reasons. Only when entrepreneurial families want to explore peripheral business opportunities outside their specific firm or industry knowledge it is when they are more willing to build external partnerships with non-family members, as illustrated, 'we consider other businesses, for example, one with my brother and another one with a friend and my wife, but it is not part of the family business' [INT15/FAM5].

While entrepreneurial families engage in the management and continuity of the core business in the family, trade-off decisions occur when exploring opportunities. In this case the family is more focused in the long-term orientation of the core family business than in other new ventures, 'There other small businesses, mainly real estate projects. We buy properties and we receive rents from them. They are just small projects because for now the family business demands most of our time. Because of that we haven't been able to develop a more active business, otherwise we would need to leave the family business and it is not an option. What we do outside is in our free time [INT31/FAM12]. This family chooses their resources at hand to focus more on the family business rather other small businesses. However, this participant admitted that they will need to look for opportunities outside the family business because 'it might not last forever [INT31/FAM12]'. The same happens with FAM14 that has a main business in the family and the rest of projects are mainly related with real state management. While enterpriseness is still present, the entrepreneurial family has to make complex decisions on how to best use the resources at hand, either on the family, the family business or peripheral businesses within the portfolio in the family. This is consistent with Litz (2008) where families strive for stability and that none of the parts in the system is compromised in the long-term. Building on Frank et al. (2019) it can be seen that the entrepreneurial family is not passive when making decisions as objectives to keep the family firm are clear; however, the paradox exists between the family and business logic. Either keep enterpriseness within the family or translate it into action in other businesses.

In entrepreneurial families, it is normal to engage simultaneously in different entrepreneurial activities, with multiple businesses in different firm life cycles. Families bundle and leverage resources depending on their needs. Members live this in a day-to-day basis part of their normal family life. As an example, a participant commenting 'It is a normal thing to see each of us in the family run a business. We live with that, is not rare [INT5/FAM1]. The family itself provides a support structure and its unity remains a priority and at the same time their decisions feed the enterpriseness within the family. This shows how the entrepreneurial family has expectations for members to keep running their firms as part of the family life. Another participant mentioning: 'we must set a sense of responsibility with our businesses and the family, for this to keep working [INT19/FAM6]'. The findings show that entrepreneurial families experience simultaneous flows, resources originated in the firms flow back to the family and subsequently converted into the support that is shown as a variety of entrepreneurial behaviour within the family. This also highlights the structures that the family puts in place for entepriseness to continue by strengthening family relationships and setting expectations and responsibilities in the entrepreneurial family.

5. Discussion

Our paper contributes to the development of the family entrepreneurship field by examining enterpriseness flows between entrepreneurial families and the business, and illuminating how enterpriseness impacts on the entrepreneurial behaviours of the family. Through our focus on entrepreneurial families we contribute to the heterogeneous nature of families as a socially constructed entity (Von Schlippe and Frank 2013) and we are able to show the consequences it has for the family business and family entrepreneurship.

Our study shows that enterpriseness changes according to the amount of capital resources available to the family and firms as a consequence of its flow (Sharma 2008). We thus build on the essence approach to enterpriseness related to decisions and behaviours by advancing the understanding of the interdependence between family and business, and examining the recent construct of enterpriseness as the enterprise's influence on family (Frank et al. 2010, 2019). We also highlight the involvement dimension of enterpriseness through the social construction of family boundaries where members without a formal business are part of the entrepreneurial family. Our study finds that enterpriseness influences the impact of business(es) on the family and in consequence on other firms in the family to keep the family entrepreneurial. Enterpriseness is contingent on the family's objectives, as well as the needs and type of entrepreneurial behaviour, while trying to keep a balance in between the family and business logic. The families show commitment to business matters, highlighting their enterpriseness, meanwhile also nurturing the family system which in turn influences the development of the firms within the family. We go a step further into deepening our knowledge on why and how the dynamics within a family are likely to influence behaviours in the family firm or other firms (Sharma 2008), this is possible by looking at the decisions on the use of resources and entrepreneurial behaviours. This contributes to unpacking the complexity of the reciprocal influence between business and family (Frank et al. 2019)

In examining entrepreneurial families, we extend the view of portfolio entrepreneurship in business families (Rosa, Howorth, and Discua Cruz 2014) and provide a more nuanced understanding of entrepreneurial behaviours, such as growing the family business, creating a portfolio of firms or creating individual ventures, found in family entrepreneurial teams (Discua Cruz et al. 2013). We find that enterpriseness influences individual family members in more ways such as: joining the core family business, diversifying the core family business, creating their own businesses either within the formal or informal economy, and supporting other businesses in the family by having official or unofficial agreements with other members.

Our findings build on Sharma's (2008) assertion that the appropriability between family and business does not limit itself to one flow from family to business, and does not limit itself only to flows of social capital. Similar to social capital resources, human capital resources are obtained in a business to serve others, for example, in the form of customers or supplier within the same or different industries. The appropriability of the entrepreneurial family brings access of networks, information, knowledge, and financial resources relevant to the business context that are easily mobilized, applied and transformed by other members for diverse purposes. These are resources which originate in the businesses and flow back to the family, subsequently turning into support to different firms in the entrepreneurial family. With this we add to knowledge beyond familiness and the different portfolio of resources (Sharma 2008), and further by unpacking the influence that the business-related resources has on the family and back into the businesses contributing to enterpriseness feeding the entrepreneurial behaviour of the entrepreneurial family itself.

Our paper finds that financial capital represents a 'safety net' in terms of opening and managing a business, but also human capital as other members of the family contribute, formally or informally, to the entrepreneurial endeavours of new entrepreneurs within the same family. In this way, human capital, which is inherent in the individual members, is transferred into social capital to benefit the wider family. Furthermore, entrepreneurial families are able to add to their human and social capital endowments, by pooling financial resources together that can provide advantages which standalone family businesses or individual entrepreneurs are not able to replicate. The enterpriseness is shown where business-related wealth goes back to the entrepreneurial family, members decide to place the accumulated wealth on other businesses demonstrating a subsequent impact. For this, family cohesion is important for the family and the business (Zahra 2012), the time spent together can also be a source to entrepreneurial behaviours (Bettinelli, Fayolle, and Randerson 2014). The consequences of these behaviours may lead members to conduct the diverse entrepreneurial activity.

The findings show that the availability and sharing of capital resources means that as a business owner it is highly valued to be a member of an entrepreneurial family. Capitals are drawn upon to ensure that the previous entrepreneurial experience of other members of the family is translated into capabilities which benefit the nascent entrepreneurs within the same family. The more experience members have dealing with the challenges of everyday business life, the more knowledge they can share across the family, providing dispersed benefits. This means that skills and training are provided to the younger generations of the family (Habbershon, Williams, and MacMillan 2003). New generations can enter businesses which complement the existing ventures within the family, this complex yet valuable sharing of resources demonstrates that entrepreneurial families conform to both structural and transactional views of the family. Clearly, the entrepreneurial families have biological ties yet they are also socially constructed by their entrepreneurial activity that brings them together, The different utilization of resources allows a more nuanced understanding of the family-related issues in family business and entrepreneurship research (Salvato and Aldrich 2012) revealing the effects of enterpriseness which result in further entrepreneurial activity. We show that the availability and ongoing sharing of the combination of human, social and financial capital in the entrepreneurial family contributes for enterpriseness to be recreating itself within this dynamic.

6. Limitations and directions for future research

We acknowledge that this research has some limitations. The empirical focus of this article is the entrepreneurial family in the capital city of the state of Mexico and involved a relatively small number of in-depth interviews with family entrepreneurs. As such, the responses of participants cannot be considered representative of the wider population. The research approach was qualitative, and while this limit the generalizability of the findings, the value of our research lies in providing in-depth insights into the notion of enterpriseness in a developing economy. These constructs are still emergent which require further research. Our focus has been on entrepreneurial families and it would be valuable to examine enterpriseness in other conceptualizations of family, we suggest further qualitative as well as quantitative studies to investigate these. Quantitative studies would be useful in examining the usages of entrepriseness in different contexts, for example, by using surveys to compare families in developed versus developing economies. In addition, surveys could be used to examine the potential negative impacts of resource (mis)allocation between family members, or restrictive enterpriseness.

7. Conclusions

This article has critically examined how family members support each other's entrepreneurial activities through shared resources and capabilities. Our contribution is to demonstrate how entrepreneurial families, where more than one member is an owner/entrepreneur who interacts with other entrepreneurs in the same family, provide each other with advantages which are not replicated in more traditional family firms or for individual entrepreneurs. This is possible due to the flow of the business-related resources to the family and to other businesses benefiting other members. The interaction of members within entrepreneurial families enables availability and use of a combination of capital resources which contribute to enterpriseness. As such, we provide a more nuanced perspective of the dynamics within families in business and move beyond comparisons of what differentiates family firms from non-family firms, to contribute to a broader conceptualization of family entrepreneurship (Randerson et al. 2015).

Through a new focus on entrepreneurial families, we are able to examine the distinct the impact that the businesses in the entrepreneurial family have on the family itself and later on the multiple firms. The entrepreneurial family provides an ideal setting to study the two-way flow of resources from the family (different entrepreneurs) to their various firms; and vice versa the use of resources acquired from different firms that serve to other entrepreneurs in the family, as such contributing to understand how enterpriseness works in entrepreneurial families.

Disclosure statement

No potential conflict of interest was reported by the authors.

References

Acemoglu, D., and J. A. Robinson. 2012. *Why Nations Fail: The Origins of Power, Prosperity, and Poverty*. New York, NY: Crown Books.

Adler, P. S., and S. W. Kwon. 2002. "Social Capital: Prospects for a New Concept." *The Academy of Management Review* 27 :17.

Aldrich, H. E., and J. E. Cliff. 2003. "The Pervasive Effects of Family on Entrepreneurship: Toward a Family Embeddedness Perspective." *Journal of Business Venturing* 18 (5): 573–596. doi:10.1016/S0883-9026(03)00011-9.

Alsos, G. A., S. Carter, and E. Ljunggren. 2014. "Kinship and Business: How Entrepreneurial Households Facilitate Business Growth." *Entrepreneurship and Regional Development* 26 (1–2): 97–122. January 8. doi:10.1080/08985626.2013.870235.

Arriagada, I. 2002. Cambios Y Desigualdad En Las Familias Latinoamericanas. *Revista De La Cepal* 77: 143–161.

Bettinelli, C. 2011. "Boards of Directors in Family Firms: An Exploratory Study of Structure and Group Process." *Family Business Review* 24 (2): 151–169. doi:10.1177/0894486511402196.

Bettinelli, C., A. Fayolle, and K. Randerson. 2014. "Family Entrepreneurship: A Developing Field." *Foundations and Trends® in Entrepreneurship* 10 (3): 161–236. doi:10.1561/0300000049.

Biernacki, P., and D. Waldorf. 1981. "Snowball Sampling: Problems and Techniques of Chain Referral Sampling." *Sociological Methods & Research* 10 (2): 141–163. doi:10.1177/004912418101000205.

Botero, I. C., and G. G. Betancourt. 2016. "Contextual Factors that Aect Selection and Use of Governance Structures in Latin American Family Enterprises." In *The Routledge Companion to Family Business* edited by F. W. Kellermanns & F. Hoy 579–596. New York: Routledge.

Bryman, A. 2012. *Social Research Methods*. 4th ed. Oxford: Oxford University Press

Chrisman, J. J., F. W. Kellermanns, K. C. Chan, and K. Liano. 2009. "Intellectual Foundations of Current Research in Family Business: An Identification and Review of 25 Influential Articles." *Family Business Review* 23 (1): 9–26.

Coleman, J. S. 1988. "Social Capital in the Creation of Human Capital." *American Journal of Sociology* 94: S95-S120. doi:10.1086/228943.

Creswell, J. W. 2013. *Qualitative Inquiry & Research Design*. Thousand Oaks, CA: Sage.

Danes, S. M., K. Stafford, G. Haynes, and S. S. Amarapurkar. 2009. "Family Capital of Family Firms: Bridging Human, Social, and Financial Capital." *Family Business Review* 22 (3): 199–215. doi:10.1177/0894486509333424.

Dibrell, C., and E. Memili. 2019. "A Brief History and A Look to the Future of Family Business Heterogeneity: An Introduction." In *The Palgrave Handbook of Heterogeneity among Family Firms* edited by E. Memili and C. Dibrell 1–15. Cham: Palgrave Macmillan.

Discua Cruz, A., C. Howorth, and E. Hamilton. 2013. "Intrafamily Entrepreneurship: The Formation and Membership of Family Entrepreneurial Teams." *Entrepreneurship Theory and Practice* 37 (1): 17–46. doi:10.1111/etap.2013.37.issue-1.

Discua Cruz, A., E. Hamilton, and S. L. Jack. 2012. "Understanding Entrepreneurial Cultures in Family Businesses: A Study of Family Entrepreneurial Teams in Honduras." *Journal of Family Business Strategy* 3 (3): 147–161. doi:10.1016/j.jfbs.2012.05.002.

Dodd, S. D., A. Anderson, and S. Jack. 2015. "The Role of Networking in the Growth Process of Entrepreneurial Family Firms." In *Family Entrepreneurship: Rethinking the Research Agenda*, edited by K. Randerson et al., 212–238. Abingdon, UK: Routledge.

Doern, R. 2009. "Investigating Barriers to SME Growth and Development in Transition Environments a Critique and Suggestions for Developing the Methodology." *International Small Business Journal* 27 (3): 275–305. doi:10.1177/0266242609102275.

Dyer, W. G., E. Nenque, and E. J. Hill. 2014. "Toward a Theory of Family Capital and Entrepreneurship: Antecedents and Outcomes." *Journal of Small Business Management* 52 (2): 266–285. doi:10.1111/jsbm.2014.52.issue-2.

Estrada-Robles, M., N. Williams, and T. Vorley. 2018. "Navigating Institutional Challenges in Mexico: The Role of Social Capital in Entrepreneurial Families." *International Journal of Entrepreneurial Behavior & Research* 26: 98–121. doi:10.1108/IJEBR-05-2017-0180.

Farrington, S. M., E. Venter, and C. Boshoff. 2012. "The Role of Selected Team Design Elements in Successful Sibling Teams." *Family Business Review* 25 (2): 191–205. doi:10.1177/0894486511426871.

Frank, H., J. Suess-Reyes, E. Fuetsch, and K. Alexander. 2019. "Introducing the Enterpriseness of Business Families: A Research Agenda." In *The Palgrave Handbook of Heterogeneity among Family Firms* edited by E. Memili and C. Dibrell 263–296. Cham: Palgrave Macmillan.

Frank, H., M. Lueger, L. Nosé, and D. Suchy. 2010. "The Concept of 'Familiness'. Literature Review and Systems Theory-Based Reflections." *Journal of Family Business Strategy* 1 (3): 119–130. doi:10.1016/j.jfbs.2010.08.001.

Gobierno Municipal Toluca. "Respalda Toluca a Sus Emprendedores; Créditos Por 2.9 MDP Entregó Alcalde Braulio Antonio Álvarez Jasso." Accessed 10 November 2015. http://www.toluca.gob.mx/respalda-toluca-sus-emprendedores-cr%C3%A9ditos-por-29-mdp-entreg%C3%B3-alcalde-braulio-antonio-%C3%A1lvarez-jasso#sthash.dLctljaN.dpuf

Granovetter, M. 2005. "The Impact of Social Structure on Economic Outcomes." *Journal of Economic Perspectives* 19 (1): 33–50. doi:10.1257/0895330053147958.

Habbershon, T. G., and M. Williams. 1999. "A Resource-Based Framework for Assessing the Strategic Advantages of Family Firms." *Family Business Review* 12 (1): 1–25. doi:10.1111/j.1741-6248.1999.00001.x.

Habbershon, T. G., M. Williams, and I. C. MacMillan. 2003. "A Unified Systems Perspective of Family Firm Performance." *Journal of Business Venturing* 18 (4): 451–465. doi:10.1016/S0883-9026(03)00053-3.

Habbershon, T.G., and J. Pistrui. 2002. "Enterprising Families Domain: Family-influenced Ownership Groups in Pursuit Of Transgenerational Wealth." *Family Business Review* 15(3): 223–237.

Hall, A., M. Nordqvist and L. Melin. 2005. "Qualitative research in family business studies: The usefulness of the interpretive approach." Paper presented at the FBN-Ifera World Academic Research Forum, EHSAL, Brussels.

Hasenzagl, R., I. Hatak, and H. Frank. 2018. "Problematizing Socioemotional Wealth in Family Firms: A Systems-theoretical Reframing." *Entrepreneurship & Regional Development* 30 (1–2): 199–223. doi:10.1080/08985626.2017.1401123.

Hatch, J. A. 2002. *Doing Qualitative Research in Education Settings*. Albany: State University of New York Press.

Hoy, F., and P. Sharma. 2010. *Entrepreneurial Family Firms*. New Jersey: Prentice Hall.

Instituto Nacional de Estadistica y Geografia. INEGI. (National Institute of Statistics, Geography and Data Processing). 2014. *Censos y Conteos de Poblacion y Vivienda*. Mexico, DF: INEGI.

Irava, W. J., and K. Moores. 2010. "Clarifying the Strategic Advantage of Familiness: Unbundling Its Dimensions and Highlighting Its Paradoxes." *Journal of Family Business Strategy* 1: 131–144. doi:10.1016/j.jfbs.2010.08.002.

Kim, P. H., H. E. Aldrich, and L. A. Keister. 2006. "Access (Not) Denied: The Impact of Financial, Human, and Cultural Capital on Entrepreneurial Entry in the United States." *Small Business Economics* 27 (1): 5–22. doi:10.1007/s11187-006-0007-x.

Koerner, A. F., and M. A. Fitzpatrick. 2002. "Toward a Theory of Family Communication." *Communication Theory* 12 (1): 70–91. doi:10.1111/comt.2002.12.issue-1.

Lambrecht, J., and J. Lievens. 2008. "Pruning the Family Tree: An Unexplored Path to Family Business Continuity and Family Harmony." *Family Business Review* 21 (4): 295–313. doi:10.1177/08944865080210040103.

Lane, P. J., and M. Lubatkin. 1998. "Relative Absorptive Capacity and Interorganizational Learning." *Strategic Management Journal* 19 (5): 461–477. doi:10.1002/(ISSN)1097-0266.

Litz, R. A. 2008. "Two Sides of a One-Sided Phenomenon: Conceptualizing the Family Business and Business Family as a Möbius Strip." *Family Business Review* 21 (3): 217–236. doi:10.1177/08944865080210030104.

Lumpkin, G.T., L. Steier, and M. Wright. 2011. Strategic Entrepreneurship in Family Business. *Strategic Entrepreneurship Journal* 5: 285–306.

Mani, Y., and L. Lakhal. 2015. "Exploring the family effect on firm performance: The impact of Internal Social Capital Dimensions on Family Firm Performance". *International Journal of Entrepreneurial Behavior & Research* (vol. 21, No. 6, pp. 898–917).

Michael-Tsabari, N., R. Labaki, and R. K. Zachary. 2014. "Toward the Cluster Model: The Family Firm's Entrepreneurial Behavior over Generations." *Family Business Review* 27 (2): 161–185. doi:10.1177/0894486514525803.

Miles, M. B., and A. M. Huberman. 1994. *Qualitative Data Analysis.* Thousand Oaks, CA: Sage.

Neergaard, H., and J. P. Ulhøi. 2007. *Handbook of Qualitative Research Methods in Entrepreneurship.* Cheltenham: Edward Elgar Publishing.

Pearson, A. W., J. C. Carr, and J. C. Shaw. 2008. "Toward A Theory of Familiness: A Social Capital Perspective." *Entrepreneurship Theory and Practice* 32 (6): 949–969. doi:10.1111/etap.2008.32.issue-6.

Plate, M., and C. Schiede, C., adn A. von Schlippe. 2010. Portfolio entrepreneurship in the context of family owned businesses. In M. Nordqvist and T. Zellweger (Eds.), Transgenerational entrepreneurship: Exploring growth and performance of family firms across generations. 96–122. Cheltenham, England: Edward Elgar.

Randerson, K., C. Bettinelli, A. Fayolle, and A. Anderson. 2015. "Family Entrepreneurship as a Field of Research: Exploring Its Contours and Contents." *Journal of Family Business Strategy* 6 (3): 143–154. doi:10.1016/j.jfbs.2015.08.002.

Randerson, K., G. Dossena, and A. Fayolle. 2016. "The Futures of Family Business: Family Entrepreneurship." *Futures* 75 (75): 36–43. doi:10.1016/j.futures.2015.10.008.

Rau, S. 2014. "Resource-based View of Family Firms." In *The Sage Handbook of Family Business* edited by L. Melin, M. Nordqvist, and P. Sharma 321–340. Thousand Oaks, CA: SAGE Publishers.

Reay, T. 2014. "Publishing Qualitative Research." *Family Business Review* 27 (2): 95–102. doi:10.1177/0894486514529209.

Rodriguez, P., C. S. Tuggle, and S. M. Hackett. 2009. "An Exploratory Study of How Potential 'Family and Household Capital' Impacts New Venture Start-Up Rates." *Family Business Review* 22 (3): 259–272. doi:10.1177/0894486509335342.

Rosa, P., C. Howorth, and A. Discua Cruz. 2014. "Habitual and Portfolio Entrepreneurship and the Family in Business." In *The Sage Handbook of Family Business* edited by L. Melin, M. Nordqvist, & P. Sharma. 364–382. London, England: Sage.

Salvato, C., and H. E. Aldrich. 2012. "'That's Interesting!' in Family Business Research." *Family Business Review* 25 (2): 125–135. doi:10.1177/0894486512446327.

Schjoedt, L., E. Monsen, A., Pearson, T., Barnett, and J. J. Chrisman. 2013. New Venture and Family Business Teams: Understanding Team Formation, Composition, Behaviors, and Performance. *Entrepreneurship Theory and Practice* 37 (1): 1–15.

Sharma, P. 2008. "Commentary : Familiness : Capital Stocks and Flows." *Entrepreneurship Theory and Practice* 2007: 971–977. doi:10.1111/j.1540-6520.2008.00266.x.

Sieger, P., T. Zellweger, R. S. Nason, and E. Clinton. 2011. "Portfolio Entrepreneurship in Family Firms: A Resource-based Perspective." *Strategic Entrepreneurship Journal* 5 (4): 327–351. doi:10.1002/sej.v5.4.

Silverman, D. 2000. *Qualitative Research: A Practical Handbook.* London: Sage.

Sirmon, D. G., and M. A. Hitt. 2003. "Managing Resources: Linking Unique Resources, Management, and Wealth Creation in Family Firms." *Entrepreneurship Theory and Practice* 27 (4): 339–358. doi:10.1111/etap.2003.27.issue-4.

Sorenson, R. L., and L. Bierman. 2009. "Family Capital, Family Business, and Free Enterprise." *Family Business Review* 22 (3): 193–195. doi:10.1177/0894486509341178.

Steier, L. P., J. J. Chrisman, and J. H. Chua. 2015. "Governance Challenges in Family Businesses and Business Families." In *Entrepreneurship Theory and Practice* 39 (6): 1265–1280.

Von Schlippe, A., and H. Frank. 2013. "The Theory of Social Systems as a Framework for Understanding Family Businesses." *Family Relations* 62 (3): 384–398. doi:10.1111/fare.2013.62.issue-3.

Zahra, S. 2012. "Organizational Learning and Entrepreneurship in Family Firms: Exploring the Moderating Effect of Ownership and Cohesion." *Small Business Economics* 38 (1): 51–65. doi:10.1007/s11187-010-9266-7.

Zahra, S. A., and P. Sharma. 2004. "Family Business Research: A Strategic Reflection." *Family Business Review* 17 (4): 331–346. doi:10.1111/j.1741-6248.2004.00022.x.

Entrepreneurial learning: the transmitting and embedding of entrepreneurial behaviours within the transgenerational entrepreneurial family

Eric Clinton, Maura McAdam, Jordan Robert Gamble and Martina Brophy

ABSTRACT

The aim of this paper is to explore how entrepreneurial behaviours are transmitted and embedded across generations within a Transgenerational Entrepreneurial Family (TEF). Although extant family business research has acknowledged the importance of learning in facilitating the transference of values, norms and attitudes, we know little about how learning embeds entrepreneurial behaviours at the family level. In order to address this, we adopted a longitudinal perspective of four TEF cases, drawing on numerous interviews, archival sources and observational instances. An iterative procedure for data analysis, which involved open coding, within-case analyses, second-order coding and cross-case analysis, was undertaken. Our findings illustrate how the implementation of entrepreneurial behaviours within TEFs was a process of negotiation and reification, informed by differences among families in response to critical incidents. Furthermore, we demonstrate how the presence of entrepreneurial behaviour enablers in each TEF has facilitated the perpetuation of entrepreneurial behaviours. Finally, we illuminate the importance of unlearning, the disregarding of prior learning to accommodate new information and behaviours, in the TEF context, where such entities are faced with unlearning paradoxes that subsequently influence their entrepreneurial behaviours.

Introduction

Entrepreneurial learning is a social phenomenon which occurs in context (Pittaway and Cope 2007) via a 'process of co-participation' whereby learning involves 'reflecting, theorising, experiencing, and action' (Taylor and Thorpe 2004, 204). This learning is often accompanied by unlearning, the process of setting aside 'prior learning in order to accommodate new information and behaviours' (Becker 2005, 661). Although the family is among the most dominant social institutions when it comes to the transference of values, norms and attitudes to its members (Berger and Luckmann 1966), little is known about how family members actually learn about the family in business (Cruz, Howorth, and Hamilton 2013; Konopaski, Jack, and Hamilton 2015). This gap in knowledge is of significance to a particular type of family, namely the Transgenerational Entrepreneurial Family (TEF) (DeWitt et al. 2015). It is frequently the case that, with these types of families, the original entrepreneurial essence of the venture has cascaded down numerous generations of the family, and manifests as a form of 'enterpriseness' within the business family (Frank et al. 2010, 124, 2019; Zellweger et al. 2012).

Despite the significance of entrepreneurial learning for TEFs, the process by which their entrepreneurial essence, through the manifestation of entrepreneurial behaviours, has been transmitted and embedded across generations of the family is a blind spot inherent in the field of family entrepreneurship (Nordqvist and Melin 2010; Randerson, Dossena, and Fayolle 2016). In keeping with recent calls for greater consideration of the family's influence on entrepreneurial processes (Randerson et al. 2017; Sarasvathy et al. 2014), this study adopts the TEF as the unit of analysis to uncover how the family operates as a social system of learning within business. In doing so, we extend understanding of the nuances of heterogeneity in family firms (Dibrell and Memili 2019). Accordingly, within this paper we adopt entrepreneurial learning as our theoretical lens in order to address this qap. Such a lens is appropriate, given that learning as a central component of entrepreneurial practice is widely recognized (Cope 2005), and that cross generational entrepreneurial practice is characteristic of TEFs (Jaskiewicz et al. 2014).

The aim of this paper is to explore how entrepreneurial behaviours are transmitted and embedded across generations within a TEF. The transmission of behaviours within organizations has been the focus of much family business research (Burke and Baldwin 1999; Randerson et al. 2015; Zhong et al. 2012). Specifically, we will investigate entrepreneurial behaviours associated with entrepreneurial learning and unlearning, in addition to critical incidents – which are defined as episodes that represent key successes or failures (Cope 2005). We achieve this aim through our adoption of a longitudinal multiple case study methodology, consisting of archival records, in-depth interviews and observations with four multi-generational TEFs in Northern Europe.

Within this paper, we make the following contributions: First, we address a research gap inherent in the field of transgenerational entrepreneurship (Randerson, Dossena, and Fayolle 2016), namely the process by which entrepreneurial behaviours are transmitted. Thus, our findings illuminate this process by illustrating how certain critical incidents have an enduring effect on the entrepreneurial behaviours embedded and sustained across generations (De Massis and Kotlar 2014). Second, we highlight that the learning processes in TEFs are bi-directional and multi-generational, involving multiple forms of co-participation from family members (Clinton and Gamble 2019; McAdam et al. 2018). This novel insight demonstrates the mutually influential relationship between individual and familial entrepreneurial behaviours (Bettinelli, Fayolle, and Randerson 2014). Third, our findings illustrate that TEFs must engage in unlearning processes to remain entrepreneurial, thus providing insights into the role of unlearning in the entrepreneurial learning process, which is currently lacking (Wang and Chugh 2014). This is significant as many entrepreneurial strategies fail due to unsuccessful navigation of paradoxical tensions between exploring new business practices and exploiting long-held assurances.

To develop these arguments, we commence by outlining the rationale for our theoretical framing, followed by a discrete analysis of entrepreneurial learning, critical incidents and unlearning in the context of entrepreneurship. We then draw these concepts together under the domain of transgenerational entrepreneurship, which forms the basis of our empirical illustration of the analysis. In the following section, we discuss our methodology. This is followed by critical evaluation of the empirical evidence from a longitudinal investigation of four cases from the Successful Transgenerational Entrepreneurship Practices (STEP)[1] project. We then critically reflect on the entrepreneurial behaviours across our cases, considering the implications for theory and practice.

Learning in an entrepreneurial context

Entrepreneurial learning is a social phenomenon (Gibb 1997) which takes place in context (Pittaway and Cope 2007) via a process of 'co-participation' (Taylor and Thorpe 2004). Given the experiential nature of this process, entrepreneurs learn through a process of action and reflection (Cope and Watts 2000; Politis 2005). One of the key mechanisms within this entrepreneurial learning process is the learning that occurs as a result of critical incidents or episodes that are either significant successes or failures (Cope 2005). Indeed, a central feature of how entrepreneurs learn is through 'major setbacks' (Minniti and Bygrave 2001) and discontinuous, contingent, and critical learning events (Cope 2005; Harmeling and Sarasvathy 2013). Empirically, critical incidents have been shown to influence family firms' innovation endeavours, with such entities not only outliving various critical incidents (e.g. succession) but using them as 'a catalyst for further radical innovation' (McAdam, Reid, and Mitchell 2010, 452).

Interestingly, the role of unlearning in the entrepreneurial learning process is relatively unexplored (Wang and Chugh 2014), despite the concept gaining considerable traction across varying managerial disciplines (Leal-Rodríguez et al. 2015). Unlearning activities may help foster entrepreneurial behaviours such as innovation (Rebernik and Širec 2007; Becker 2010), internationalization (Casillas, Moreno, and Barbero 2010) and strategic renewal (Volberda, Baden-Fuller, and Van Den Bosch 2001). Thus, unlearning is especially apposite for the TEF as they repeatedly engage in entrepreneurship across multiple generations (Jaskiewicz, Combs, and Rau 2015). This provides a learning opportunity whereby family members accumulate experience that is transmitted to future generations (Cucculelli and Bettinelli 2016; Zahra 2012). However, Becker (2005) argues that embedded knowledge is more difficult to unlearn than newly acquired information. This is particularly relevant to the TEF context as 'the feelings and emotions related to change are likely to be deeper and more intense than those in nonfamily businesses' (Dyer 1994, 125).

Thus, TEFs are presented with a paradox, which involves balancing the familiarity of past behaviours with the uncertainty of the future (Chrisman et al. 2015; De Massis, Vittorio, and Frattini 2016). According to Hamilton (2011,19), 'discontinuity and new practice' in TEFs 'are as important as continuity and enduring practices'. However, many entrepreneurial strategies fail because family members are unable to manage the paradoxical tensions that exist between exploring novel approaches and exploiting embedded practices (Cegarra-Navarro, Sánchez-Vidal, and Leiva 2011).

The transgenerational entrepreneurial family

Within the family business field, the TEF is considered distinctive from traditional families in business, which are often considered conservative and risk-averse (Miller and Le Breton-Miller 2005). This distinction has resulted in increased attention afforded to the role of family influence in transgenerational entrepreneurship (Chrisman et al. 2015; Zellweger et al. 2012). Indeed, those families that possess strong transgenerational succession intentions and extensively seek external knowledge have the potential to engage in a high level of corporate entrepreneurship (Randolph, Li, and Daspit 2017). Transgenerational entrepreneurship is the 'processes through which a family uses and develops entrepreneurial mind-sets and family influenced capabilities to create new streams of entrepreneurial, financial, and social value across generations' (Habbershon, Nordqvist, and Zellweger 2010, 1). Such mindsets are the beliefs and attitudes which are the 'oxygen that feeds the fire of entrepreneurship' within the TEF (Rogoff and Heck 2003, 559).

Hence, what makes the phenomenon of entrepreneurial learning especially relevant for the TEF is not only multigenerational involvement, but also the adoption of an entrepreneurial mindset with a long-term orientation (McCann, Leon-Guerrero, and Haley 2001; Lumpkin, Brigham, and Moss 2010). Within such a context, longitudinal entrepreneurial performance and entrepreneurial learning are more accurately investigated when the TEF is the unit of analysis rather than a particular business entity (Habbershon and Pistrui 2002, 239). Thus, the TEF's long-term horizons facilitate a repository of learning and hub of entrepreneurial activity (Miller and Le Breton-Miller 2005; Zellweger 2007). Accordingly, we respond to calls for positioning the family at the centre of research exploring the entrepreneurship function of family firms (Nordqvist and Melin 2010; Randerson et al. 2017). This adoption of a family-centred perspective will facilitate insights into the entrepreneurial behaviours of the TEF, which is currently lacking in family business research (Zellweger et al. 2013). However, such an approach is essential to uncovering the transmission of these behaviours across time and generations.

Methodology

Research design

Given the nature of our research aim, a comparative case study methodology is deemed apposite (Yin 2009). Such an approach aligns with the entrepreneurial learning domain, which relies largely on qualitative analyses (Cope 2011). Within this line of inquiry, it has been suggested that the adoption of multiple data collection procedures (e.g. archival and participant observation) may facilitate 'a deeper and more nuanced understanding of how material practices influence the development of collective interpretations' (Stigliari and Ravasi 2016, 445). In family business research, case studies facilitate theoretical expansion, thus enhancing our understanding of family behaviour (Clinton, McAdam, and Gamble 2018; De Massis and Kotlar 2014). In addition, we adopt a longitudinal stance, consisting of primary data collection at multiple points across a six-year period[2] (2011–2017) and archival sources dating from 1919–2016. All four TEFs share the same geographical location in Northern Europe. Whilst there is no optimal number of cases per multiple case study design, Eisenhardt (1989) recommends between four and ten cases. Accordingly, four cases are deemed appropriate for this exploratory investigation in order to adhere to replication logic and to pursue distinct patterns of theoretical replications (Yin 2016).

Sampling

Our sampling was purposeful in that we sought and selected richly detailed cases that related to our aim (Palinkas et al. 2015). Our sample of TEFs was chosen from a pool of case studies in adherence with the STEP project case study protocol. We purposely selected TEFs of multiple and varying generations to account for the transgenerational aspect of the study. In acknowledging the role of family heterogeneity in the transgenerational transmission of entrepreneurial behaviours, additional family-specific criteria were applied to our sampling strategy. For each TEF, we sought information on the number of group members and living generations, the geographical dispersion of TEF members and the frequency of meetings among members. In addition, we sought TEFs that had experienced different types of family ownership transitions (Gersick et al. 1997). An overview of each case is provided in Table 1 and case vignettes can be viewed in Appendix 1.

Data collection

Archival records

We gathered hundreds of items of evidence that were either publicly available or provided by the TEFs. These archival records (345 pieces of evidence in total) allowed the research team to trace the four TEFs back almost a century. Archival sources ranged from reports and published corporate histories to newspaper articles and blog posts. Furthermore, we cross compared the records with interviews and observations to confirm findings, reach consensus, and achieve triangulation, thereby enhancing the credibility of our findings (Yin 2016). See Table 2 for a review of all archival sources.

Interviews

Our semi-structured interviews, averaging 51 minutes in duration, were conducted with 32 participants across the four TEFs over a four-year period (2011–2015). Of the interviews conducted, eight were with family owner/MD/Chairman/Board members, eight were with next generation members, and 16 were with non-family managers, advisors, and other stakeholders. Consistent with Eisenhardt (1989, 536) who claims that 'a priori specification of constructs can shape the initial design of theory building research', the STEP guide posed pre-set questions relating to family business and entrepreneurship constructs. The questions most pertinent to our research aim related to the business family history, externalities, and culture that might indicate critical incidents throughout the business family's life (See Appendix 2 for the list of questions). This round of questioning preceded follow-up

Table 1. Overview of cases.

Case	TEF A	TEF B	TEF C	TEF D
Industry	Timber processing; sawmilling	Food (oat-based branded cereals)	Wastewater treatment	Farm machinery manufacturer and supplier
Year founded	1913	1785	1968	1963
Age/Generation	104/Third	232/Seventh	49/Second	54/Second
Employees/Turnover[a]	380/€127 million	55/€20 million	300/€72 million	50/€10 million
Family MD/Chairman	Yes (Co-MDs)	Yes	Yes	Yes
Family ownership	100%	100%	100%	100%
No. of TEF members	5	6	12	5
No. of living generations	1	2	2	2
Geographical dispersion of TEF members[b]	4/1	5/1	9/3	5/0
Frequency of meetings[c]	FC: 4/BM: 4	FC: 4/BM: 4	FC: 6/BM: 4	FC: 4/BM: 4
Most recent ownership transition type	Recycled	Devolutionary	Evolutionary	Evolutionary
Familial Relationships	*Brothers(G3)* Managing Director* + Managing Director* + Board Member*+	*Parents(G6)* Managing Director*+ Non-Exec Director *Children(G7)* Int. Business Dvlpt. Manager*+ Financial Controller*+ Brand Manager +	*Brothers(G1)* Managing Director*+ Board Director* Board Director* + *Cousins(G2)* Deputy MD*+ Commercial Director*	*Parent(G1)* Executive Chairman* *Children(G2)* General Manager* Business Dvlpt. Manager* Sales & Marketing Director* Manager*

[a]Sourced through the national companies register, as accessed through the FAME database of Bureau van Dijk.
[b]National/international.
[c]Family Council (FC)/Board Meetings (BM) per annum.
* Denotes members interviewed.
[+]Denotes members observed.

Table 2. Archival sources*.

Year	TEF A	TEF B	TEF C	TEF D
Pre-1920	MA (4), GD (2)	MA (2), GD (3)		
1921–1930	MA (3), GD (2)	GD (3)		
1931–1940	MA (1)	GD (1)		
1941–1950	CR (1), GD (4)	GD (2)		
1951–1960	CR (1), MA (3)	MA (1)		
1961–1970	CR (1), VTR (1), GD (2), MA (1), OF (1)	CR (1), OF (1), GD (1)	MA (2), GD (3)	
1971–1980	CR (1), VTR (1), MA (6), OF (1)	CR (2), VTR (1), OF (1)	OF (1), GD (3), MA (2)	
1981–1990	CR (1), MA (18), GD (1), OF (1)	CR (2), MA (2), VTR (1), OF (1)	OF (1), MA (2), CR (2), VTR (2)	MA (3)
1991–2000	CR (1), VTR (2), MA (15), OF (1)	CR (1), VTR (3), OF (1), GD (1), CP (1)	OF (1), MA (6), CR (4), CP (1), VTR (1), GD (1)	MA (6)
2001–2010	CR (1), MA (14), CP (2), GD (2), OF (1)	CR (2), VTR (8), OF (1), GD (1), CP (1)	OF (1), MA (9), CR (10), CP (2)	MA (4), VTR (2), PR (15)
2011–2016	CR (1), VTR (3), MA (30), CP (3), GD (2), OF (1)	CR (2), MA (2), VTR (8), OF (1), CP (4)	OF (1), MA (14), CR (20), CP (6), VTR (5), GD (2)	MA (5), PR (10)
Total	**136**	**62**	**102**	**45**

*MA = media articles, CR = Corporate reports, VTR = video, television, radio, CP = corporate presentations, GD = government document, OF = official filings (companies register), PR = press release.

interviews which served to clarify, refine, and bolster the data. The interviews were transcribed verbatim resulting in 548 pages of transcript from approximately 27 hours of tape.

Observations

In order to achieve within-method triangulation (Bekhet and Zauszniewski 2012), we used observations as our third data collection method. In total, 27 observational instances, ranging from family council meetings to plant tours, were observed over a six-year period (2011–2017). As suggested by Yin (2016), the data collection procedure for observations required the researcher to note the time and location, the participants present and the type of observation. Two research team members acted as participant observers who kept field notes while generating observations. See Table 3 for a comprehensive review of interview and observation data.

Data analysis

In keeping with our inductive approach, our data analysis was an iterative process between the data and the emerging theory (Eisenhardt 1989). Analysis was carried out by two members of the research team who were both highly familiarized with the case firms. The initial phase of analysis involved compiling and documenting all textual data including interview transcriptions, field notes, observations, and archival evidence on each of the four TEFs. As a result of this process, a case study database was formed (De Massis and Kotlar 2014). This provided the basis for our structured process for data analysis (Miles and Huberman 1994) comprising of open coding, within-case analyses, second-order coding, and cross-case analysis.

Open coding

Two researchers coded the data for critical incidents, resulting in a list with an accumulative total of 34 critical incidents. Given the subjective, retrospective nature of critical incident retelling (Cope and Watts 2000), we sought to enhance the credibility of our findings (Lincoln and Guba 1985) by including only the occurrences deemed critical as corroborated by evidence from at least one major data source (i.e. 'A', evidence from 4+ interviewees; or 'C', evidence from 4+ archival types) and one minor data source (i.e. 'a', evidence from 2+ interviewees; or 'c', evidence from 2+ archival types).

Within-case analyses

Case descriptions were written to enhance our understanding of the family in business and its rich history and allow for within-case patterns to emerge (Eisenhardt 1989). We then uncovered patterns in the data whereby a critical incident was followed by a learning outcome (Yin 2009). This was

Table 3. Interview and observation data.

	TEF A		TEF B		TEF C		TEF D	
Interviews*	A	B	A	B	A	B	A	B
Chairman	-	-	-	-	-	-	1	1G
Board Member (BM)	1	3G	-	-	2	1G; 1G	-	-
Family advisor	-	-	-	-	-	-	2	Non
Financial Controller (FC)	1	Non	1	7G	-	-	-	-
General Manager (GM)	-	-	-	-	-	-	1	2G
Managing Director (MD)	2	3G; 3G	1	6G	1	1G	-	-
Other Director	-	-	-	-	2	2G; 2G	-	-
Other Manager	2	Non	2	Non; 7G	2	Non	1	2G
Sales/Marketing Director	1	Non	1	Non	-	-	1	2G
Business Development Officer (BDO)	-	-	-	-	-	-	1	2G
Other	-	-	-	-	1	Non	5	Non
Total	7	3	5	3	8	5	12	5

Observations	TEF A	TEF B	TEF C	TEF D
Plant tours	3	3	2	2
Family dinner	2	-	-	3
Corporate presentations	4	2	3	1
Family council meetings	-	1	1	-
Total	**9**	**6**	**6**	**6**

*Column A signals no. of interviewees/interviews. Column B signals no. of family members and their generation. 'Non' denotes non-family members (Adapted from Marchisio et al. 2010).

conducted by two members of the research team who acted as independent raters, with both raters meeting periodically to discuss their analysis and resolve any discrepancies. A third member of the research team acted as an independent referee (Sieger et al. 2011). These learning outcomes formed our first-order codes.

Second-order coding

In the next phase of analysis, we searched for second-order codes that could group these learning outcomes into themes. Thus, five distinct entrepreneurial behaviours (e.g. opportunity seeking/ recognizing; risk-taking; striving for efficiency; strategic regenerating; and diversifying products and/or markets) were identified. Our five identified behaviours were subsequently corroborated with evidence from secondary sources (e.g. financial accounts filed with the National Companies Register). Consistent with the theory building process, this stage of analysis was an iterative cycle between the data, emerging theory, and existing literature (Elsenhardt and Graebner 2007).

Cross-case analysis

In the final phase of coding, we searched for themes that could explain how these entrepreneurial behaviours were transmitted and embedded across generations as a result of the critical incidents and learning outcomes. A cross-case comparison technique was conducted whereby certain categories were used to determine patterns of similarity and difference across the cases (Eisenhardt 1989). This led to the identification of four aggregate dimensions or entrepreneurial behaviour enablers. These enablers (e.g. entrepreneurial education and experience; predecessor legacy building; entrepreneurial mentoring; family legacy unification and emulation) facilitated the transmission and embedment of entrepreneurial behaviours across generations. The use of enablers to enhance entrepreneurial vitality has been advocated by other management scholars (see Kuratko, Montagno, and Hornsby 1990; Yamada 2004), who acknowledge that they can exert a range of heterogeneous effects on entrepreneurial capabilities and behaviours (Mwasalwiba, Dahles, and Wakkee 2012). All four entrepreneurial behaviour enablers can be viewed in Appendix 3 and the data analysis procedure followed for each TEF can be viewed in Table 4.

Findings

We now present findings, in which our identified entrepreneurial behaviours are explored in detail and illustrated with fragments of the narrative or 'power quotes' (Pratt 2008, 501).

Critical incidents

According to one of the Co-MDs (G3) in TEF A, a major critical incident for the family was the home plant fire that occurred in 2004 (see Table 4). The G3 Co-MD recounted the night of the fire, with 'people coming up and looking for a sense of direction. I have inherited the responsibility of their families'. Subsequently, the brothers needed to make a strategic decision regarding the future of the home plant and those it employed: 'What matters [is] giving a sense of localness, being part of the community' (BD G3). Our interview data collected during the initial research period revealed that the decision to forgo the home plant and focus efforts on the secondary plant and other opportunities for growth (e.g. international acquisitions) was considered by the G3 Co-MDs to be 'a difficult one but it was the right decision'. This opportunity seeking behaviour subsequently resulted in success and acclaim when the brothers later won the Ernst & Young Industry Entrepreneur of the Year Award (Press release 2010). The Co-MDs also drew from past experiences: their father and first-generation MD sought and acquired supply from a neighbouring country. Indeed, the interview data collected during the initial research period, corroborated by more recent archival sources, indicate that the Co-MDs later unified and aligned the objectives of their

Table 4. TEF A-D Data Analysis.

	Identify Critical Incidents							Entrepreneurial Behaviours		
TEF	Year	Critical Incidents	Evid-ence	Ext./ Int.	Gen/s	Learning Outcomes	Entrepreneurial Behaviour Enablers	Behaviour	Value	Perpetuation
A	1968	Hurricane hits neighbouring country and creates extensive damage to forests.	aC	Ext.	G2	-Secure materials internationally. -Establish long-term supply.	Predecessor legacy building.	Opportunity recognition and risk-taking.	Ent. + Eco.	G3
A	2004	Serious fire destroys home plant.	AC	Ext.	G3	-Prioritise business survival over family needs. -Manage adversity. -Witness loyalty of workforce.	Predecessor legacy building.	Strategic regeneration.	Ent. + Soc.	-
B	1985	Entry to the cold cereals market.	aC	Ext.	G6	-Stick to core area. -Taking well-measured risks.	Entrepreneurial education and experience. Entrepreneurial mentoring.	Diversifying and risk-taking.	Ent. + Eco.	G7
B	1997	First non-family directorship.	AC	Int.	G6	-Adopt non-family expertise. -Develop marketing strategy.	Entrepreneurial mentoring. Predecessor legacy building.	Strategic regeneration.	Ent. + Eco. + Soc.	G7
B	2007	Seventh generation joins the firm.	AC	Int.	G6 G7	- Apply best practice gained from outside experience to family business.	Entrepreneurial education and experience. Predecessor legacy building.	Striving for efficiency.	Ent. + Eco.	G7
C	1973	Decision to leave electrical goods and focus on pumps.	aC	Ext.	G1	-Develop a strong core product offering. -Geographically expand operations. -Be adaptive.	Predecessor legacy building.	Diversifying	Ent. + Soc.	G2
C	1981	Non-family technical director receives 10% equity on appointment.	aC	Ext.	G1	-Adopt non-family expertise. -Share ownership privilege with non-family.	Entrepreneurial mentoring.	Opportunity seeking and recognizing.	Ent. + Eco.	-
D	2012	Executive Chairman returns and begins restructuring the company.	AC	Int.	G1 G2	-Manage adversity. -Be adaptive. -Resolve family tensions.	Predecessor legacy building.	Strategic regeneration and striving for efficiency.	Eco. + Ent.	G2

father's legacy by acquiring firms in this particular country: 'Dad always said, "it is ok to make mistakes, you need to try"' (Co-MD G3).

Our second-round interviews revealed that, in TEF B, the current Managing Director's (G6) attempted diversification into 'ready to eat' cereals was a critical incident that led to failure (see Table 4). This failure offset both learning and unlearning as the family discarded their previous assumptions about diversifying: 'We failed, learned from it and moved on' (MD G6). Notably, the family only diversified within the core product offering. These findings echo a similar measured risk-taking strategy by TEF A as a response to a critical incident of £30 million worth of trees felled by a hurricane, after which the second-generation MD 'bought enough timber to supply the mill in [the home plant] for two years' (excerpt from the TEF A's Biographical Book).

According to a Board Member (G1) in TEF C, a prominent critical incident was the decision to withdraw from the electrical goods market and focus on pumps as the core product offering (see Table 4). As the G1 Co-Founder explained, 'We took the decision to get out of all brown goods, white goods, and all that'. Interview data collected during the initial research period revealed that this incident allowed the TEF to 'change the whole market [both nationally and abroad] and bring in new products' (DMD G2). The TEF embraced these learnings and even became flexible in their personal lives: 'We got the agency on the condition that we open two branches: one in the Midlands and one in the West. I was dispatched to the West' (MD G1).

For TEF D, a key critical incident was when the Executive Chairman (G1) returned from a period of illness in 2012 and began restructuring the company (see Table 4). He explained: 'I looked at a lot of companies, but [Firm D] fitted very simple criteria'. A non-family Legal Advisor provided a further insight into the Executive Chairman's restructuring goals for the firm: 'He is hoping to have a sustainable capable business where – either directly or indirectly, the family would get a return from their efforts.' It appears that his attainment of this goal involved a long experiential learning process of trial and error: 'The Executive Chairman has this concept about a shared or collective governance structure' (Auditor non-family). The other critical incident for TEF D was the establishment of the family holdings group, which was strategically created to instil entrepreneurial learning through the insourcing of advice from 'two separate entities outside of TEF D' (GM G2).

Bi-directionality and co-participation

Our findings reveal insights into co-participation and bi-directionality in family entrepreneurial behaviours in TEF C (see Table 4), notably when the second-generation Deputy Managing Director was mentored by a non-family, shareholding director. This embedded opportunity-seeking behaviour resulted in the formulation of an intra-firm consortia and first-to-market contracts. A learning that emerged from this incident is the significance of thinking long-term regarding 'big growth and opening up more opportunities' (DMD G2) – an entrepreneurial behaviour that has been transmitted across the two generations of the family. Whereas in TEF A, the second-generation Co-MDs embarked on their first acquisition, the family's most prominent example of risk-taking (see Table 4), with the continued backing and advice of their father 'who understood deeply that this was the defining event in the transition to the next generation'. Furthermore, according to archival sources, they were 'increasingly becoming key decision makers in the business' (Excerpt from the TEF's Biographical Book).

In TEF D, as a serial entrepreneur, the Executive Chairman demonstrated an 'enterpriseness' (Frank et al. 2010, 124) that was characterized by heightened risk-taking and 'maximisation of available assets' (EC G1). These entrepreneurial behaviours were evident in the second-generation members of TEF D who, via the family holdings group, personally developed, embraced risk-taking, and created their own space in the market: 'There is definitely going to be diversification but not necessarily within [TEF D]' (GM G2). A prominent example of diversification also occurred in 2014 with the establishment of their online marketplace that 'helps farmers and contractors secure the best prices' (Website 2017).

For TEF B, their infusion of bi-directionality and co-participation in entrepreneurial behaviours is grounded in their acknowledgement of differing opinions and approaches (see Table 4).

The unlearning paradox

As evidenced in two stages of interviews and in-depth observations (board meeting, family council meeting) during the closing research period, the sixth generation MD of TEF B implemented a policy whereby all next generation members had to obtain prior external experience: 'Once you see good practice in operation, that's what you aspire to' (BDO G7). Thus, the next generation acquired entrepreneurial education and experience that has not only offset learning but also unlearning through the disregarding of previous operational approaches (see Table 4). In turn, the next generation members have imparted learnings to the incumbent generation regarding best practices obtained from international work experience (e.g. computerization), as well as unlearning in relation to outdated practices. In addition to their policy of new generations gaining external experience to inform their learning (and unlearning), the TEF has bolstered this with a research driven approach to new product development i.e. focus groups. These two motivations for learning/unlearning insights have subsequently embedded efficiency behaviours, in addition to value enrichment for the TEF due to the evidence of predecessor legacy building: 'Dad would not want to let it get out of the family. It is part of the family history' (FC G7). In contrast with TEF C, there was no such employment conditions for next generation, as indicated by the second-generation Deputy Managing Director who obtained a basic third level college degree before entering the business (see Table 4).

As evidenced by archival and early-stage interview data, paradoxical tensions emerged in TEF A following the home plant fire (see Table 4). The brothers were devastated by the incident with 'the only solace being that [their father] was not alive to see the destruction' (Excerpt from the TEF's Biographical Book). Nevertheless, the brothers effectively changed their approach by unlearning their engrained belief that they must preserve the home plant: 'It really broke my heart to say it, but we said [rebuilding is] not the right solution' (Co-MD G3).

The unlearning paradox was also evident in TEF B on the entry of the seventh generation to the firm: 'None [of the next generation] should go back in directly. So, [my children] have both got experience in other fields in other countries' (MD G6). Following this work experience, the next generation attempted to diversify by introducing new product flavours (see Table 4). However, closing interviews revealed that certain organizational members preferred a more calculated approach to these introductions, so that new product development processes could be effectively implemented: 'You will need a lot of lead time before any new products are brought out' (FC G7). In TEF C, early to midway interviews revealed that the family chose to unlearn their policy on exclusive family ownership when a key non-family member requested shares (see Table 4), as the recruitment of this Technical Director played a 'major role' in growing the company (News article 2012).

In TEF D, unlearning by the individual family members played a major part in company restructuring (see Table 4). Contemporary archival data and early-stage interviews with second generation management reveal that when the Executive Chairman returned to the company, the TEF experienced an unlearning paradox: 'My dad got sick for a while, he was outside of the business. So, I just had to fill that gap' (BDO G2). They could either retain their current 'tried and tested' business practices or unlearn and embrace a new emphasis on consolidating the product range and maximizing efficiency. As evidenced by archival data, striving for efficiency is a behaviour embedded in the next generation; in 2007, the New Business Development Manager (G2) implemented a new ERP system and fostered greater technology usage to minimize costs. 'It's very advanced and the machine runs incredibly smoothly .... It's going to be way ahead of the competition' (GM G2).

Discussion and propositions

In alignment with other research into entrepreneurial families (De Massis and Kotlar 2014; Lechner and Dowling 2003), we now present the discussion of our empirical findings along with theoretical propositions for entrepreneurial learning in TEFs.

The relevance of critical incidents for entrepreneurial learning in TEFs

This study demonstrates how entrepreneurial learning triggered by critical incidents is a key mechanism in understanding how entrepreneurial behaviours are transmitted and embedded across generations within a TEF. From our empirical findings, we have observed how TEFs, in the event of disaster-based critical incidents, learn to use their sense of 'family protectiveness' with all employees, and how this responsibility to provide direction informs their subsequent regeneration. We now also understand that in specific circumstances, it is necessary for TEFs to change their approach by disregarding one entrepreneurial behaviour (such as strategic regeneration after a critical incident) as an antecedent for the embedment of another (such as opportunity seeking for growth and acquisition), because they collectively believe that it is the right decision for them as a family. Azadegan and Dooley (2010, 3) argue that entrepreneurial learning is informed by incidents of the past and incidents yet to emerge as entrepreneurial families 'teeter on the exploratory or totter on the exploitative sides of a learning see-saw'. If no precedent is set for a critical incident, then the learning that arises is largely explorative and based on the probability that such actions will save them. Our findings reveal that being opportunity-seeking, resourceful and risk-taking are entrepreneurial behaviours that can be transferred from first to subsequent generations of a TEF through predecessor legacy building. This longitudinal learning progression is reminiscent of the theoretical underpinnings of exploitative learning, as defined by Li et al. (2014, 275) as deriving from 'the knowledge and skills that are familiar with the firms' current experiences.' Our findings advance this theoretical position by demonstrating that the exploitation of not only current but also preceding experience in TEFs has led to three distinct learning outcomes: first, the prioritization of business over non-financial interests (including family-related); second, sustaining the workforce; and third, seeking new means of growth.

Proposition 1: Within TEF contexts, as a result of the behaviour enabler of *family legacy unification and emulation*, longitudinal and exploitative learning may be integral to the embedment of entrepreneurial behaviours, in particular, strategic regeneration and opportunity recognition.

Minniti and Bygrave (2001) argue that entrepreneurial learning can emerge from an action learning process, in which the entrepreneur repeats choices that have been fruitful and disregards options that have amounted to failure. This action learning process, according to Waddill and Marquardt (2011), is grounded in theoretical perspectives of adult learning, in which reflective inquiry favours a cognitivist approach. Our findings advance this theoretical approach to entrepreneurial learning by revealing two salient learning outcomes for TEFs: first, they should persevere with the core product offering in which the family specializes; and second, they should take more measured risks in the future by conducting market research. The comparison of our historical and contemporary archival findings demonstrates that, despite a conservative approach, innovation is still a major part of the TEF's approach.

Proposition 2: From the perspective of TEFs, the behaviour enabler of *entrepreneurial mentoring* can forge strong relationships between failure-driven learning outcomes and the subsequent transmission of entrepreneurial behaviours, namely diversification and risk-taking, even when implemented in a calculative and measured way.

Cope (2005) postulates that entrepreneurial learning processes involving radical change can facilitate 'higher-level' learning outcomes, which in turn create the capacity for differentiated actions. In adherence with Kolb's (1984) theory of experiential learning, this process of entrepreneurial learning entails experience, reflection, cogitation and action. Our findings expand upon these theoretical concepts by showing how three distinct higher-level learning outcomes can emerge from radical changes in TEF entrepreneurial behaviour, when combined with subsequent experiential learning to achieve desired goals: first, develop a strong product offering; second, grow the business through geographical expansion; and third, become adaptive to difficult market conditions. As indicated by our empirical data, learning outcomes can remain relevant if senior family members handle recessionary challenges by continuing to grow through innovation, risk-taking and internationalization.

Proposition 3: In TEFs, the family's involvement impacts not only the behaviour exhibited by the TEF but also the rationale behind family and firm decision making.

Furthermore, the TEF's resultant 'enterpriseness' (Frank et al. 2010, 124) may then manifest in another entrepreneurial behaviour – namely diversification – which is a cornerstone of firm strategy (Garg and Eisenhardt 2017).

Bi-directionality and co-participation in TEF entrepreneurial behaviours

In line with entrepreneurial learning theory, Cope (2005) conceptualizes social characteristics as a dynamic and integrative approach to entrepreneurial learning. Building on this construct, García-Álvarez, López-Sintas, and Saldaña Gonzalvo (2002, 196) consider entrepreneurial mentoring to be a form of these social characteristics, which is 'reserved only for founders' potential successors and begins when successors work full time in the business'. This occurs when the incumbent generation provides autonomy and support to the next generation in pursuing entrepreneurial endeavours. Non-family managers often assume a mentoring position with next generation members (Poza 2010). Hamilton (2011) states that 'the next generation have the knowledge of how to run the business having developed a skilled identity'. Our findings show that the learning processes in a TEF are not only bi-directional and multi-generational (Clinton and Gamble 2019), but also socially constructed as they involve multiple forms of 'co-participation of entrepreneurial learning' (Taylor and Thorpe 2004, 204) from external members of the family.

Proposition 4: Due to behaviour enabler of *entrepreneurial education and experience*, TEFs should adopt a more receptive and combinative approach to family-based and externally-based knowledge acquisition as a means to facilitate multi-generational long-term opportunities and diversification.

Getz and Carlsen (2005, 242) describe a successful family in business as one which may 'allow children a degree of autonomy and to take risks'. Hence, it is evident from our findings that subsequent generations of a TEF not only learn from participation but apply their own venturing knowledge to the group, thus making the learning process and behaviour transmission bi-directional. The salient learning outcomes of this critical incident are as follows: first, allow the next generation space to build an entrepreneurial portfolio; and second, grow the business via diversification. As uncovered here, this type of entrepreneurship is of particular pertinence to TEFs, as it can provide multiple opportunities and income sources for a large next-generation family management cohort (Carter and Ram 2003; Sieger et al. 2011).

Proposition 5: Diversification behaviours in TEFs are enabled by unlearning via the *predecessor legacy building behaviour* enabler and are a result of the bi-directionality of internal/external knowledge transmission combined with learning outcomes.

The unlearning paradox in transgenerational entrepreneurial families

Another distinctive feature of our TEFs is multi-generational family involvement, which brings diverse opinion and input, in turn fostering entrepreneurial ideation (Kellermanns et al. 2008). García-Álvarez, López-Sintas, and Saldaña Gonzalvo (2002, 194) argue that formal education and training are components of a family socialization process experienced by the next generation. They suggest that this formal period of education and training is coupled with entrepreneurial learning and training, which together facilitate 'strong emotional aspects and cognitive learning that are the basis for a descendant's identification with his or her own family'. In our study, the data reveal that the next generation managers of a TEF attain a higher level of education and more external work experience than their predecessors. Resultantly, this affords them 'a greater ability to engage in analysing markets and competitors in order to find room for new entrepreneurial activities' (Cruz and Nordqvist 2012, 37), thus facilitating the incoming transfer of learned entrepreneurial behaviours (i.e. opportunity recognition and diversification). This approach is consistent with Costello's (1996) interpretation of entrepreneurial learning theory through a combination of constant and habitual learning, in which pre-established knowledge is applied to new problems. In our study, the next generation family members of a TEF can impart past learnings to the incumbent generation regarding best practices obtained from work experience, as well as unlearnings in relation to outdated practices to mitigate against future issues. This can subsequently embed efficiency behaviours, in addition to value enrichment for the TEF due to the evidence of predecessor legacy building from the family.

Proposition 6: The opportunities facilitated by external learning via qualifications, as well as unlearning via legacy building behaviour enablers, lead to the transfer and embedding of entrepreneurial behaviours in TEFs that are more inward-facing (i.e. striving for internal operation efficiency and value enhancement) as opposed to outward-facing (i.e. diversifying with new products or markets).

These insights advance entrepreneurial learning theory by extending findings from García-Álvarez, López-Sintas, and Saldaña Gonzalvo (2002), who suggest that founders who view the firm as a means for the family are likely to have a next generation with a lower level of formal education and whom at a young age join the firm at an entry-level position.

While it is necessary for TEFs to transmit and embed entrepreneurial behaviours across family generations, Becker (2010, 265) proposes that unlearning is the overlooked aspect of 'ensuring that individuals relinquish, or at the very least refine, existing knowledge and behavior' that can result in more efficient learning and change processes. It is essential that TEFs unlearn and uncover new business practices; however, Chirico and Nordqvist (2010, 6) assert that the culture of some families makes them 'inflexible, resistant to change and inclined to stick to path-dependent traditions'. This, according to Ingram et al. (2016), creates paradoxical tensions that pervade TEFs and in some cases can cause the diminishment of innovative firm behaviours. Sole and Wilson (2002, 4) have stated that unlearning is fundamentally challenging because 'we need to unlearn practices and mental frames that we don't even realize we rely on'. Our findings advance this statement by demonstrating how the families' decisions to unlearn a mindset on which their entire viewpoint is shaped is not only arduous but essential if entrepreneurial behaviours (e.g. risk-taking and strategic renewal) are to be embedded. These insights lend weight to the theoretical suggestion by Wang and Chugh (2014) that entrepreneurial families are prone to a higher level of exploratory unlearning, compared to their non-entrepreneurial counterparts.

Proposition 7: Due to the behaviour enabler of *family legacy unification and emulation*, TEFs are not invariably inflexible to changing path-dependent family traditions, as they have shown to exhibit strategic use of unlearning and alternative regeneration approaches as part of their crisis management process.

Resistance to change is reflective of older organizations where repeat practices become embedded and thus their perpetuation is legitimized (Tsang and Zahra 2008). Schuman, Stutz, and Ward (2010) theorize that business families can manage the unlearning paradox by not substituting one demand for another. Resulting from our empirical findings, we now also know that the TEF can unlearn the mindset about keeping the core product unaltered, whilst retaining the quality and authenticity of their product.

Unlearning is not an end in itself; rather it leads to the embedding of new knowledge and behaviours (Becker 2010) and as evident in this case, an increased appetite for opportunity exploration. Klein (1989) argues that the original learning is still available, and the individual chooses the knowledge and behaviour that fits the current context. Our findings build on this logic by demonstrating that this mindset can re-emerge when shareholding stakes are returned to the TEF.

Proposition 8: Where a TEF chooses to unlearn their policies on exclusive family ownership, the paradoxical tension between unlearning and retaining the mindset of safeguarding family control and influence emerges.

As evidenced by our study, striving for efficiency is a behaviour embedded in later generations of a TEF. Akgün et al. (2007, 800) state that unlearning differs from the broader concept of organizational change, in that it serves as 'a stage or catalyst [...] in the change process to make it a dynamic process'. Our longitudinal findings thereby indicate that, for TEFs, the change is not instigated by the unlearning process itself, but by the implementation of the entrepreneurial behaviours as a corollary of family and non-family members forgoing their taken-for-granted assumptions of business management.

Resulting from the above discussion and propositions, we now present our theoretical model (see Figure 1 below), in which our eight propositions are visually depicted in terms of their relationship to each other and to the constructs of our research paradigm.

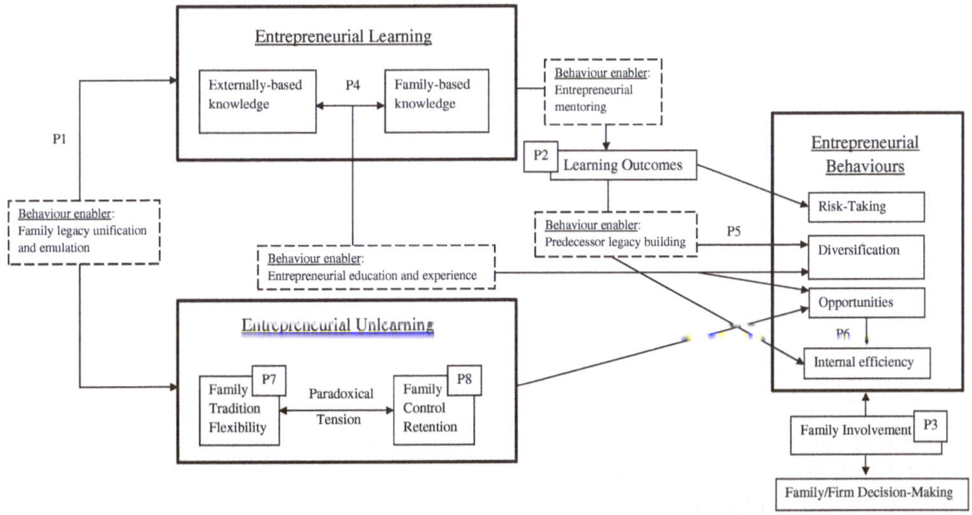

Figure 1. Theoretical model with propositions.

Conclusion

Within this paper, we make the following theoretical contributions. Our first contribution is to the entrepreneurial learning domain, where we advance knowledge of how collective learning occurs among entrepreneurial families (Wang and Chugh 2014) by demonstrating how entrepreneurial learning, triggered by critical incidents, is a key mechanism in understanding how entrepreneurial behaviours are transmitted and embedded across generations within a TEF. As showcased by our findings and discussion, all generations in the TEF have the potential to transmit entrepreneurial behaviours via learning as stimulated by critical incidents (Cope and Watts 2000). This is especially relevant during critical incidents relating to entry of the next generation to the firm, when new members may possess valuable venturing knowledge and experience. We suggest that TEFs should adhere to a more open and multi-faceted approach to external and internal knowledge acquisition as a catalyst for multi-generational long-term diversification and opportunistic behaviour.

Our second contribution is to the family entrepreneurship literature by extending a theoretical model and propositions for the transmission and embedment of entrepreneurial behaviours in TEFs (Randerson, Dossena, and Fayolle 2016). Accordingly, by addressing calls to prioritize the family in the study of family firm entrepreneurship (Nordqvist and Melin 2010; Randerson et al. 2017), we highlight that the transfer of entrepreneurial behaviours in a TEF is represented by a bi-directional, co-participative and multi-generational learning process (McAdam et al. 2018). Specifically, we demonstrate that subsequent generations of a TEF not only learn from participation but apply their own venturing knowledge to the group via portfolio entrepreneurship, thus demonstrating the bi-directional transmission of risk-taking and diversification. This novel insight discounts the assumption within the literature that the transmission of entrepreneurial behaviours between generations is one directional (Randerson et al. 2015), while also empirically highlighting the bi-directional relationship between individual and family entrepreneurial behaviours (Bettinelli, Fayolle, and Randerson 2014).

Our third contribution relates to unlearning and its role in the entrepreneurial learning process, which requires greater attention (Wang and Chugh 2014). Interestingly, our study shows that for TEFs to be entrepreneurial, members must engage with an unlearning paradox: a dual process of retaining practices that work and unlearning practices that are non-economical, obsolete, or misleading. Hence, we conclude that unlearning via legacy building in TEFs may result in the embedment of more inward-facing entrepreneurial behaviours such as value enhancement and internal operation efficiency as opposed to external behaviours such as diversification (García-Álvarez, López-Sintas, and Saldaña Gonzalvo 2002). We have also demonstrated that TEFs are more flexible than previously thought in terms of their strategic use of unlearning and unorthodox regeneration approaches, which can have positive implications for their crisis management processes and enabling the transfer of entrepreneurial behaviours. Moreover, we conclude that it is not the unlearning process itself that directly enables change processes in TEFs, but rather the embedding of the entrepreneurial behaviours that arise when both family and non-family executives relinquish their taken-for-granted assumptions surrounding business (Becker 2010).

Managerial implications

Given the importance of developing applicative knowledge from family business research (Frank and Landström 2016), we extend some practical implications based on this study. First, in order for TEFs to evolve into an agile learning organization, they must effectively manage and navigate the unlearning paradox, using a 'both-and' rather than an 'either-or' approach (Schuman, Stutz, and Ward 2010). However, it may be particularly difficult for older TEFs to engage in unlearning due to established practices (Tsang and Zahra 2008). In this case, non-family professional advisors and managers may be better positioned to identify and lead organizational change initiatives.

Second, as demonstrated by our study, certain enablers can pre-suppose the transmission of entrepreneurial behaviours between TEF members. While we do not claim that the enablers relevant to this study will apply to every transgenerational entrepreneurial family, we note their importance to the transmission of entrepreneurial behaviours between generations. In particular, our findings suggest that TEFs should consider a less complex ownership structure which may secure family influence and foster diversification and business growth.

Finally, in acknowledging that entrepreneurial behaviours vary and 'respond to different mechanisms' (Bettinelli et al. 2017, 522), we show that longitudinal and exploitative learning may be central to the embedment of entrepreneurial behaviours, in particular, strategic regeneration and opportunity recognition. Moreover, in keeping with the action learning process (Minniti and Bygrave 2001), we highlight the connection between failure-driven learning outcomes and the subsequent transmission of entrepreneurial behaviours, namely diversification and risk-taking. Finally, we show how TEF members engage with higher-level learning outcomes and experiential learning to achieve goals, thus showing that the family's involvement impacts not only the behaviour exhibited by the TEF but also the rationale behind family and firm decision making.

Limitations and future research

In addressing the limitations of this research, we also suggest avenues for future work. For instance, our study concentrated on a single geographical context (a region of Northern Europe). Although this has enabled us to control for cultural variation (Salvato and Corbetta 2013), future research could explore the entrepreneurial learning process within TEFs across various cultural contexts. Our understanding of the cyclical relationship between learning and unlearning could be greatly enriched by the adoption of an institutional perspective. Another limitation of our study is that our results are affected by survivor bias. We acknowledge that our results are biased by our selection of TEFs that have proven successful in the phenomena under investigation (Zellweger et al. 2012). Future research could track the entrepreneurial learning of TEFs over a longer period, including firms that were sold or dissolved.

This study has also contributed to theory-building as no definitive theory exists for the transmission and embedment of entrepreneurial behaviours within TEFs (Randerson, Dossena, and Fayolle 2016). Our theoretical model and propositions could be used as a foundation from which to test quantitatively a number of hypotheses relating to the relationship between critical incidents and the entrepreneurial process; the influence of TEF heterogeneity on the transmission of entrepreneurial behaviours; and the unlearning paradox in TEFs.

It was our aim in this paper to contribute theoretical knowledge of how entrepreneurial behaviours are transmitted across generations of TEFs via entrepreneurial learning, offset by critical incidents. In doing so, we believe this study provides a significant contribution both to family entrepreneurship and entrepreneurial learning domains, in addition to the emerging field of transgenerational entrepreneurship.

Notes

1. The STEP project was created in 2005 by Babson College in collaboration with six academic affiliates in Europe. It is a global research initiative that aims to uncover how entrepreneurial mindsets and capabilities are passed across generations, enabling them to create new streams of value. As of 2015, STEP has grown to include 40 institutions with over 175 scholars across five global regions.
2. This data collection period from 2011–2017 was chosen as it marked the aftermath of a worldwide economic downturn and an increase in entrepreneurial activity in this region (OECD 2017).
3. Only questions relevant to this study.
4. Follow-up questions not included in original STEP interview guide.

Disclosure statement

No potential conflict of interest was reported by the authors.

References

Akgün, A. E., J. C. Byrne, G. S. Lynn, and H. Keskin. 2007. "Organizational Unlearning as Changes in Beliefs and Routines in Organizations." *Journal of Organizational Change Management* 20 (6): 794–812. doi:10.1108/09534810710831028.

Azadegan, A., and K. J. Dooley. 2010. "Supplier Innovativeness, Organizational Learning Styles and Manufacturer Performance: An Empirical Assessment." *Journal of Operations Management* 28 (6): 488–505. doi:10.1016/j.jom.2010.02.001.

Becker, K. 2010. "Facilitating Unlearning during Implementation of New Technology." *Journal of Organizational Change Management* 23 (3): 251–268. doi:10.1108/09534811011049590.

Becker, K. L. 2005. "Individual and Organisational Unlearning: Directions for Future Research." *International Journal of Organisational Behaviour* 9 (7): 659–670.

Bekhet, A. K., and J. A. Zauszniewski. 2012. "Methodological Triangulation: An Approach to Understanding Data." *Nurse Researcher* 20 (2): 40–43. doi:10.7748/nr2012.11.20.2.40.c9442.

Berger, P., and T. Luckmann. 1966. *The Social Construction of Reality: A Treatise in the Sociology of Knowledge*. London: Penguin.

Bettinelli, C., A. Fayolle, and K. Randerson. 2014. "Family Entrepreneurship: A Developing Field." *Foundations and Trends® in Entrepreneurship* 10 (3): 161–236. doi:10.1561/0300000049.

Bettinelli, C., S. Sciascia, K. Randerson, and A. Fayolle. 2017. "Researching Entrepreneurship in Family Firms." *Journal of Small Business Management* 55 (4): 506–529. doi:10.1111/jsbm.2017.55.issue-4.

Burke, L. A., and T. T. Baldwin. 1999. "Workforce Training Transfer: A Study of the Effect of Relapse Prevention Training and Transfer Climate." *Human Resource Management* 38 (3): 227–241. doi:10.1002/(ISSN)1099-050X.

Carter, S., and M. Ram. 2003. "Reassessing Portfolio Entrepreneurship." *Small Business Economics* 21 (4): 371–380. doi:10.1023/A:1026115121083.

Casillas, J. C., A. M. Moreno, and J. L. Barbero. 2010. "A Configurational Approach of the Relationship between Entrepreneurial Orientation and Growth of Family Firms." *Family Business Review* 23 (1): 27–44. doi:10.1177/0894486509345159.

Cegarra-Navarro, J. G., M. E. Sánchez-Vidal, and D. Leiva. 2011. "Balancing Exploration and Exploitation of Knowledge through an Unlearning Context: An Empirical Investigation in SMEs." *Management Decision* 49 (7): 1099–1119. doi:10.1108/00251741111151163.

Chirico, F., and M. Nordqvist. 2010. "Dynamic Capabilities and Trans-generational Value Creation in Family Firms: The Role of Organizational Culture." *International Small Business Journal* 28 (5): 487–504. doi:10.1177/0266242610370402.

Chrisman, J. J., J. H. Chua., A. De Massis, F. Frattini, and M. Wright. 2015. "The Ability and Willingness Paradox in Family Firm Innovation." *Journal of Product Innovation Management* 32 (3): 310–318. doi:10.1111/jpim.12207.

Clinton, E., and J. R. Gamble. 2019. "Entrepreneurial Behavior as Learning Processes in a Transgenerational Entrepreneurial Family." In *Entrepreneurial Behaviour: Individual, Contextual and Microfoundational Perspectives*, edited by M. McAdam and J. A. Cunningham, 237–260. London: Palgrave MacMillan.

Clinton, E., M. McAdam, and J. R. Gamble. 2018. "Transgenerational Entrepreneurial Family Businesses: An Examination of the Business Model Construct." *Journal of Business Research* 90: 269–285. doi:10.1016/j.jbusres.2018.04.032.

Cope, J. 2005. "Toward a Dynamic Learning Perspective of Entrepreneurship." *Entrepreneurship Theory & Practice* 29 (4): 373–397. doi:10.1111/etap.2005.29.issue-4.

Cope, J. 2011. "Entrepreneurial Learning from Failure: An Interpretative Phenomenological Analysis." *Journal of Business Venturing* 26 (6): 604–623. doi:10.1016/j.jbusvent.2010.06.002.

Cope, J., and G. Watts. 2000. "Learning by Doing–an Exploration of Experience, Critical Incidents and Reflection in Entrepreneurial Learning." *International Journal of Entrepreneurial Behavior & Research* 6 (3): 104–124. doi:10.1108/13552550010346208.

Costello, N. 1996. "Learning and Routines in High-tech SMEs: Analyzing Rich Case Study Material." *Journal of Economic Issues* 30 (2): 591–597. doi:10.1080/00213624.1996.11505823.

Cruz, A. D., C. Howorth, and E. Hamilton. 2013. "Intrafamily Entrepreneurship: The Formation and Membership of Family Entrepreneurial Teams." *Entrepreneurship Theory & Practice* 37 (1): 17–46. doi:10.1111/etap.2013.37.issue-1.

Cruz, C., and M. Nordqvist. 2012. "Entrepreneurial Orientation in Family Firms: A Generational Perspective." *Small Business Economics* 38 (1): 33–49. doi:10.1007/s11187-010-9265-8.

Cucculelli, M., and C. Bettinelli. 2016. "Corporate Governance in Family Firms, Learning and Reaction to Recession: Evidence from Italy." *Futures* 75: 92–103. doi:10.1016/j.futures.2015.10.011.

De Massis, A., and J. Kotlar. 2014. "The Case Study Method in Family Business Research: Guidelines for Qualitative Scholarship." *Journal of Family Business Strategy* 5 (1): 15–29. doi:10.1016/j.jfbs.2014.01.007.

De Massis, D., A. Vittorio, and F. Frattini. 2016. "Mastering Innovation in Family Firms: How to Resolve the Ability Vs. Willingness Paradox." In *The European Business Review*. Accessed 8 January 2019. https://www.europeanbusinessreview.com/mastering-innovation-in-family-firms-how-to-resolve-the-ability-vs-willingness-paradox/

DeWitt, R., N. Auletta, M. J. Parada, M. Yusof, and P. Sharma. 2015. "Developing Next Generation Leaders." In *Developing Next Generation Leaders for Transgenerational Entrepreneurial Family Enterprises*, edited by S. Pramodita, N. Auletta, R.-L. DeWitt, M. J. Parada, and M. Yusof, 1–20. Northampton: Edward Elgar Publishing .

Dibrell, C., and E. Memili. 2019. "A Brief History and A Look to the Future of Family Business Heterogeneity: An Introduction." In *The Palgrave Handbook of Heterogeneity among Family Firms*, edited by E. Memili and C. Dibrell, 1–15. Cham: Palgrave Macmillan.

Dyer, W. G. 1994. "Potential Contributions of Organizational Behavior to the Study of Family-owned Businesses." *Family Business Review* 7 (2): 109–131. doi:10.1111/j.1741-6248.1994.00109.x.

Eisenhardt, K. M. 1989. "Building Theories from Case Study Research." *Academy of Management Review* 14 (4): 532–550. doi:10.5465/amr.1989.4308385.

Eisenhardt, K. M., and M. E. Graebner. 2007. "Theory Building from Cases: Opportunities and Challenges." *Academy of Management Journal* 50 (1): 25–32. doi:10.5465/amj.2007.24160888.

Frank, H., J. Suess-Reyes, E. Fuetsch, and A. Kessler. 2019. "Introducing the Enterpriseness of Business Families: A Research Agenda." In *The Palgrave Handbook of Heterogeneity among Family Firms*, edited by E. Memili and C. Dibrell, 263–296. Cham: Palgrave Macmillan.

Frank, H., and H. Landström. 2016. "What Makes Entrepreneurship Research Interesting? Reflections on Strategies to Overcome the Rigour–relevance Gap." *Entrepreneurship & Regional Development* 28 (1–2): 51–75. doi:10.1080/08985626.2015.1100687.

Frank, H., M. Lueger, L. Nosé, and D. Suchy. 2010. "The Concept of "Familiness": Literature Review and Systems Theory-based Reflections." *Journal of Family Business Strategy* 1 (3): 119–130. doi:10.1016/j.jfbs.2010.08.001.

García-Álvarez, E., J. López-Sintas, and P. Saldaña Gonzalvo. 2002. "Socialization Patterns of Successors in First-to Second-generation Family Businesses." *Family Business Review* 15 (3): 189–203. doi:10.1111/j.1741-6248.2002.00189.x.

Garg, S., and K. M. Eisenhardt. 2017. "Unpacking the CEO–board Relationship: How Strategy Making Happens in Entrepreneurial Firms." *Academy of Management Journal* 60 (5): 1828–1858. doi:10.5465/amj.2014.0599.

Gersick, K. F., M. M. Hampton, I. Lansberg, and J. A. Davis. 1997. *Generation to Generation: Life Cycles of the Family Business*. Harvard, MA: Harvard Business Press.

Getz, D., and J. Carlsen. 2005. "Family Business in Tourism: State of the Art." *Annals of Tourism Research* 32 (1): 237–258. doi:10.1016/j.annals.2004.07.006.

Gibb, A. A. 1997. "Small Firms' Training and Competitiveness. Building upon the Small Business as a Learning Organisation." *International Small Business Journal* 15 (3): 13–29. doi:10.1177/0266242697153001.

Habbershon, T. G., M. Nordqvist, and T. Zellweger. 2010. "Transgenerational Entrepreneurship." In *Transgenerational Entrepreneurship: Exploring Growth and Performance in Family Firms across Generations*, edited by M. Nordqvist and T. Zellweger, 1–38. Cheltenham: Edward Elgar.

Habbershon, T. G., and J. Pistrui. 2002. "Enterprising Families Domain: Family-influenced Ownership Groups in Pursuit of Transgenerational Wealth." *Family Business Review* 15 (3): 223–237. doi:10.1111/j.1741-6248.2002.00223.x.

Hamilton, E. 2011. "Entrepreneurial Learning in Family Business: A Situated Learning Perspective." *Journal of Small Business and Enterprise Development* 18 (1): 8–26. doi:10.1108/14626001111106406.

Harmeling, S. S., and S. D. Sarasvathy. 2013. "When Contingency Is a Resource: Educating Entrepreneurs in the Balkans, the Bronx, and Beyond." *Entrepreneurship Theory & Practice* 37 (4): 713–744. doi:10.1111/etap.2013.37.issue-4.

Ingram, A. E., M. W. Lewis, S. Barton, and W. B. Gartner. 2016. "Paradoxes and Innovation in Family Firms: The Role of Paradoxical Thinking." *Entrepreneurship Theory & Practice* 40 (1): 161–176. doi:10.1111/etap.2016.40.issue-1.

Jaskiewicz, P., J. G. Combs, and S. B. Rau. 2015. "Entrepreneurial Legacy: Toward a Theory of How Some Family Firms Nurture Transgenerational Entrepreneurship." *Journal of Business Venturing* 30 (1): 29–49. doi:10.1016/j.jbusvent.2014.07.001.

Jaskiewicz, P., J. H. Block, D. Miller, and J. G. Combs. 2014. "Founder versus Family Owners' Impact on Pay Dispersion among non-CEO Top Managers Implications for Firm Performance." *Journal of Management* 43 (5): 1524–1552. doi:10.1177/0149206314558487.

Kellermanns, F. W., K. A. Eddleston, T. Barnett, and A. Pearson. 2008. "An Exploratory Study of Family Member Characteristics and Involvement: Effects on Entrepreneurial Behavior in the Family Firm." *Family Business Review* 21 (1): 1–14. doi:10.1111/j.1741-6248.2007.00107.x.

Klein, J. I. 1989. "Parenthetic Learning in Organizations: Toward the Unlearning of the Unlearning Model." *Journal of Management Studies* 26 (3): 291–308. doi:10.1111/joms.1989.26.issue-3.

Kolb, A. 1984. *Experiential Learning: Experience as the Source of Learning and Development*. Englewood Cliffs, NJ: Prentice-Hall.

Konopaski, M., S. L. Jack, and E. Hamilton. 2015. "How Family Business Members Learn about Continuity." *Academy of Management Learning & Education* 14 (3): 347–364. doi:10.5465/amle.2014.0244.

Kuratko, D. F., R. V. Montagno, and J. S. Hornsby. 1990. "Developing an Intrapreneurial Assessment Instrument for an Effective Corporate Entrepreneurial Environment." *Strategic Management Journal* 11 (Summer): 49–58.

Leal-Rodríguez, A. L., S. Eldridge, J. L. Roldán, A. G. Leal-Millán, and J. Ortega-Gutiérrez. 2015. "Organizational Unlearning, Innovation Outcomes, and Performance: The Moderating Effect of Firm Size." *Journal of Business Research* 68 (4): 803–809. doi:10.1016/j.jbusres.2014.11.032.

Lechner, C., and M. Dowling. 2003. "Firm Networks: External Relationships as Sources for the Growth and Competitiveness of Entrepreneurial Firms." *Entrepreneurship & Regional Development* 15 (1): 1–26. doi:10.1080/08985620210159220.

Li, Y., H. Chen, Y. Liu, and M. W. Peng. 2014. "Managerial Ties, Organizational Learning, and Opportunity Capture: A Social Capital Perspective." *Asia Pacific Journal of Management* 31 (1): 271–291. doi:10.1007/s10490-012-9330-8.

Lincoln, Y. S., and E. G. Guba. 1985. *Naturalistic Inquiry*. Newbury Park, CA: Sage Publications.

Lumpkin, G. T., K. H. Brigham, and T. W. Moss. 2010. "Long-term Orientation: Implications for the Entrepreneurial Orientation and Performance of Family Businesses." *Entrepreneurship & Regional Development* 22 (3–4): 241–264. doi:10.1080/08985621003726218.

Marchisio, G., P. Mazzola, S. Sciascia, M. Miles, and J. Astrachan. 2010. "Corporate Venturing in Family Business: The Effects on the Family and Its Members." *Entrepreneurship & Regional Development* 22 (3–4): 349–377. doi:10.1080/08985621003726168.

McAdam, M., E. Clinton, M. Brophy, and J. R. Gamble. 2018. "A Multilevel Perspective of Organizational Learning in the Transgenerational Entrepreneurial Family Firm." Paper presented at the European Academy of Management Conference, Reykjavik, Iceland, June 19–22.

McAdam, R., R. Reid, and N. Mitchell. 2010. "Longitudinal Development of Innovation Implementation in Family-based SMEs: The Effects of Critical Incidents." *International Journal of Entrepreneurial Behavior Research* 16 (5): 437–456. doi:10.1108/13552551011071887.

McCann, J. E., III, A. Y. Leon-Guerrero, and J. D. Haley Jr. 2001. "Strategic Goals and Practices of Innovative Family Businesses." *Journal of Small Business Management* 39 (1): 50–59. doi:10.1111/0447-2778.00005.

Miles, M. B., and A. M. Huberman. 1994. *Qualitative Data Analysis: An Expanded Sourcebook*. Beverly Hills, CA: Sage Publications.

Miller, D., and I. Le Breton-Miller. 2005. *Managing for the Long Run: Lessons in Competitive Advantage from Great Family Businesses*. Boston: Harvard Business Press.

Minniti, M., and W. Bygrave. 2001. "A Dynamic Model of Entrepreneurial Learning." *Entrepreneurship Theory & Practice* 25 (3): 5–16. doi:10.1177/104225870102500301.

Mwasalwiba, E., H. Dahles, and I. Wakkee. 2012. "Graduate Entrepreneurship in Tanzania: Contextual Enablers and Hindrances." *European Journal of Scientific Research* 76 (3): 386–402.

Nordqvist, M., and L. Melin. 2010. "Entrepreneurial Families and Family Firms." *Entrepreneurship & Regional Development* 22 (3–4): 211–239. doi:10.1080/08985621003726119.

OECD. 2017. "Global Interim Economic Outlook, March 2017." *OECD*. Accessed 14 March 2017. http://www.oecd.org/eco/outlook/economic-outlook/

Palinkas, L. A., S. M. Horwitz, C. A. Green, J. P. Wisdom, N. Duan, and K. Hoagwood. 2015. "Purposeful Sampling for Qualitative Data Collection and Analysis in Mixed Method Implementation Research." *Administration and Policy in Mental Health and Mental Health Services Research* 42 (5): 533–544. doi:10.1007/s10488-013-0528-y.

Pittaway, L., and J. Cope. 2007. "Simulating Entrepreneurial Learning: Integrating Experiential and Collaborative Approaches to Learning." *Management Learning* 38 (2): 211–233. doi:10.1177/1350507607075776.

Politis, D. 2005. "The Process of Entrepreneurial Learning: A Conceptual Framework." *Entrepreneurship Theory & Practice* 29 (4): 399–424. doi:10.1111/etap.2005.29.issue-4.

Poza, E. J. 2010. "Late Stage Entrepreneurial Activity: What Students Should Know about Family -owned and Family-controlled Companies." In *Entrepreneurship and Family Business*, edited by J. Katz and A. C. Corbett, 359–366. Bingley, UK: Emerald Group Publishing Limited.

Pratt, M. G. 2008. "Fitting Oval Pegs into Round Holes: Tensions in Evaluating and Publishing Qualitative Research in Top-tier North American Journals." *Organizational Research Methods* 11 (3): 481–509. doi:10.1177/1094428107303349.

Randerson, K., C. Bettinelli, A. Fayolle, and A. Anderson. 2015. "Family Entrepreneurship as a Field of Research: Exploring Its Contours and Contents." *Journal of Family Business Strategy* 6 (3): 143–151. doi:10.1016/j.jfbs.2015.00.002.

Randerson, K., G. Dossena, and A. Fayolle. 2016. "The Futures of Family Business: Family Entrepreneurship." *Futures* 75: 36–43. doi:10.1016/j.futures.2015.10.008.

Randerson, K., H. Frank, C. Dibrell, and E. Memili. 2017. "Special Issue: 'From Family to Families: Pushing Family Entrepreneurship Forward' Call for Papers." *Entrepreneurship & Regional Development*.

Randolph, R. V., Z. Li, and J. J. Daspit. 2017. "Toward a Typology of Family Firm Corporate Entrepreneurship." *Journal of Small Business Management* 55 (4): 530–546. doi:10.1111/jsbm.2017.55.issue-4.

Rebernik, M., and K. Širec. 2007. "Fostering Innovation by Unlearning Tacit Knowledge." *Kybernetes* 36 (3/4): 406–419. doi:10.1108/03684920710747039.

Rogoff, E. G., and R. K. Z. Heck. 2003. "Evolving Research in Entrepreneurship and Family Business: Recognizing Family as the Oxygen that Feeds the Fire of Entrepreneurship." *Journal of Business Venturing* 18 (5): 559–566. doi:10.1016/S0883-9026(03)00009-0.

Salvato, C., and G. Corbetta. 2013. "Transitional Leadership of Advisors as a Facilitator of Successors' Leadership Construction." *Family Business Review* 26 (3): 235–255. doi:10.1177/0894486513490796.

Sarasvathy, S., K. Kumar, J. G. York, and S. Bhagavatula. 2014. "An Effectual Approach to International Entrepreneurship: Overlaps, Challenges, and Provocative Possibilities." *Entrepreneurship Theory & Practice* 38 (1): 71–93. doi:10.1111/etap.12088.

Schuman, A., S. Stutz, and J. Ward. 2010. *Family Business as Paradox*. Basingstoke, UK: Palgrave Macmillan.

Sieger, P., T. Zellweger, R. S. Nason, and E. Clinton. 2011. "Portfolio Entrepreneurship in Family Firms: A Resource-based Perspective." *Strategic Entrepreneurship Journal* 5 (4): 327–351. doi:10.1002/sej.v5.4.

Sole, D., and D. G. Wilson. 2002. "Storytelling in Organizations: The Power and Traps of Using Stories to Share Knowledge in Organizations." 1–9. New York, NY: LILA Harvard University.

Stigliari, I., and D. Ravasi. 2016. "Combining Qualitative Methods to Study Collective Cognition in Organizations." In *Handbook of Qualitative Organizational Research: Innovative Pathways and Methods*, edited by K. D. Elsbach and R. M. Kramer, 444–453. USA: Routledge.

Taylor, D. W., and R. Thorpe. 2004. "Entrepreneurial Learning: A Process of Co-participation." *Journal of Small Business and Enterprise Development* 11 (2): 203–211. doi:10.1108/14626000410537146.

Tsang, E., and S. Zahra. 2008. "Organizational Unlearning." *Human Relations* 61 (10): 1435–1462. doi:10.1177/0018726708095710.

Volberda, H., C. Baden-Fuller, and F. Van Den Bosch. 2001. "Mastering Strategic Renewal: Mobilising Renewal Journeys in Multi-unit Firms." *Long Range Planning* 34 (2): 159–178. doi:10.1016/S0024-6301(01)00032-2.

Waddill, D., and M. Marquardt. 2011. "Adult Learning Theories and the Practice of Action Learning." In *Action Learning in Practice*, edited by M. Peddler, 415–427. Farnham, UK: Gower Publishing.

Wang, C. L., and H. Chugh. 2014. "Entrepreneurial Learning: Past Research and Future Challenges." *International Journal of Management Reviews* 16 (1): 24–61. doi:10.1111/ijmr.2014.16.issue-1.

Yamada, J. 2004. "A Multi-dimensional View of Entrepreneurship: Towards A Research Agenda on Organisation Emergence." *Journal of Management Development* 23 (4): 289–320. doi:10.1108/02621710410529776.

Yin, R. K. 2009. *Case Study Research: Design and Methods. Essential Guide to Qualitative Methods in Organizational Research*. Thousand Oaks, CA: Sage.

Yin, R. K. 2016. *Qualitative Research from Start to Finish*. New York: Guilford Press.

Zahra, S. A. 2012. "Organizational Learning and Entrepreneurship in Family Firms: Exploring the Moderating Effect of Ownership and Cohesion." *Small Business Economics* 38 (1): 51–65. doi:10.1007/s11187-010-9266-7.

Zellweger, T. 2007. "Time Horizon, Costs of Equity Capital, and Generic Investment Strategies of Firms." *Family Business Review* 20 (1): 1–15. doi:10.1111/j.1741-6248.2007.00080.x.

Zellweger, T. M., F. W. Kellermanns, J. J. Chrisman, and J. H. Chua. 2012. "Family Control and Family Firm Valuation by Family CEOs: The Importance of Intentions for Transgenerational Control." *Organization Science* 23 (3): 851–868. doi:10.1287/orsc.1110.0665.

Zellweger, T. M., R. S. Nason, M. Nordqvist, and C. G. Brush. 2013. "Why Do Family Firms Strive for Nonfinancial Goals? an Organizational Identity Perspective." *Entrepreneurship Theory & Practice* 37 (2): 229–248. doi:10.1111/etap.2013.37.issue-2.

Zhong, E., W. Fan, J. Wang, L. Xiao, and Y. Li 2012. "Comsoc: Adaptive Transfer of User Behaviors over Composite Social Network." In *Proceedings of the 18th ACM SIGKDD international conference on Knowledge discovery and data mining*, 696–704, Beijing, China, August 12. doi:10.1177/1753193412442290.

Appendix 1. Case vignettes

FIRM A

Since 1913, Firm A have been operating as a family-owned sawmilling business both nationally and internationally, as overseen by three generations of the founding family. Joint managing directors, and brothers, work to supply products for the construction, pallet wood and fencing industries. They are the third sibling partnership to co-own and manage the family business, taking the reins from their father, in the mid-1990s. Firm A is currently the country's leading timber processor (turnover of €127m). Originally established by the banks of the river in their local town, the modest sawmill has expanded and evolved to include six plants across two countries with over 380 employees and another 190 indirectly employed by means of harvesting and haulage. Acquiring a second plant in 1998 helped to drive the growth of the company, leading the way for a further four acquisitions in later years. The brothers invested €27m in developing this plant into a state of the art facility, with one of the most technologically advanced production lines in the world. Despite promising expansion and prosperity, the company has not experienced a linear growth path, and experienced a huge fire in 2004 that destroyed the primary plant and production line. Heritage, loyalty to their employees and strong family ties have ensured the survival and rebuilding of Firm A. The brothers understand that sustainability is of utmost importance in forestry and the timber industry. Thus, the company has committed to implementing environmentally responsible methods and choosing quality suppliers to assure the conservation of woodlands.

FIRM B

A seventh generation family business, the founding family have been milling oats since 1785, making them the oldest native family company presently operating in the national food sector. Specializing in the manufacture of oat products, Firm B have operated from a single site for over two hundred years, creating revenue believed to exceed €20 million. With 45 lines of products, their range is derived from the staple and traditional ingredient of oats, extending into the organic and bakery markets. Although a national household name, Firm B have been building their international presence in recent years with exports to sixteen different countries worldwide accounting for approximately twenty-five per cent of the total sales. Despite competition from other global players, Firm B's story, reputation and renowned entrenchment in the local and national community have distinguished them among competitors. Ethical performance also proves to be of significant value at Firm B; using on-site wind and water turbines, they generate sixty per cent of the electricity used for their operations. The company was incorporated in 1940; then in the 1990s, the current Managing Director (G6) acquired the shareholdings of his cousins and brother to obtain total ownership. He and his wife make up two of the six directors at present with three of their six children – the seventh generation of the family to be involved – working among the company's seventy employees. Demonstrating commitment to maintaining family ownership, their son, works in exports while their two daughters work in finance and marketing respectively.

FIRM C

Firm C, a second generation company specializing in water and wastewater management, was founded under a previous name in 1968. Established as a partnership between two co-founders, the ownership of Firm C was later divided among one founder and his three siblings, when the other founder later sold his shareholding stake. Reincorporated in 1973 as Firm C, it has since grown under the guidance of the family for almost 49 years. Despite changing its primary focus from the supply of electrical appliances, Firm C developed to become the largest national family owned water/wastewater treatment and pumping products firm. Only recently, the sibling quartet has given way to the next generation of ownership, a group consisting of siblings and cousins. The Managing Director (G2) leads the current team of both family and non-family directors. Despite this complex structure, Firm C generates over €72m in turnover. Designing solutions which vary from the complex municipal and industrial projects to the single domestic units, Firm C serves clients ranging from homeowners to large multinational and municipal authorities. Delivering services to the municipal, industrial, commercial, agricultural and domestic sectors, Firm C operates on both a national and international level, with many of its clients located abroad. Headquartered locally, the company serves from its eight branches and employs around four hundred people (including subsidiaries) and presently exports to over thirty different countries worldwide. With plans for further expansion, Firm C maintains and accelerates the ambition shown by its founding partnership in 1968.

FIRM D

Firm D is a family owned and run business that was acquired by serial entrepreneur, the current Executive Chairman (G1), in 1963. In its 54-year existence, Firm D has grown from manufacturing light engineering products to now specializing in the widest range of agricultural silage wrapping machinery in the world. The company exports to over 30 countries worldwide, generates approximately €10 million in turnover, and has a domestic headquarters where 50 employees are based. The General Manager (G1) was joined by his eldest son in 2003, who worked in a financial role within the company initially. The second generation of the family is now firmly integrated in Firm D, with four of the founder's five children now working in management roles. There are currently four shareholders in the business, three of whom are family and one who is non-family. At the time of interview, the General Manager, (G1) was gradually relinquishing control to the next generation and anticipated his own retirement in the short-term future. Firm D pride themselves as innovators within the bale wrapping industry, with their first to market approach. The General Manager (G1) has also provided space for the next generation to learn and grow entrepreneurially via their family holdings group. Armed with the necessary resources and knowledge, two members of the next generation have led diversification efforts, and developed a new entrepreneurial venture – a cross comparison farm machinery purchasing website.

Appendix 2. STEP semi-structured interview guide[3]

History and Externalities

(a) Who and what are the key people and strategic events that have made a difference in what you do today or in whom you are?
(b) Outline the key innovations, new ventures, new markets or renewal activities that have made a difference in what you are today or in whom you are?
(c) Describe the major *strategic and/or entrepreneurial events and initiatives* during your history that have made you what you are today – think in terms of 20, 15, 10, and 5 year blocks.

Entrepreneurial Performance

(a) What are the most important entrepreneurial outcomes to the ownership and management of the business or group?
(b) How has the workforce (number of employees) evolved over the last three years (increase/decrease)?
(c) How would you describe your market share/position in the market over the last three year in relation to your competitors (increase/decrease)?
(d) What are the expenses for research and development as a percent of total sales and how have they evolved during the last 3 years?

Entrepreneurial Orientation

Would you describe the *owner-family* as entrepreneurial? Why or why not?

The answer should cover, if relevant, the following issues:

(a) The main attributes that you think makes the family entrepreneurial?
(b) The main attributes that you think are lacking for it to be entrepreneurial?
(c) How the family ownership is a resource for entrepreneurship?
(d) How it has changed over time?
(e) Is continuity in and of itself transgenerational/entrepreneurial (i.e. existing for a long period of time)?

Entrepreneurial Learning[4]

(a) What were the key learnings of this incident?
(b) What was your initial response to this incident?
(c) What were the entrepreneurial responses to this incident?
(d) How did entrepreneurial behaviours change as a result of this incident?

Appendix 3. Entrepreneurial behaviour enablers

Entrepreneurial behaviour enabler	Description
Predecessor legacy building	Examples where the family have made strategic decisions or undertaken new explorative practices in order to build upon their predecessor's legacy.
Entrepreneurial mentoring	Evidence of mentoring the next generation upon entering the business; providing resources and autonomy to next generation in pursuing entrepreneurial endeavours; supporting next generation in decision-making and introducing changes.
Entrepreneurial education and experience	*Formal* Statements about family members attaining qualifications (e.g. degree level); studying areas that relate to the family business; obtaining work experience (at home or abroad) that relates to the family business industry. *Informal* Statements about family members learning about the industry/family business through trade fairs, business trips, meetings, 'on the job' training etc.
Family legacy unification and emulation	Statements that demonstrate unified efforts by the family to recreate and perpetuate the family legacy

Transgenerational entrepreneurship in entrepreneurial families: what is explicitly learned and what is successfully transferred?

Junsheng Dou, Emma Su, Shengxiao Li and Daniel T. Holt

ABSTRACT

Research has suggested that the interaction between older and younger generation family members plays a pivotal role in the development of the younger generation's entrepreneurial practices. Little is known, however, what the older generation transfers to younger generation family members and what is explicitly applied by the younger generation in new entrepreneurial settings. Drawing on multiple case studies with Chinese business families, we identify the elements of knowledge that are passed between the two generations to include moral values, competence values, and cognitive heuristics. Moreover, we show that values rather than heuristics are further transferred in new entrepreneurial settings.

There is a growing recognition that understanding the family, as an entity, is important to understand how individuals' entrepreneurial activities are nurtured and incubated (Bettinelli, Fayolle, and Randerson 2014; Bettinelli et al. 2017; Marchisio et al. 2010; Randerson et al. 2015). As such, within entrepreneurial families, the family holds great potential for understanding the next generation's entrepreneurial behaviours (Aldrich and Cliff 2003; Matthews, Schenkel, and Hechavarria 2009). Social learning theory has provided the theoretical framework to explain how families shape entrepreneurial behaviours (Bandura 1986), positing that the continuous, reciprocal interactions with others through socialization and role modelling serve as active examples to be emulated, thereby motivating behavioural patterns (Chlosta et al. 2012; McKeever, Anderson, and Jack 2014). Thus, family business owners' offspring learn through observation and interaction wherein the parents' behaviour to include entrepreneurial behaviour, is observed and imitated.

Whereas social learning theory offers a meaningful explanation of how entrepreneurship is nurtured within entrepreneurial families through observation and interaction, it fails to examine the content of the interactions to identify what specifically is learned from the older generation and what specifically is transferred to new entrepreneurial settings. To address these shortcomings, we use an inductive theory-building approach from multiple cases to identify the elements of knowledge that are passed across generations to nurture entrepreneurial behaviours and what elements of knowledge are subsequently transferred to new entrepreneurial settings (Edmondson and McManus 2007; Eisenhardt and Graebner 2007). We conduct our investigation within a unique cultural setting – Chinese business families.

We contribute to the growing conversation regarding the interactions between entrepreneurship, the family, and the family business (Randerson et al. 2015). Whereas previous work has explored these issues at the family- and firm-level (Bettinelli et al. 2017; Fletcher 2006), we narrow the level of analysis to explore interactions at the individual level. This is important because families and firms by themselves do nothing – even the most collective activities taking place within families and firms are an amalgamation of the activities of individuals; therefore, family businesses and business families are entrepreneurial through individuals' actions. According to social learning theory, the entrepreneurial actions of the second-generation would be influenced by the within-family transmission of information, beliefs, and resources that facilitate entrepreneurial learning and assist in the development of an entrepreneurial posture. If the content of these interactions is understood, it is possible to test how to transmit knowledge to the second-generation so it can be applied, furthering our understanding of the interactions between entrepreneurship, the family, and family businesses (Randerson et al. 2015).

Entrepreneurship and the family

Although there has been considerable theorizing about the interaction between entrepreneurship, the family, and business families, empirical research has largely examined the relationship between entrepreneurship and the family, focusing on how an individual's propensity to become an entrepreneur is shaped by his or her family (Bettinelli, Fayolle, and Randerson 2014; Dyer and Handler 1994; Nordqvist and Melin 2010). As noted, social learning theory (Bandura 1986) offers an explanation as to why an individual's propensity to become an entrepreneur would be linked to his or her family (Matthews, Schenkel, and Hechavarria 2009). According to social learning theory, individuals are motivated to make certain decisions, behave in specific ways, and pursue certain goals based on the visible, active examples provided by those around them (Chlosta et al. 2012). Because children are especially exposed to their parents' behaviours, parents significantly influence the child's subsequent choices (Chung and Gale 2009) to include the engagement in entrepreneurial actions (e.g. Mathews and Moser 1995).

While it is beyond our scope to comprehensively review the literature that has explored the links between family and entrepreneurship, the theory suggests that individuals' entrepreneurial attitudes and activities are strongly rooted in the influence of entrepreneurial parents through socialization and role modelling (Steyaert and Katz 2004). Indeed, empirical findings indicate that children are more likely to develop entrepreneurial behaviours if they grow up with parents who are entrepreneurs, learning from their parents' entrepreneurial experiences and internalizing their parents' behaviour as norms for their own (Schmitt-Rodermund 2004). Beyond the environmental stimuli that the parental entrepreneurs provide, these children are said to obtain key information resources for entrepreneurial activities (Carsrud, Gaglio, and Olm 1987) where parents transfer knowledge from their own entrepreneurial experience and provide an informal introduction to things like business models (e.g. Mueller 2006), through story-telling (Bettinelli, Fayolle, and Randerson 2014; Jaskiewicz, Combs, and Rau 2015).

Within wine-making families, Jaskiewicz, Combs, and Rau (2015) found, through interviews of family members, that a family's senior generation engaged the younger generation in strategic education, entrepreneurial bridging, and strategic transitions to purposefully encourage entrepreneurship of the latter. Strategic education provided the younger generation with the necessary human capital to prepare them entrepreneurially. This ensured the proper university education was attained while providing work experience within the family firm. Entrepreneurial bridging enhanced the younger generation with mentorship, decision authority, and resources for firm-related innovations that younger generations directed. Finally, strategic transitions involved steps to actively integrate the next generation's current family (i.e. spouse and children) into his or her original family (i.e. parents and siblings).[1]

Collectively, this suggests that social interactions work to influence the attitudes, motivations, values, and cognitions of the younger family members which subsequently helps them develop an understanding of entrepreneurship and the associated behavioural expectations (Cabrera-Suárez, De Saá-Pérez, and García-Almeida 2001). Although illuminating, this research has largely focused on the process where language, history, symbols, and any other verbal or nonverbal communication, are leveraged with other activities (i.e. acquiring human capital). Consequently, the younger generation may develop a shared framework and pattern of understanding such that family members develop homogenous perceptions towards entrepreneurship. Nonetheless, the content of the communications between parents and children has been largely overlooked, suggesting that little is known about what specific knowledge is transferred and what further applied in new entrepreneurial settings. This led to the following research questions: (a) what knowledge is learned by the second-generation family member from the first-generation family member in an entrepreneurial family? and (b) what elements of this knowledge are transferred to new entrepreneurial settings?

Methods

We address our questions with a multiple-case study design (Edmondson and McManus 2007; Eisenhardt and Graebner 2007). This allowed comparisons and contrasts between cases such that similarities and differences between them could be captured while each case served to (dis)confirm the inferences drawn from others. This approach is typically better grounded theoretically and more generalizable, providing robust results (e.g. Taura and Watkins 2014).

Setting and sample

Chinese business families from Shaoxing city participated. These firms were identified through recommendations made by the Secretary-General of the *Association of Young Entrepreneurs of Shaoxing City*, a not-for-profit organization that provides networking and knowledge-sharing opportunities for young entrepreneurs. Shaoxing has one of the most vibrant entrepreneurship communities in China. Given our interest in entrepreneurial knowledge learned and applied in new entrepreneurial settings by the younger generation of the family, we purposefully selected family firms that had (a) at least 50% of shares held by the controlling family[2]; (b) at least two family members currently (or in the past) employed as significant owners, top managers, or directors; (c) at least one second-generation family member currently employed as a significant owner, top manager, or director (Arregle et al. 2012). The median percentage of shares owned by the controlling family was 91.88. On average, four family members were involved in middle-to upper-level management and second-generation family members had worked in the firm over ten years.

Further, family firms where the second-generation family member had successfully initiated entrepreneurial activities were sampled. All entrepreneurial activities by the second-generation took place less than six months prior to data collection, mitigating concerns regarding recall. In addition, four firms were involved in their entrepreneurial activities of the younger generation during data collection. This allowed us to incorporate retrospective thoughts with real-time data, allowing both efficiencies in data collection by increasing the number of cases and improved richness by learning how events evolve in real-time.

The firms represented various industries, including real estate, solar energy, and manufacturing (see Table 1). These industries have faced pressure to engage in entrepreneurial endeavours; yet, they differed along key dimensions such as the knowledge needed to launch entrepreneurial initiatives. As such, a diverse sample of family firms was represented, enhancing the sample's representativeness and the generalizability of results.

Data sources

Data sources included: (1) qualitative data, including semi-structured interviews with first-generation family members, second-generation family members, or management team members; (2) archival data, including company web sites, annual reports, and press releases; (3) public news reports, including interviews with local media, as well as speeches given by first- or second-generation family

Table 1. Case descriptions.

Family firm	Industry	Number of employees	Percentage of shares owned by the family	Number of family members in middle- to upper-level management	Years second-generation worked in the firm	Informants	Additional data	Entrepreneurial activities initiated by the second-generation
SHGF	Manufacturing (HVAC & auto parts); Real estate; Solar energy	13,200	51.96%	3	15	General manager (founder's son); Founder's assistant	Press releases; media reports; MBA thesis	Entered solar energy industry
LBJT	Manufacturing (Electrical components; machinery) Copper and aluminium processing	760	58.28%	2	4	President (founder); General manager (founder's son)	Media reports	Developed new products (high-tech copper)
HGJT	Dyeing; Clothing; Real estate	1280	100%	4	11	General manager (founders' daughter); Founder's assistant	Media reports; speech	Entered international market
ZSJS	Construction; Real estate	2100	100%	4	13	Vice president (founder's daughter)	Media reports; news interview	Entered real estate venture
HJJT	Manufacturing (chain equipment); Printing	2016	88.75%	4	14	President (founder's son)	Media reports	Entered international market
JCRE	Real estate	1300	95%	4	15	President (founder's daughter); Founder's assistant	Media reports; news interview	Entered real estate venture & hotel industry

To ensure the anonymity, pseudonyms were used throughout. HVAC refers to heating ventilation and air conditioning.

members; (4) observations, including visits to each firm; (5) emails and phone communications, including follow up interviews.

Interviews lasted from 75 to 135 minutes. Where it was possible, two or more informants were interviewed. Over 19 months, 10 interviews were conducted with second- and first-generation family members as well as the founder's executive assistant.[3] Interviews followed the same format with appropriate modifications made based on the informant's role. Specifically, interview questions with the second-generation family members addressed (a) basic information related to the family firm (e.g. firm history, size, sales), (b) basic information related to the informant (e.g. age, education background, experience), (c) knowledge acquired from the first-generation family member, (d) a description of the most recent entrepreneurial activity (e.g. product launch or internationalization), (e) a description of the knowledge learned from the first-generation that has been applied in the new entrepreneurial initiative, and (f) a description of similarities and differences between themselves and the first-generation in dealing with people and issues.

Further, we asked direct and indirect questions to the second-generation to trace answers to the first research question – *what knowledge is explicitly learned by the second-generation family member from the first-generation family member in an entrepreneurial family?* This approach provided a strong grounding of theoretical insights and mitigated bias. Direct questions included: '*What components of knowledge have you learned from your parents?*' Indirect questions included: '*In what ways have your parents helped you with business-related issues?*'

The first-generation and, in a few cases, the founder's executive assistant provided his or her perspective on many of the same issues. This was done to triangulate the findings and complement the second-generation's perspective (Eisenhardt and Graebner 2007). Like the second-generation, the first-generation provided basic information related to the firm, but were asked to expand on this to share the motivations to start the business. In addition, a description of the most recent entrepreneurial activity was provided by the first-generation and assistants. The first-generation explained their role, while the first-generation and assistants both explained what made it successful. Also, the first-generation and assistants described the similarities and differences in the ways first- and second-generation dealt with people and issues.

Data analysis

A central aspect of data analysis was our triangulation between interviews and archival data collected from press releases, media reports, and business documents. This led to the development of a case story for each firm that was used for within- and cross-case analyses and represented a rich, reliable account of each firm (Lee 1999). These case stories, used in the within-case analysis, focused on developing what the second-generation learned from the first-generation through interactions and observations and what knowledge was transferred to new entrepreneurial settings. A core aspect of this inductive process was that constructs emerged from the data during this process, rather than being guided by specific hypotheses. Though similarities and differences were noted among cases during the within-case analysis, further analysis was not completed until case write-ups were completed independently such that each case would serve as a distinct, stand-alone analytic unit (Eisenhardt and Graebner 2007).

After each case was written and analysed, similar constructs and ideas across cases were identified. Using cross-case analysis techniques, we generated first-order concepts that captured individuals' responses to what knowledge was learned from the first-generation; similar first-order concepts were grouped and second-order themes that parsimoniously described the understanding and knowledge were developed (Gioia, Corley, and Hamilton 2013). During the process of analysing the participants' understanding, we drew upon ideas from the values and learning literature; applying this literature provided a framework to structure the construct categories that emerged and identify unexpected, vicariously learned and transferred elements. Thus, theory elaboration and theory generation approaches were used (Lee 1999).

We then iterated between theory and data to clarify the findings, enhance internal validity, and improve the robustness of our theoretical arguments. We refined emerging relationships through replication logic, revisiting the data to see if each separate case demonstrated the same pattern. The process was iterative and lasted six months, leading to second-order themes that captured the components of knowledge shared by the individuals, which fed into the aggregate theoretical dimensions.

With regards to the first research question (i.e. knowledge explicitly learned), the second-generation largely provided answers. Each thought mentioned by the second-generation was recorded (Corbin and Strauss 1998), and then used in a constant comparative analysis to aggregate similar content into second-order themes (Gioia, Corley, and Hamilton 2013), namely, moral values, competence values, and cognitive heuristics. Figure 1 illustrates the first-order concepts, second-order themes, and aggregate dimensions.

To identify what elements of knowledge had been transferred to new entrepreneurial settings, we identified the key success factors (KSFs) for the recent entrepreneurial activities that had been initiated by the second-generation. These KSFs were compared to the components of knowledge the second-generation indicated that they had learned from the first-generation. When common factors emerged, the preliminary conclusion was that the knowledge was transferred. These preliminary conclusions were verified by comparing the results with the answers given by the second-generation – *'Are there any of the KSFs for the entrepreneurial activity related to what you have learned from your entrepreneurial parents? If yes, what are they?'*

Findings

What is explicitly learned by the second-generation family member from the first-generation family member in entrepreneurial families?

The data revealed that the specific knowledge acquired by the second-generation entrepreneurs could best be characterized as *values*. Values are core beliefs about what is important and represent guiding principles of what is moral, desirable, or just (Rokeach 1973; Sorenson 2013). Drawing on Rokeach's (1973) conceptualization of values, two value categories emerged. *Moral values* were concerned with evaluations of abstract ideas such as integrity, respect, and responsibility. Moral values guide day-to-day business and life and how to sustain interpersonal relationships. *Competence values* were related to personal achievements such as being ambitious, capable, and forward-looking.

Moral values

Among the second-generation entrepreneurs (and consistent with social learning theory), participants were deeply influenced by their entrepreneurial parents' moral values. For example, a second-generation family member of firm JCRE said, *'What I have learned most from my father are his life values and ways of conducting himself and dealing with issues. Through talking to our father on a regular basis, my brother and I have learned these valuable principles'*. Similarly, a second-generation son (LBJT) mentioned, '[My father] *has set a good example in so many aspects for me to follow. He always told me it is more important to learn to be a responsible and decent person than to run a successful business. I know some entrepreneurs are very successful in their businesses, but they are not necessarily the most successful in terms of being a noble person. That is very unfortunate'*. Furthermore, a second-generation daughter (ZSJS) said, *'My father's notion of 'being a good person is more important than running a successful business' is deeply rooted in my mind. He has been telling me this since I was little'*.

In addition, most of the second-generation entrepreneurs mentioned that they learned the values needed to sustain interpersonal relationships, for example, being loyal, valuing friendship, and

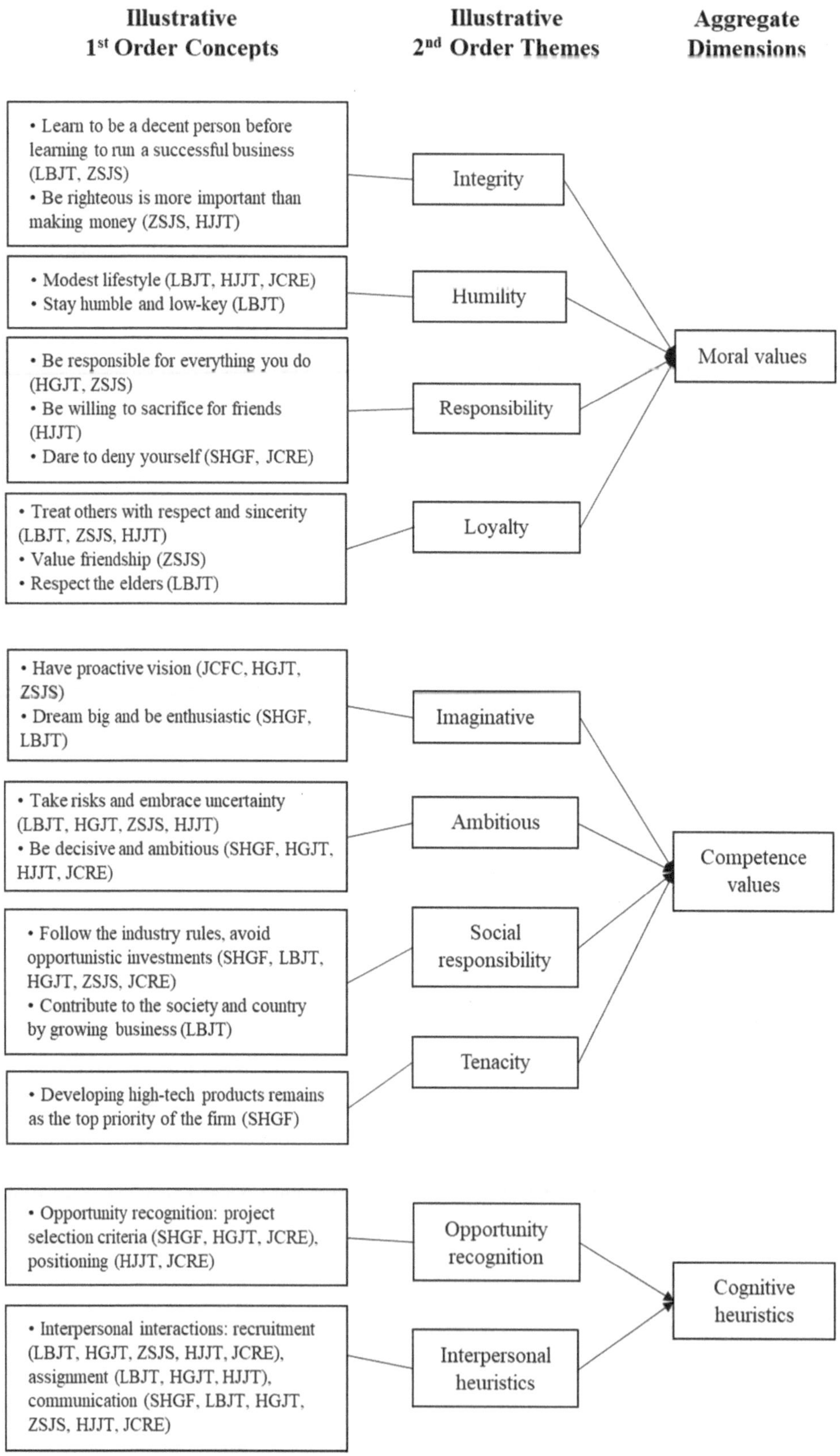

Figure 1. First- and second-order constructs.

sacrificing for friends. One second-generation daughter (ZSJS) said, her father taught her *'how to be loyal to our friends and relatives'*. The son of a founder (LBJT) said, *'It is important to have the right attitudes in dealing with people and things. My father has set a good example on this aspect. My father is always honest with the employees. His attitudes and beliefs are, to a certain extent, reflected in the business'*. Similarly, the second-generation family member (HJJT) mentioned, *'My father is a well-respected person in our community. He shares the traits that a successful entrepreneur has in Shaoxing. He is always willing to sacrifice himself for his friends. These traits help him run a successful business in Shaoxing'*. Moreover, LBJT's founder told his son, *'If you want others to respect you, you need to first respect them. You need to talk to them frequently and set a good example in front of them so that they are willing to follow you.'*

The importance of values was repeatedly emphasized. For example, the daughter of HGJT's founder repeatedly mentioned that her father had taught her how to become a noble person, which was consistent with the typical thinking rooted in the Chinese culture. According to Confucian's 'the Great Learning', an important part of an individual's life should be dedicated to the cultivation of moral values. According to Confucian principles, *' … people need to rectify their hearts if they wish to become a noble person; people need to become a noble person if they wish to regulate their families … '* The importance of moral values can be formally stated:

***Proposition 1*: The second-generation family member acquires moral values from the first-generation, including integrity, humility, responsibility, and loyalty.**

Competence values

The second category of values being transmitted across generations was related to competence. In comparison to their western counterparts, family firms in China usually do not have a long history with most being founded after the implementation of China's Open Door Policy (1978). As such, family firms are not professionalized and the first-generation, founding entrepreneur typically serves in several roles (i.e. leader and manager). Thus, the first-generation transmitted values that stressed how to become a successful entrepreneurial leader rather than procedural skills or know-hows. Specifically, values related to being persistent and resilient were cited most frequently, with interviewees stressing that being persistent, to a certain extent, contributed to becoming a successful entrepreneurial leader. For example, the second-generation of firm LBJT said, *'My father is always persistent on the way our business shall be conducted. He is keen to continue to invest in production lines (also known as the 'real economy' in China) which many other firms have already given up doing. He believes that 'real economy' is the future of our country. I have learned from my father to stick with the core value of our business'*. Other values dealt with risk, emergencies, and difficulties. Specifically, several second-generation entrepreneurs mentioned the importance that risk-taking played in entrepreneurial success was learned from the first-generation.

Data collected from ZSJS and HGJT also revealed that entrepreneurial parents explicitly instilled the importance of positive thinking in the face of difficulties and uncertainties. For example, the second-generation of firm ZSJS said, *'What I have learned most from my father is I shall always stay calm, trust myself, and try to find solutions to solve the problems regardless of what kind of situation I am facing. When you are calm, more solutions are likely to come to mind'*. This view is confirmed by the daughter of HGJT's founder who said, *'My mom is very calm when she comes to handle difficult situations. I am learning from her every day on how to stay calm under any circumstances.'* In addition to the values of persistence and poise, the second-generation mentioned other values including forward-thinking and dreaming as integral parts of entrepreneurial success.

These findings, to a certain extent, support arguments made in the literature regarding the importance of risk-taking (Brockhaus and Horowitz 1986), tolerance for ambiguity (Begley and Boyd 1987), and self-efficacy (Chen, Greene, and Crick 1998) to an individual's entrepreneurial success. In addition, constant encouragement from the first-generation entrepreneur played an important role in developing the second-generation to become competent entrepreneurial leaders. For example, a father's encouragement played a pivotal role in his son's delivering a successful speech and answering strategic questions (firm SHGF). The importance of competence values can be formally stated:

***Proposition 2*: The second-generation family member acquired competence values from the first-generation, including creativity, ambition, social responsibility, and tenacity.**

Heuristic portfolio

The second-generation also learned a series of heuristics that helped them manage interpersonal relationships and identify entrepreneurial opportunities. While the first-generation typically gained their diverse experiences by taking multiple roles within the business (Gersick et al. 1997), the second-generations' management experience varied based on when they joined the business. Thus, the heuristics, learned from their parents, guide them in the management of the firm. Heuristics are cognitive shortcuts that emerge when information, time, and processing capacity are limited (Newell and Simon 1972). The heuristics are transmitted as a set of principles and steps for problem analysis and solving. Responses were coded as cognitive heuristics when they were mentioned as rules of thumb for choosing whom they can trust or which project or market opportunities should be pursued.

Among the second-generation family members, learned heuristics were related to interpersonal relationships. Specifically, such heuristics include how to recognize trustworthy subordinates and customers, and how to communicate and negotiate. The second-generation member of LBJT further highlighted the importance of heuristics in the transmission of knowledge between generations, '*I remember one time when the contract negotiation with one of our clients did not go well, my father told me that "you need to have a good understanding of the other party before you enter the room to negotiate the contract." Without a good understanding of the client, you will face the difficulty of implementing the contract even if the contract was successfully signed. The clients can always come back and change their mind and nullify the contract*'. Further, the second-generation family member of HJJT provided another example of heuristics that he learned about how to handle customers' complaints. He said, '*Whenever there is a complaint from our customers, my father will first evaluate the real intention behind the customer. He told us, "the complaints from our European or American customers are most likely related to the quality of our products and we usually need to address their complaints immediately. Complaints from our South-East Asian clients are more likely to have something to do with the price of goods. It's not unusual for this group of clients to use price to bargain for other things." We need to have different strategies to deal with complaints from customers of different regions*'.

Heuristics related to opportunity-recognition were important elements that the second-generation learned from the first-generation. Such heuristics included rules-of-thumb regarding which opportunities should be pursued, how to prioritize opportunities, when it was best to explore new opportunities, as well as when it was best to stop pursuing an opportunity. For instance, the second-generation of firm SHGF's applied intuition and heuristics that he learned from his father when he successfully diversified the firm. According to the son, '*Due to the economic crisis in 2012, our company was constrained by the availability of opportunities to grow. My father asked me to explore some new opportunities for the firm to grow. With the assistance of my father, we set three criteria for developing new products: new energy, water processing, and smart grid. Also based on the principle of "using limited resources to explore the unlimited market," we then spent 15 million USD and started a new project in the solar energy industry. This project is currently going well. I think the kinds of heuristics related to decision-making that I have learned from my father has largely contributed to the success of this project. Most of the time these kinds of heuristics cannot be articulated, but they play an important role in identifying opportunities*'. The daughter of JCRE's founder also mentioned her father's rules of thumb to make decisions and select construction sites for commercial and residential properties. She told us, '*The main principle that my father applies in choosing a construction site for developing new properties is that "the construction site does not necessarily need to be in the downtown area, however, the surrounding environment must have the potential for future growth."'* Further, the son of SHGF told us, *'Doing business can be very fun when you use heuristics and insights to deal with business-related issues. We cannot make decisions just based on rational thinking. Our experience told us that decisions based on heuristics often are the best decisions'*.

Although the literature often describes heuristics as dysfunctional 'rules of thumb' that may lead to errors (Busenitz and Barney 1997), our findings revealed that entrepreneurs use heuristics as mechanisms to exercise business judgement. These findings were also consistent with Bingham and Eisenhardt (2011) argument that heuristics help identify opportunities and implement strategies. Heuristics are often used in unique situations and particularly in situations where information and time are limited (Newell and Simon 1972).

Further, heuristics were often said to be more accurate than other decision-making methods. According to the daughter of HGJT who said, *'I found my mother often uses her intuition or heuristics to make decisions. I am still learning from her how to use heuristics. My mother is no more involved in the day-to-day business management. But when she stops by the office and runs into a new customer, she usually can tell instantly if this customer will be our next big customer. My mother has a very good sense of judgment in terms of identifying our next big customers.'* A similar point of view was shared by the son of SHGF's founder, *'My father makes many decisions based on his intuition and these decisions are often proved to be the best decisions'*. The importance of heuristics related to one's professional development can be formally stated:

***Proposition 3*: The second-generation entrepreneur has acquired cognitive heuristics from the first-generation including opportunity recognition and interpersonal heuristics.**

What elements of knowledge that the entrepreneurial children have learned from the first-generation entrepreneur are further transferred to new entrepreneurial settings?

Interestingly, data showed that values rather than cognitive heuristics were more likely to be transferred to new entrepreneurial settings. For example, the founder and the son of firm LBJT mentioned shared values that guided running the business. Using the son's words, *'I think I am growing more and more like my father. There might be some differences between us in the past, but I am growing more and more like my father every day. For example, both of us are very passionate about our business. Under the influence of my father, I have recently started a new high-tech project to follow my father's footprint to venture new business which has great potential to succeed'*. The founder of LBJT further confirmed this view by suggesting, *'My employees often told me the little boss (i.e. the son) is growing more and more like the big boss (i.e. the father); they told me we are like two peas in a pod'*. As another example, the son of SHGF's founder started a project by acquiring 30% ownership from an Israel-based company. This initiative shows the second-generation family member's commitment to carry on the founder's values towards running their business which is *'be the leader in the field'*. The executive assistant to the founder of SHGF further confirmed, '*... both the father and the son are open-minded.*' and '*... the big boss and the little boss have similar leadership and management styles and they are willing to take risks to grow the business in order to become the leader in the industry ...*'. With regards to the elements of values being transferred, the daughter of HGJT's founder said *'Most of my mother's values are very valuable to me, including her hard-working spirit and her strong sense of responsibility toward people and many things ... these values are especially important in the current downturn economy. I have learned to apply these values in expanding our business into international markets.'*

Regarding the cognitive heuristics, although some second-generation members mentioned that their entrepreneurial parents used 'rules of thumb', and they had learned to apply heuristics in their own work, most did not give detailed descriptions that explained how they applied heuristics in new entrepreneurial settings, sharing only abstract principles. For example, the daughter of HGJT's founder told us, *'My mother taught me how to use intuition and heuristics to make business decisions'*.

The daughter of ZSJS's founder also said, *'What I have accomplished at work in the past few years is largely due to the improvement that I've made in my interpersonal skills, which I have learned greatly from my father. My father taught me to be sincere and loyal to my friends. These also contribute to my success in running the business.'*

These findings suggested that cognitive heuristics were applied in day-to-day management activities, while values were more important as new entrepreneurial activities are evaluated and pursued. Because the second-generation typically worked as senior executives, few were involved in the day-to-day management of the business. As a result, the second-generation was more likely to use values that they acquired from their entrepreneurial parents rather than cognitive heuristics that were often tailored to practical issues.

Moreover, the absence of a complete definition of 'entrepreneurial activities' in the current literature may also, to a certain extent, explain our finding that values are more likely to be transferred to new entrepreneurial contexts. Our study shows that the second-generation entrepreneur often considers entrepreneurial activities as the recognition and evaluation of opportunities rather than the subsequent activities following recognition and evaluation of the opportunity where opportunity recognition and evaluation required values more than heuristics.

Lastly, heuristics may be too complicated or tacit to be clearly articulated by entrepreneurs. As the son of HJJT's founder mentioned, *'It has been two years since I became the board chair for the firm. I finally came to notice that my father made many decisions based on his intuitions and heuristics which he has gained over all the years of hard-work. However, these intuitions and heuristics cannot be articulated'*. The second-generation of LBJT shared a similar thought. He used a term 'grassroots stuff' to express the tacit nature of the heuristics. He said, *'The grassroots stuff (acquired from my father) is invaluable to help me successfully run the business'*. When we asked him to elaborate on the contents of such 'grassroots stuff', he said, *'It is more like the rules of thumb used in running businesses in the unique institutional environment in China'*.

These findings align with key elements of learning theory which explain what learning is transferred and when. Gray and Orasanu (1987) suggest learning can be applied to more far-reaching and novel areas when it is more general. General knowledge, in contrast to specific knowledge, refers to attitudes and methods, or as general principles and general modes of attack. This knowledge is applied more easily to situations dissimilar to those where the original learning occurred. Consistent with this, second-generation learns general principles and modes of attack (i.e. moral and competence values; cognitive heuristics) from their entrepreneurial parents and carry-over values to new entrepreneurial activities.

The founder genuinely hoped the young generation family member could carry on the values, a good way for the young generation to win the old generation's support is to learn and apply the old generation's values. For example, the founder of firm LBJT said, *'I am thrilled to observe my son is growing to be more like me and inherited my business philosophy and leadership style. I am often told that we (he and his son) are like two peas in a pod'*. Moreover, according to Collins and Porras (1994), the preservation of core values is critical for a firm's long-lasting success. Since the core values of the enterprise are usually formed based on the founder's values and ideas (Schein 1984), the continuation of the founder's values across generations is important to the continuation of the core values in the business. Thus, the idea that entrepreneurial parents' core values are continued on to the second-generation and this continuation appeals to the second-generation can be formally stated:

***Proposition 4*: In new entrepreneurial settings, the second-generation entrepreneur is more likely to apply values (to include moral and competence values) rather than cognitive heuristics that they have learned from the first-generation.**

Discussion

The importance of research at the intersection between entrepreneurship and the family, and family firms has been emerging (e.g. Bettinelli et al. 2017). At the intersection of all three, the continuity of

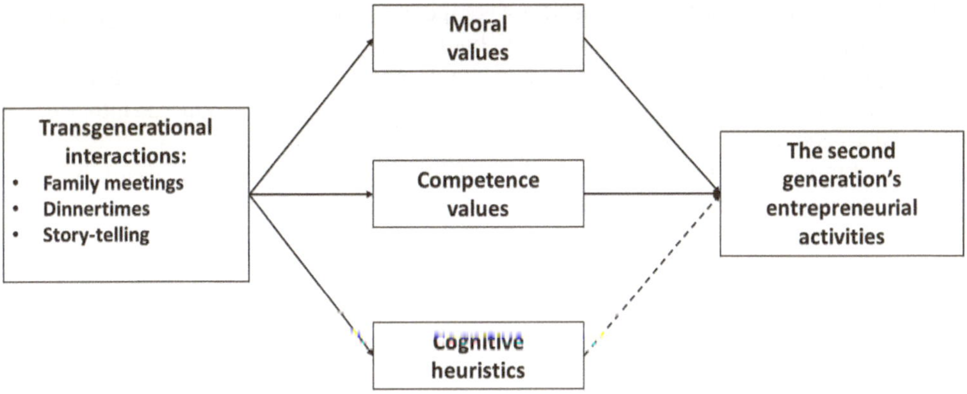

Figure 2. Conceptual model of main findings.

Cognitive heuristics were not transferred to new entrepreneurial activities, whereas moral and competence values were transferred.

entrepreneurial activities across generations is particularly salient as these entrepreneurial activities are crucial for the transgenerational continuity and longevity of family firms (Zellweger, Nason, and Nordqvist 2012), and entrepreneurial outcomes of business families. Indeed, findings suggest that the family, especially the parents, influence children's entrepreneurial behaviours (Bettinelli, Fayolle, and Randerson 2014; Matthews, Schenkel, and Hechavarria 2009). Nonetheless, the elements of knowledge the second-generation entrepreneur learns from the first-generation and what elements are further transferred in new entrepreneurial settings remains a mystery. Our multiple-case study, including six Chinese business families, found the second-generation learned values (moral and competence) and cognitive heuristics from the first-generation. Further, values, whether moral or competence, were most transferred to new entrepreneurial settings (see Figure 2 for a summary of the main findings).

By studying the content of learning and what content is applied to new entrepreneurial settings, we make several contributions to the dialogue regarding the intersection between entrepreneurship, the family, and family firms. Our findings, consistent with social learning theory, support the long-held idea that experienced parental entrepreneurs are an important source of young entrepreneurs' learning (Cabrera-Suárez, De Saá-Pérez, and García-Almeida 2001; Schmitt-Rodermund 2004). We extend this thinking further by identifying the elements that are explicitly learned from parental entrepreneurs through interactions and socialization and which of these elements are transferred to subsequent entrepreneurial contexts. This individual-level focus, as indicated by our data and results, suggests opportunities to begin testing how to best transmit these elements as well as how the next generation initiates and carries out entrepreneurial activities in the core family firm or elsewhere.

In addition, our study has practical implications for family firms engaging in entrepreneurship, and responds to calls for creating applicable knowledge in entrepreneurship (Frank and Landström 2016). Our findings, for instance, address shortcomings in the guidance available to senior generations who are trying to groom younger generations' entrepreneurial activities. Specifically, the extant prescriptions that describe the ways of grooming later generations are often (a) too vague (e.g. role model) or (b) too context-specific to offer help. Knowing that younger generations learn values and cognitive heuristics and the values rather than heuristics have been further transferred to subsequent entrepreneurial activities can better guide families in creating an environment that can facilitate the learning of such values and the transferring of the values to achieve the continuation of entrepreneurial activities across generations.

Contributions aside, this study has several limitations that represent additional opportunities for future research. First, while we focus on transgenerational entrepreneurship in entrepreneurial families, researchers can explore the extent to which transmitted values and cognitive heuristics influence intrafamily succession. McMullen and Warnick (2015), for instance, theorize that parent-founders can promote child-successors' psychological needs for competence and relatedness within the family firm, which encourages the next generation family member to engage in succession. From this, one would expect competence values to be instrumental in the second-generation's decision to succeed the previous. This, however, is an empirical question that may be driven by a more nuanced interaction that includes moral values and cognitive heuristics.

Second, our retrospective narratives limit the conclusions that can be drawn about the application of values in new entrepreneurial settings and the extent to which this application leads to success across cultures, leaving opportunities to observe the implications that might arise. In fact, several studies have further reinforced the potential in gaining a contextualized, culturally embedded understanding of values and heuristics and how they are used by the younger generation. Koiranen (2002), for instance, found that moral values (i.e. honesty and credibility) and competence values (i.e. hard work) were important in Finnish family firms as well as being important characteristic of successors in Canadian family firms. Thus, we encourage further exploration of how transferred values are applied and the results that emerge within entrepreneurial families when these values are applied by the younger generations.

Conclusions

Socialization and role modelling are crucial in the development of next generation as entrepreneurs in entrepreneurial families. Looking at these interactions and the socialization between generations, we provide some answers to the questions related to what is acquired by the younger generation and what is applied to new entrepreneurial activities. Data indicated that (1) the second-generation acquired moral values, competence values, and terminal values from the first-generation entrepreneur; (2) cognitive heuristics related to opportunity recognition which help the second-generation entrepreneurs' professional development as managers, are important components that need to be transmitted across generations; (3) values, rather than cognitive heuristics, transmitted across generations, are applied in new entrepreneurial activities.

Notes

1. *The current family* is the family context in which an individual currently lives, whereas *the family of origin* is the family context in which an individual grew up (Jaskiewicz et al. 2017).
2. In China, families typically own at least 50% of their firms (Dou, Su, and Wang 2017).
3. In China, a founder's executive assistant often helps facilitate the communication between two generations by transferring important information from the founder to the second-generation.

Disclosure statement

No potential conflict of interest was reported by the authors.

Funding

This research is funded by the National Natural Science Foundation of China [Grant Numbers 71672173].

References

Aldrich, H. E., and J. E. Cliff. 2003. "The Pervasive Effects of Family on Entrepreneurship: Toward a Family Embeddedness Perspective." *Journal of Business Venturing* 18 (5): 573–596. doi:10.1016/S0883-9026(03)00011-9.

Arregle, J. L., L. Naldi, M. Nordqvist, and M. A. Hitt. 2012. "Internationalization of Family-controlled Firms: A Study of the Effects of External Involvement in Governance." *Entrepreneurship Theory and Practice* 36 (6): 1115–1143. doi:10.1111/j.1540-6520.2012.00541.x.

Bandura, A. 1986. *Social Foundations of Thought and Action: A Social Cognitive Theory*. Englewood Cliffs, NJ: Prentice-Hall.

Begley, T. M., and D. P. Boyd. 1987. "A Comparison of Entrepreneurs and Managers of Small Business Firms." *Journal of Management* 13 (1): 99–108. doi:10.1177/014920638701300108.

Bettinelli, C., A. Fayolle, and K. Randerson. 2014. "Family Entrepreneurship: A Developing Field." *Foundations and Trends® in Entrepreneurship* 10 (3): 161–236. doi:10.1561/0300000049.

Bettinelli, C., S. Sciascia, K. Randerson, and A. Fayolle. 2017. "Researching Entrepreneurship in Family Firms." *Journal of Small Business Management* 55 (4): 506–529. doi:10.1111/jsbm.2017.55.issue-4.

Bingham, C. B., and K. M. Eisenhardt. 2011. "Rational Heuristics: The 'Simple Rules' that Strategists Learn from Process Experience." *Strategic Management Journal* 32 (13): 1437–1464. doi:10.1002/smj.965.

Brockhaus, R., and P. Horowitz. 1986. "The Psychology of the Entrepreneur." In *The Art and Science of Entrepreneurship*, edited by D. Sexton and R. Smilor. Cambridge, MA: Ballinger.

Busenitz, L. W., and J. B. Barney. 1997. "Differences between Entrepreneurs and Managers in Large Organizations: Biases and Heuristics in Strategic Decision-making." *Journal of Business Venturing* 12 (1): 9–30. doi:10.1016/S0883-9026(96)00003-1.

Cabrera-Suárez, K., P. De Saá-Pérez, and D. García-Almeida. 2001. "The Succession Process from a Resource-and Knowledge-based View of the Family Firm." *Family Business Review* 14 (1): 37–46. doi:10.1111/j.1741-6248.2001.00037.x.

Carsrud, A. L., C. M. Gaglio, and K. W. Olm. 1987. "Entrepreneurs–mentors, Networks, and Successful New Venture Development: An Exploratory Study." *American Journal of Small Business* 12 (2): 13–18. doi:10.1177/104225878701200201.

Chen, C. C., P. G. Greene, and A. Crick. 1998. "Does Entrepreneurial Self-efficacy Distinguish Entrepreneurs from Managers?" *Journal of Business Venturing* 13 (4): 295–316. doi:10.1016/S0883-9026(97)00029-3.

Chlosta, S., H. Patzelt, S. B. Klein, and C. Dormann. 2012. "Parental Role Models and the Decision to Become Self-employed: The Moderating Effect of Personality." *Small Business Economics* 38 (1): 121–138. doi:10.1007/s11187-010-9270-y.

Chung, H., and J. Gale. 2009. "Family Functioning and Self-differentiation: A Cross- Cultural Examination." *Contemporary Family Therapy* 31 (1): 19–33. doi:10.1007/s10591-008-9080-4.

Collins, J. C., and J. I. Porras. 1994. *Built to Last: Successful Habits of Visionary Companies*. Harper Business.

Corbin, J. M., and A. L. Strauss. 1998. *Basics of Qualitative Research: Techniques and Procedures for Developing Grounded Theory*. Newbury Park, CA: Sage Publications.

Dou, J., E. Su, and S. Wang. 2017. "When Does Family Ownership Promote Proactive Environmental Strategy? the Role of the Firm's Long-term Orientation." *Journal of Business Ethics* 1–15.

Dyer, W. G., Jr., and W. Handler. 1994. "Entrepreneurship and Family Business: Exploring the Connections." *Entrepreneurship Theory and Practice* 19 (1): 71–83. doi:10.1177/104225879401900105.

Edmondson, A. C., and S. E. McManus. 2007. "Methodological Fit in Management Field Research." *Academy of Management Review* 32 (4): 1155–1179. doi:10.5465/amr.2007.26586086.

Eisenhardt, K. M., and M. E. Graebner. 2007. "Theory Building from Cases: Opportunities and Challenges." *Academy of Management Journal* 50 (1): 25–32. doi:10.5465/amj.2007.24160888.

Fletcher, D. 2006. "Entrepreneurial Processes and the Social Construction of Opportunity." *Entrepreneurship & Regional Development* 18 (5): 421–440. doi:10.1080/08985620600861105.

Frank, H., and H. Landström. 2016. "What Makes Entrepreneurship Research Interesting? Reflections on Strategies to Overcome the Rigour–relevance Gap." *Entrepreneurship & Regional Development* 28 (1–2): 51–75. doi:10.1080/08985626.2015.1100687.

Gersick, K. E., K. E. Gersick, J. A. Davis, M. M. Hampton, and I. Lansberg. 1997. *Generation to Generation: Life Cycles of the Family Business*. Harvard Business Press.

Gioia, D. A., K. G. Corley, and A. L. Hamilton. 2013. "Seeking Qualitative Rigor in Inductive Research: Notes on the Gioia Methodology." *Organizational Research Methods* 16 (1): 15–31. doi:10.1177/1094428112452151.

Gray, W. D., and J. M. Orasanu. 1987. "Transfer of Cognitive Skills." *Transfer of Learning: Contemporary Research and Applications* 183–215.

Jaskiewicz, P., J. G. Combs, and S. B. Rau. 2015. "Entrepreneurial Legacy: Toward a Theory of How Some Family Firms Nurture Transgenerational Entrepreneurship." *Journal of Business Venturing* 30 (1): 29–49. doi:10.1016/j.jbusvent.2014.07.001.

Jaskiewicz, P., J. G. Combs, K. K. Shanine, and K. M. Kacmar. 2017. "Introducing the Family: A Review of Family Science with Implications for Management Research." *Academy of Management Annals* 11 (1): 309–341. doi:10.5465/annals.2014.0053.

Koiranen, M. 2002. "Over 100 Years of Age but Still Entrepreneurially Active in Business: Exploring the Values and Family Characteristics of Old Finnish Family Firms." *Family Business Review* 15 (3): 175–187. doi:10.1111/j.1741-6248.2002.00175.x.

Lee, T. W. 1999. *Using Qualitative Methods in Organizational Research*. Thousand Oaks, CA: Sage.

Marchisio, G., P. Mazzola, S. Sciascia, M. Miles, and J. Astrachan. 2010. "Corporate Venturing in Family Business: The Effects on the Family and Its Members." *Entrepreneurship & Regional Development* 22 (3–4): 349–377. doi:10.1080/08985621003726168.

Mathews, C. H., and S. B. Moser. 1995. "Family Background and Gender: Implications for Interest in Small Firm Ownership." *Entrepreneurship & Regional Development* 7 (4): 365–378. doi:10.1080/08985629500000023.

Matthews, C. H., M. T. Schenkel, and D. M. Hechavarria. 2009. "Family Background and Influence on Nascent Entrepreneurs." In *New Firm Creation in the United States*, 51–67. New York, NY: Springer.
McKeever, E., A. Anderson, and S. Jack. 2014. "Entrepreneurship and Mutuality: Social Capital in Processes and Practices." *Entrepreneurship & Regional Development* 26 (5–6): 453–477. doi:10.1080/08985626.2014.939536.
McMullen, J. S., and B. J. Warnick. 2015. "To Nurture or Groom? the Parent-founder Succession Dilemma." *Entrepreneurship Theory and Practice* 39 (6): 1379–1412.
Mueller, P. 2006. "Entrepreneurship in the Region: Breeding Ground for Nascent Entrepreneurs?" *Small Business Economics* 27 (1): 41–58.
Newell, A., and H. A. Simon. 1972. *Human Problem Solving*. Vol. 14. Englewood Cliffs, NJ: Prentice-Hall.
Nordqvist, M., and L. Melin. 2010. "Entrepreneurial Families and Family Firms." *Entrepreneurship & Regional Development* 22 (3–4): 211–239. doi:10.1080/08985621003726119.
Randerson, K., C. Bettinelli, A. Fayolle, and A. Anderson. 2015. "Family Entrepreneurship as a Field of Research: Exploring Its Contours and Contents." *Journal of Family Business Strategy* 6 (3): 143–154. doi:10.1016/j.jfbs.2015.08.002.
Rokeach, M. 1973. *The Nature of Human Values*. New York: Free Press.
Schein, E. H. 1984. "Coming to a New Awareness of Organizational Culture." *Sloan Management Review* 25 (2): 3–16.
Schmitt-Rodermund, E. 2004. "Pathways to Successful Entrepreneurship: Parenting, Personality, Early Entrepreneurial Competence, and Interests." *Journal of Vocational Behavior* 65 (3): 498–518. doi:10.1016/j.jvb.2003.10.007.
Sorenson, R. L. 2013. "How Moral and Social Values Become Embedded in Family Firms." *Journal of Management, Spirituality & Religion* 10 (2): 116–137. doi:10.1080/14766086.2012.758050.
Steyaert, C., and J. Katz. 2004. "Reclaiming the Space of Entrepreneurship in Society: Geographical, Discursive and Social Dimensions." *Entrepreneurship & Regional Development* 16 (3): 179–196. doi:10.1080/0898562042000197135.
Taura, N. D., and D. Watkins. 2014. "Counteracting Innovative Constraints: Insights from Four Case Studies of African Knowledge-intensive Metalworking and Automotive Clusters–'the Akimacs'." *Entrepreneurship & Regional Development* 26 (3–4): 313–336. doi:10.1080/08985626.2014.904004.
Zellweger, T. M., R. S. Nason, and M. Nordqvist. 2012. "From Longevity of Firms to Transgenerational Entrepreneurship of Families Introducing Family Entrepreneurial Orientation." *Family Business Review* 25 (2): 136–155. doi:10.1177/0894486511423531.

Index

Note: Figures are indicated by *italics*. Tables are indicated by **bold**. Endnotes are indicated by the page number followed by 'n' and the endnote number e.g., 20n1 refers to endnote 1 on page 20.